DREXEL UNIVERSITY
HEALTH SCIENCES LIBRARIES
HAHNEMANN LIBRARY

D0217737

Storymaking in Bereavement

Dragons Fight in the Meadow

of related interest

Reflections on Therapeutic Storymaking
Alida Gersie
ISBN 1 85302 272 1

Dramatic Approaches to Brief Therapy
Edited by Alida Gersie
ISBN 1 85302 271 3

Storymaking in Education and Therapy
Alida Gersie and Nancy King
ISBN 1 85302 519 4 hb
ISBN 1 85302 520 8 pb

Children, Bereavement and Trauma
Nurturing Resilience
Paul Barnard, Ian Morland and Julie Nagy
ISBN 1 85302 785 5

The Forgotten Mourners, 2nd edition
Guidelines for Working with Bereaved Children
Susan C. Smith
ISBN 1 85302 758 8

Helping Children to Manage Loss
Positive Strategies for Renewal and Growth
Brenda Mallon
ISBN 1 85302 605 0

Talking with Children and Young People about Death and Dying
A Workbook
Mary Turner, illustrated by Bob Thomas
ISBN 1 85302 563 1

Interventions with Bereaved Children
Edited by Susan C Smith and Sister Margaret Pennells
ISBN 1 85302 285 3

Living Through Loss
A Training Guide for Those Supporting People Dealing with Loss
Fay W Jacobsen, Margaret Kindlen and Allison Shoemark
ISBN 1 85302 395 7

Grief and Powerlessness
Helping People Regain Control of their Lives
Ruth Bright
ISBN 1 85302 386 8

Good Grief 1
Exploring Feelings, Loss and Death with Under Elevens, 2nd edition
Barbara Ward and Associates
ISBN 1 85302 324 8

Good Grief 2
Exploring Feelings, Loss and Death with Over Elevens and Adults
Barbara Ward and Associates
ISBN 1 85302 340 X

**DREXEL UNIVERSITY
HEALTH SCIENCES LIBRARIES
HAHNEMANN LIBRARY**

Storymaking in Bereavement

Dragons Fight in the Meadow

Alida Gersie

Foreword by Ofra Ayalon

Jessica Kingsley Publishers
London and Philadelphia

The author and the publishers gratefully acknowledge permission to reprint the following:

The poem 'Burying a Child' (R.B., 1969–1974), published in *Uncarving the Block* by Barry Goldensohn, Vermont Crossroads Press, 1978 is reprinted by kind permission of the author.

The extract from the poem 'The Mourners', published in *The Thether* by Lorrie Goldensohn L'Epervier Press, 1983 is reprinted by kind permission of the author.

The extract from 'Autobiography' Part One, 3, from *Collected Poems* (London: Allison & Busby, 1986) by Adrian Henri is reprinted by permission of Rogers Coleridge and White Ltd.

The extracts from *The Treasures of Darkness* (1976) by Thorbald Jacobsen are reprinted by permission of Yale University Press.

The extracts from *The Sumerians: Their History, Culture and Character* (1963) by S.N. Kramer have been reprinted by permission of The University of Chicago Press.

The extracts from *Mythologies of the Ancient World* (1961) by S.N. Kramer have been reprinted by permission of Doubleday & Company (New York) Publishers.

The extract from *The Epic of Gilgamesh*, translated by N.K. Saunders (Penguin Classics, Revised Edition, 1964) is reproduced by permission of Penguin Books Ltd.

The extract from the poem 'The Deathbed' by Siegfried Sassoon is reprinted by permission of George Sassoon.

The extracts from *Inanna, Queen of Heaven and Earth* (1983) by D. Wolkstein and S.N. Kramer have been reprinted by permission of D. Wolkstein.

All rights reserved. No paragraph of this publication may be reproduced, copied or transmitted save with written permission or in accordance with the provisions of the Copyright Act 1956 (as amended), or under the terms of any licence permitting limited copying issued by the Copyright Licensing Agency, 33–34 Alfred Place, London WC1E 7DP. Any person who does any unauthorised act in relation to this publication may be liable to criminal prosecution and civil claims for damages.

The right of Alida Gersie to be identified as author of this work has been asserted by her in accordance with the Copyright, Designs and Patents Act 1988.

First published in the United Kingdom in 1991 by
Jessica Kingsley Publishers Ltd
116 Pentonville Road
London N1 9JB, England
and
325 Chestnut Street
Philadelphia, PA19106, USA

www.jkp.com

Second impression 1996
Third impression 2000

BF
575
.G7
G381s
1991

Copyright © 1991 Alida Gersie
Library of Congress Cataloging in Publication Data
A CIP catalog record for this book is available from the Library of Congress
British Library Cataloguing in Publication Data
Gersie, Alida
Storymaking in bereavement
1. Bereaved persons. Counselling
I. Title
362.8
ISBN 1 85302 065 6
Printed and Bound in Great Britain by
Athenaeum Press, Gateshead, Tyne and Wear

In memory of Emma Admiraal-Stoffels

'Joy comes softly'

Acknowledgements

Without the people who allowed me to share their times of grief, this book could not have been written. I am deeply grateful for the trust I was given and I sincerely hope that I have done justice to these experiences with family and friends, students, colleagues and clients. Thank you all.

Professionally I am indebted to my first clinical supervisors, Alan Shuttleworth, the Tavistock Clinic and Michael Mercer, then with the Family Welfare Association. I also treasure the stimulating hours spent with Jean Thomson and Dr Stewart Katzmann, both Jungian Analysts. They guided my work in so many ways.

Dr Ofra Ayalon and Dr Mooli Lahad are the friends and colleagues who cajoled and nourished me into accepting that the work with storymaking in bereavement counselling had to be recorded. Warm thanks to you!

The sustaining love of Rosie Gibb, Simon Markson, Olivia Lousada and Rhea and Nigel Short-Karageorgiou helped me to keep on writing. I am grateful for your buoyant enthusiasm as we discussed yet another idea about loss and death. Janet Tucker, Dr Audrey Insch and Ann Winn shared with me what it means to celebrate life today as well as tomorrow. Their lived example inspires much of this writing. Whilst the steady nourishment received from Marina Jenkyns and Mel Hofstead helped me to move beyond several hurdles which came my way.

I much appreciate the support received from my colleagues at Hertfordshire College of Art and Design, Phil Jones and Ditty Dokter. My sincere thanks for your extra work and care during my sabbatical absence and for the pleasure I gain from being there with you.

I also want to express thanks beyond words to my mother and to my sister, Ditty and to Therese and Antoine. Your healing from grief and your love of life, has given and gives me so very much.

Last but not least I want to say a heartfelt 'dankjewel' to Cees Roos and Bart van Hulzen, both of whom helped me to retrieve lost files in so many more ways than one.

Without Jessica Kingsley's enthusiasm, which supported me throughout the various stages and moods of writing, I might not have had the courage to find the words to describe bereavement experiences. Thank you, Jessica.

Contents

Myths and Stories

Foreword

Not so many years ago, when I started to experiment with (or should I rather say 'tamper with') the subject of death education with a group of teachers, I had to confront an indirect but rather blatant accusation from my students: 'Since we started on your course, the death rate in our school communities has noticeably increased'.[1] The underlying trepidation was quite obvious, almost palpable. It was a clear reflection of the apprehension we experience for violating one of our culture's most revered taboos.

The 'Death' taboo operates along the Denial line, namely, 'If I don't think of it, it will never happen' (commonly expressed by proverbs like 'let sleeping dogs lie' or 'don't call the devil'). As a therapist I have been painfully aware of the psychological price some people pay for the denial of death; namely, unconsummated grieving processes, fear of life, avoidance of intimacy, curtailed creativity and looming depressions. Since I acknowledged the difficulty of looking death straight in the face, my concern has been to find risk-safe ways of helping people to get in touch with the potentially healing dimensions of death.

But who shall speak the unspeakable? Who may break the taboo and still go unharmed?

Sharing these concerns with Alida, I have been rewarded by her following insight.

As 'saying the unspeakable' has been denied to ordinary people by force of this taboo, it became the prerogative of some strange characters, such as the 'wise' fool, who in other disguises is the story-teller, the shaman, or the ancient Biblical prophet. They share the freedom to say publicly the most outrageous things under the protecting immunity called 'poetic license'. They are able to tell a story that seduces us with the passion and promise inherent in a narrative, and quietens the inner critic in us.

It is partly through language, myth and ritual that we attempt to explain and to cope with the potential threat of death, as we learned from Bruno Bettleheim.[2] The acknowledgement of death is paramount to the full awakening of the person to adult maturity, symbolically portrayed in myth, legend and folk tales.

By creating a backdrop of familiar scenes and images, storytellers create a semblance of a stable and secure environment into which they will later introduce the foreboding elements that carry the message or the bit of unbearable knowledge that has to be imparted to the audience.

The working out of a crucial conflict, such as arises from issues around death, will not be possible unless we can provide a safe enough atmosphere for trying it out. The story provides this safety by containing within its framework the two seemingly contradictory elements of *distancing* and *involvement*, introduced in Michael Shiryon's rationale for Literatherapy.[3]

The need for distancing is recognised by myth, legends and folk tales and is reflected by common beginnings such as 'once upon a time, in Never-Never Land' and the 'heroes' being royalty, personified animals or supernatural creatures. While these elements allow for safe distancing it is also important to create in the audience the necessary involvement with the situation at hand, in order to achieve personal identification with the characters, ideas and emotional experiences of the story.

Using these elements the story becomes a metaphorical reflection on life's pain and grievances. Like any other metaphor, the story provides us with multi-level images that by definition defy an intellectual analysis of interpretation. Paul Watzlavic[4] believes that information transmitted through metaphors rather then by direct communication is much more effective in creating a change in the mind and the behaviour; it is absorbed by the 'right brain' which has the ability to grasp complex relationships, patterns and structures holistically.

Thus a story well chosen provides the necessary distancing, yet this very same 'safe distance' allows involvement through the process of identification; this includes projection, ie the readers or listeners attribute their own motives and emotions to the one or more of the characters featured in the story, be it human, beast, tree or a supernatural (imaginary) being. Catharsis (uncensored and spontaneous release of emotions) and insight (the awareness of motivations previously unnoticed by their bearer) will complete the therapeutic impact of the story. The widely experienced consequence of this healing process is a combination of diminished anxiety and increasing self esteem, which may be the gain of those who not only will read this book but will also take the benefit of its therapeutic suggestions.

Throughout this book Alida is making a conscious and serious attempt to stay faithful to the origins of her carefully selected stories. She does this out of reverence to the indigenous cultures from which she, very lovingly, borrows their oral traditions. She treats these traditional expressions with the same respect and concern which she shows toward the easily damaged fauna and flora of our tattered ecology. In her own words, 'only those who created and transmitted the stories through the ages have the right to change, edit and bring them up to date according to their own needs'. But the pains she takes to heed to her preservation principles are rewarded by the way the stories open up to her, disclosing their innermost secrets. Contained within each and every story we find a problem exposition and a problem solving method. Alida succeeds in translating the embedded themes and structures of a story into a universal psychological quest for inner knowledge. This she does by weaving into the storytelling sequential tasks and exercises that turn the readers of her book from passive audience to active participants, eliciting their own images and creating their own myth. Her 'structures' are effective because they take the reader on a personal journey which parallels the story's journey. Thus ancient and remote stories are filled with immediate and personal relevance.

The reader of *Storymaking in Bereavement* will not find 'theoretical' interpretations of the story's themes. Alida, who devoted many years to the study of comparative mythology, does not belong to the school of 'this means that', but believes that '"this" means "that" to me today, and may overlap with what it means to you today.' She follows in the footsteps of Joseph Campbell[5] in looking into myth and stories for 'the emerging patterns across time'.

Campbell also suggested that 'the secret cause of all suffering is mortality itself, which is the prime condition of life. It cannot be denied if life is to be affirmed.' In the same spirit, Alida's book on death, loss and bereavement serves as a tool in the hand of the skilled group-worker to help reach this goal of the affirmation of life. It is designed to accomplish the greatest task of all, namely 'coming to grips with mortality.'

Dr Ofra Ayalon

References

1. Ayalon, O. (1987). *Rescue! Community Oriented Preventive Education*. Haifa: Nord Publications.

Ayalon, O. (1990). *Crisis & Coping With Suicide & Bereavement*. Haifa: Nord Publications.

2. Bettleheim, B. (1975). *The Uses of Enchantment*. New York: Alfred Knopf.

3. Shiryon. M. (1978). 'Literatherapy: Theory and Application', in Rubin, R. J., (Ed.) *Bibliotherapy Sourcebook*. New York: Oryx Press.

4. Watzlavic, P. (1978). *Language of Change*. New York: Basic Books.

5. Campbell, J. (1988). *The Power of Myth*. London: Doubleday.

We saw it in each other's eye,
And wished in every half-breathed sigh,
To speak, but did not.

Thomas Moore

Introduction

This is a book about love and loss; not about the loss to life when people who once loved one another go their different ways, but about loss through death. When someone we love has died, we know that we shall never be able to hear their voice again like we used to. We shall not play with them, be hugged, or irritated in the old familiar ways. All that has ended and will not return. If we believe in afterlife or patterns of reincarnation, we may find comfort in the thought of a possible re-encounter. However, we still need to come to grips with death's finality in this life. To find a way of expressing our loss which will lead to the healing of our pain.

A man whose eight year old son was killed in an accident said, shortly after the event: 'It's not until they die that you realise how much you love them. I can't get back to any kind of normality. Something is dead inside me and nothing means anything any more.'

We recognise his words. Those of us who had to cope with the death of a young person, or with sudden or painfully slow death, probably spoke them ourselves. Words do not suffice to convey such grief; yet we also know that our life and well-being depend on the expression of feelings, on finding the words to say it.

In this book I try to find words for the experience of profound grief and to offer various ways in which we may help ourselves and others to express our feelings, especially when mourning is difficult.

Because I love stories and have found great comfort in ancient folktales and myths, I have over the years shared such stories with friends, family, clients and students. Often I told the stories in times of pleasure, sometimes in times of transition and also in times of sorrow. Grief has touched the life of many people I know and love, and it entered my own life more than once. During such times of mourning I shared the stories at first hesitantly, not wishing to intrude upon the private territory of grief. When the story-listeners encouraged me not only to tell more tales but also said that they told the stories to other people in case they too might find them comforting, my confidence grew.

Meanwhile, I was teaching comparative mythology and worked freelance, offering workshops in 'therapeutic storymaking'. In this work and in my other role at that time as a family social worker and student-trainer, I encountered again and again the consequences of withheld sorrow. The devastating effect of grief which had not been given expression became increasingly clear. The impact of stuck mourning on family life cried out to be noted. In my work with adolescents who had attempted suicide, I noticed how their plea for help with issues of 'life, death and mourning' had often been ignored. We silence grief at our peril.

This book is the outcome of my work- and life-experience with themes of love, life and death. Its structure and style reflect these twin roots. The book is divided into six parts, each with different chapters.

Part One is devoted to an exploration of the themes evoked by love and death. In Chapter One the reader is introduced to the complexities of intimate relationships and how our felt ambiguities hamper the expression of grief. Key-aspects of saying farewell are noted and the basic tasks of grief and mourning are indicated. As such this chapter sets out the basics, which are explored in greater depth in subsequent chapters.

In Chapter Two I explore how we acquire our ideas about death, and how life-experience intertwines with our developing death-concept. Various explanations for adult reluctance to discuss issues of death and dying with their children and with each other, are offered. This leads to a discussion of the price we pay for not bringing death into our awareness. I also touch upon the way in which stories help the process of reflecting on the circumstances of our life, particularly when this circumstance is one of profound sorrow.

Having created some demarcation points as regards death and life, I then describe in Chapter Three some of the experiences which commonly occur in the time between the actual death and the burial or cremation. When discussing this chapter with people who had lived through bereavements, I was encouraged to convey some details of what we may feel at such a time. One of the most frequently heard statements was: 'If only I had known that the way I felt was normal, perfectly average. I was so frightened I was going crazy...'

I am aware that I did justice only to some of the ways we feel at that time. The essence of what happened to you may well have been quite different. However, I hope that it will serve the function of bringing your memories of those days freshly into your awareness, thereby creating a further opportunity for sharing, and, I hope, healing.

Part Two of the book is entitled *A Tracery of Connections through Mourning and Myth*. There are seven chapters in this part of the book. Each one is constructed in a similar way. I set out the main themes evoked by the chapter title. Then I weave my way around the theme through a mixture of discussion, reflection and by telling ancient myths and folktales, which are pertinent to the theme. As such, these chapters are an abundant resource of Folktales and Myths. It is important to note that I have selected the stories because they matter to me personally, and because I have shared the tales with people who were living through their mourning. A story's relevance to these actual life-experiences determined whether or not it was included in the book.

The stories were given birth amongst many different tribes and in many different countries. They were selected not only because they are beautiful and movingly concise, but also because many people in the West are unfamiliar with these tales. Today the life of native people all over the world is threatened, their way of life undermined by our Western life-style. If these stories were to help us to put on the brakes even a little and actively to support the fight for the rights of tribal people I shall be well rewarded.

I used several 19th and 20th century source-books and articles in order to find a number of recorded versions of each tale. The 'common' tale could then be traced. I re-told this tale in as sparse a style as possible, trying to be truthful to the common components and stylistic characteristics. In the reference sections I have listed a contemporary source for every story, not only so that the reader has immediate access to two versions of each tale, but also because those particular books invariably contain other interesting material. I trust this is of use.

The first chapter in this section introduces the reader to stories about the way death came into the world. The various explanations people give are closely connected with the way we relate to death and grief. I lift some of these connections to the fore. Through the discussion of the stories I also aim to introduce the reader to various methods of reflecting on ancient stories.

In subsequent chapters I explore major themes in relation to our response to bereavement. Sooner or later most of us struggle with these themes, not necessarily in this sequence and not necessarily with equal intensity for each theme. However, within the context of the book it was important to give each one attention, to ponder its characteristics and to weave a pathway through the mourning-process.

This part of the book can best be seen as a map of sorts. We use maps in our own way and to our own end, hastening along some aspects of the journey, dwelling longer in other places. Those who wish to become guides to other people's travel do, however, need to be thoroughly familiar with the various routes and the details of the landscape. I therefore strongly recommend that you carefully read these chapters, especially if you work with bereavement-counselling groups and would like to use these stories in your practice.

The third part focuses on death within the intimate circle of our life: the death of a parent, child or life-partner. Though there is a degree of overlap between these chapters and the points noted in Part One and Two, the attention given to the specificity of each loss has allowed for more detailed reflection on the issues raised, and above all permitted the introduction of story-material pertinent in those situations.

Part Four includes two chapters, which are grouped under the title: *When a Tyrant Spell has Bound Us*. Experience suggests that our journey through bereavement presents two great dangers. The first is the embrace of profound depression, the second is the decision that life is not worth living, can no longer be lived and that therefore the attempt to end one's life has to be made.

I discuss these two dangers within the context of therapeutic storymaking. The reader who is interested in depression and para-suicide/suicide attempts has access to an abundance of literature. I have therefore refrained from discussing these predicaments in the usual way, but have persisted in using stories to reflect upon these life-difficulties and to use life-experience in order to reflect upon the stories. When working with profoundly depressed clients I have often found it helpful to reinterpret the lived experience as an attempt to enter a dark world which shows parallels with the heroic attempt to enter into the underworld in search of renewal. I therefore introduce the reader to a discussion of the Inanna-myth and its importance to the bereavement process.

The chapter on death's dangerous pull explores at length the connections I have noted between heroic journeys and the recovery of the will to life. I describe in detail the form such work takes, and discuss why the creation of heroic tales along ancient story-patterns may be important. The reader who works with stories in a therapeutic way, will find much in these chapters which is relevant to such work.

Part Five is devoted to a discussion of therapeutic work with stories in bereavement-counselling. Having introduced many stories in earlier chapters, and having shared key aspects of the bereavement-journey, the time has come to speak about the stories *per se*.

In the first chapter in this section I introduce the reader to basic concepts related to myths and stories and note some issues which matter when retelling ancient tales. Though I do not quote Joseph Campbell and Mircea Eliade, their teachings are of fundamental importance to my work and permeate much of the thinking about mythology and storytelling.

In the chapter devoted to storymaking in bereavement counselling groups I discuss the fundamental characteristics of such groups, their aims, purpose and boundaries. I also introduce elements of facilitator-style and explore specific characteristics of the storymaking groups. The reader who is interested in a more detailed discussion of the concepts and ideas which underpin the creation of story-making structures is referred to the book *Storymaking in Education and Therapy* written by me and Nancy King, which is also published by Jessica Kingsley Publishers.

Part Six contains twelve myths and tales and thirty six storymaking structures.

It is important to note that the tales have been retold in accordance with the method described above. It is also crucial to remember that the stories are *not* arranged in a purposefully sequential manner. As such they do not constitute a course of treatment. Each storymaking structure is no more and no less than a stepping stone towards healing grief. When used carefully and at the appropriate time the structure can be trusted to facilitate this process.

A closing comment. As you will later notice, I refer only rarely to client case-material. I arrived at this decision because the bereavement experience will affect us all if we are lucky enough to live a long life and to create bonds with people who matter. I therefore elected to write using the plural form.

At times this irritated me for it led to an excessive use of 'maybe's. However, I stuck by my choice because we all travel the road of love and grief, and because all other styles felt wrong.

Finally I imagined that the users of the book might be people who lived through the loss of a person they love and therefore that you are one of these people. I sincerely hope that I have done justice to several aspects of your grief, though I imagine that much was also left unsaid, as the experience of grief is unique to each of us. I have tried to bear honest witness to the experiences which came my way, some intimately and directly, some from time immemorial through stories and tales.

As such, this book is the work of many people whose names are not mentioned, but whose vital presence was always felt.

Part One

Themes of Love and Death

'I will complain, yet praise;
I will bewail, approve;
And all my sour-sweet days,
I will lament and love.'

George Herbert

CHAPTER ONE

Acknowledging the work of separation and mourning

We are born and we shall die, sooner or later. It is a simple truth. Most of us know it; few are willing to discuss it. In our culture we rarely talk about death. Afterlife is mentioned a great deal more often than the end of our actual life, even though we die feigned deaths to each other in our divorces, redundancies and shunnings. Such deaths we may endure or generate with great frequency, hoping to be brought to life again through a promising new beginning, another job, a new partner, different friends.

We have discovered the validity of Sir Edward Dyer's words, written several centuries ago:

> The firmest faith is found in fewest words,
> The turtles do not sing, and yet they love;
> True hearts have ears and eyes, no tongues to speak;
> They hear and see, and sigh, and then they break.[1]

Many of us have lived through times of heart-breaking. However, we also know that we suffered because we actually experienced the profound rewards and wordless satisfactions of an intimate relationship, and reaped the thousand and one blessings which came our way when least expected.

Thus we break our heart and try to mend it, or we dare not break our heart and need not mend it, because we did not give it away. We are still in trouble, for we tend to lose that which we try to preserve. We may bitterly acknowledge that our attempt to keep our heart well-protected has resulted in great lonesomeness. The refusal to permit other people entry into the intimate web of our daily life creates the suffering of self-generated isolation. None of us can avoid the reality that sooner or later 'love' presents itself as an issue in our life. Our relationships with our parents and partners, friends and children make us die numerous little deaths and equally make us live through numerous resurrections long before we encounter death itself.

When we experience life's little deaths we discover what it means to witness the disillusion of the dreams which are of our own making. A disillusionment during which we feel the pain of withholding silences, of looks which meet with animosity. Then we stand face to face with our angry reluctance to hold the person whom we once so tenderly embraced. We experience that our bonds have become unstitched. Does this too deserve the name of love?

How can we ever find a place for real dying within such inner turmoil? How to grieve over someone's actual death when our feelings are so full of poignant contradictions? Did not the turmoil inflicted by our love make us long for death from time to time? When living was a pain, most of us occasionally imagined that death might be a pleasure.

Then we became bereaved and we sorely remember the earlier sense that the days and nights with such soul-destroying love were not worth living. How come then that we now miss them so much - the man, the woman, the child or friend about whom we had deeply ambivalent feelings. It does not seem to make sense.

An explanation might be that although our marriage did not live up to expectations, it was still our marriage, for better and for worse. Our relationship with our partner may have been troubled, but we lived together. These days we climb into our bed alone. Our child might have caused us a whole lot of trouble but we never ceased to love him or her. Since their death the sight of the bike or a last bit of make-up reduces us to tears.

It takes courage to admit to ourselves how confused we often are. Torn between love and hate, birth and death, renewal or destruction. There is so much we desire and for many of us only so few of our desires become reality. When we grow up we soon discover that we have to surrender many of our longings, only then to find that life yields a different kind of harvest. One which we had not expected. As the years pass by we learn that we have to embrace the understandings and the misunderstandings which are part and parcel of all intimate relationships. To admit our wishes, to surrender our grievances. We learn and then the person with whom and around whom our learning happened, died. Did we have time to say good-bye? Truly to say good-bye? Or did the doorbell ring and did we hear the news brought by a stranger. 'Your father died. Your son has had a serious accident. I'm afraid he is no longer alive.' Words which we will remember years later. Experiences which need to be integrated into the intimate fabric of our existence. But how?

Whenever we bid a serious farewell, and death is the most serious of all farewells, there are four phases which need to be experienced:

- It has to be acknowledged that an important bond exists. Then we have to accept that this bond is unavoidably altered by any prolonged absence and irrevocably changed by death.

- Outstanding major issues need to be settled; the decks cleared. Having shared what could be shared, and with our hearts and minds more or less at peace, we can prepare for the actual separation.

- Seeing the other person in some respects possibly for the 'first' time, it is even harder to let go. It pains us all the more. But the awareness of the depth of our bond enables us to be genuine. We can offer and accept each other's blessing. This is the third stage.

- Then the actual separation follows. We grant the other and ourselves true permission to embark upon our different journeys. We turn away from one another and at last the separation is a reality.

The death of someone we love creates an encounter with the reality of these four stages. Some aspects of this we may have lived through, others we have denied. Our actual experiences and above all those we did not have, become part and parcel of the work of grief, 'Work' which involves the speaking of the unspoken and ample space for those feelings which were earlier withheld. Consequently, we shall find that the tasks of grief are fourfold:-

- We mourn the life which we actually lived.

- We mourn the life which we did not live, but which we can imagine we would have lived if only circumstances had been different.

- We mourn the future which we imagined to be an extension of our actual life, the future which we could have reasonably expected.

- We mourn the 'possible' future, the life which might have been ours, if only our imagined past had become a reality.

Whenever we experience a serious bereavement we grieve over the loss of these four dimensions of our life. This is our cross. These actual and potential lives need to be brought into our awareness because each contains important aspects of our relationship with the person who died.

Seeing our life with such clarity is a difficult experience. More often than not, the acknowledgment of the realities of the 'lost dream of life' causes us a substantial amount of pain. Yet we need to transcend the constraints of the old dreams. Only when we know the full measure of our longings and experiences can newness arise. Remembering, we can then forget and thereby be remembered.

Death is the great expected unexpected. It is the anticipated yet unknown journey. How can we possibly be prepared for its impact? We know that our intimate relationships offer us a daily chance to encounter the force of our wants and needs, our disappointments and longings. As such they present a continuous challenge, the recurring opportunity to practice both commitment and acceptance. Such practice is not easy. Who said it was? But the more we become aware of the complexity of our ways of being, the greater our willingness to accept that life and death are twin-born. Love weaves a colourful thread between them.

We fear that we lose this love when we become bereaved. We know that if we lose such love, we lose life. Therefore we are in danger. Bereavement is at first a terrifying experience. The journey also offers us new healing - but that is much later.

Let us explore some aspects of our experience of mortality and thereby ease our willingness to grieve.

References

1. Extract from, Dyer, Sir Edward, (c. 1545-1607), 'The Lowest Trees have Tops'.

'But yet, alas, but seldom I
do think indeed that I must die.'

Robert Southwell

CHAPTER TWO
Coming to grips with mortality

We become bereaved through the death of a person who matters to us. If someone is not important in our life we note their dying, but above all the fact of death. The gap which they leave in our life is negligible. When our colleague tells us that his neighbour, whom he hardly knew, suddenly died the night before, we might say: 'Sorry to hear it'. Are we sorry that his neighbour died? Sorry that our colleague was so near and yet so far removed from someone's death, or do we regret that death is a reality?

If we have a minute to spare we might talk a little about the vagaries of life, then continue our work. Unless we recently suffered a major loss. Then the news about the unknown neighbour's death resonates with our own pain, summoning these woes into poignant presence. When such resonance occurs we may well send a spoken or unspoken wish to the unknown neighbour's family. Wishing them strength, just in case they too loved wholeheartedly or ambivalently. But nonetheless loved and lost.

The etymological dictionary tells us that centuries ago in Old English the word 'Bereaved' conveyed the meaning that one had been robbed of someone's presence. The dead person had been violently taken away. The Anglo-Saxons understood that therefore life was spoiled. More literally, they knew that the death of someone we love leaves us standing naked before life. The term 'bereaved' suggested that clothes and armour had been forcibly removed. We recognise the echoes of this meaning, for the death of someone we love initially seems to remove our protective layers. Thus we are twice violated:

— First because death has taken away the person we love and probably need.

— Secondly the death of the loved one has left us feeling naked and unprotected.

This dual robbery causes a rupture in the life we have known. A rupture which needs mending, but how to heal that which has been irrevocably lost and what exactly does irrevocable loss mean?

We cannot come to grips with the loss endured in bereavement unless we are willing to explore our relationship with death both as an experience and as a concept. We have to ask ourselves what we understand by 'death', and how we acquired our ideas. In order to do this we shall begin at the beginning and discuss how children develop ideas about death.

Some theoreticians believe that the child's observations of nature lead to the formulation of thoughts about death. They suggest that upon seeing a dead insect, animal, or plant the child starts to ask questions. Sooner or later, these questions involve the death of people, and finally, his or her own death (Mitchell, 1967). Others propose that the child's experience of death-like events, such as separations and hospitalizations, form the basis for the understanding of death, and that through generalization, the child extends these experiences to those of all living beings (Anthony, 1971).

Maybe my young friend had seen a dead bird in the park. Maybe it mattered that she had not seen me for a few weeks. But one Autumn afternoon, when I came to visit, she enthusiastically lay down on the carpet, calling triumphantly: 'Alida, I'm dead. I'm dead'. She tried to lie perfectly still. Nothing stirred; even her breathing became very quiet. I knelt down beside her, felt her body and said something like: 'My lovely Rachel has died. I wish she would be alive ... Ooooh. Oooh.' Then I burst into very believable make-believe tears. A satisfied smile grew around her lips - the louder my wailing, the happier the smile. She suddenly woke up, flung her arms around me, and said most comfortingly: 'I'm not dead.' To be followed by an immediate: 'Do it again. Do it again.' Thus we played at being dead and sobbing until she had enough of it. Which took a while.

This little three year old knew that death was connected with 'not' moving, trying not to breathe, and closing your eyes. When dead, you are cut off from activity and sensory experience. She had also learned that the death of an important person must be followed by weeping and moaning. The quality of the sobs mattered to her. They had to be intense. Also, the more the better. Then she knew beyond doubt that her resurrection would be welcome. She loved that moment. Surprise, surprise. Cease your wailing, halt your moaning. She, whom you thought dead, has returned to life. Some of us might think: 'If only it were this easy in real life'.

Rachel is still too young to ask questions about the whys and wherefores of death. At present it is no more than a momentary state, voluntarily entered into and abandoned when the game is finished. Death is something to play around with. But the day will come when she too will wonder:

— Why is that fly dead?
— Why did the rabbit die?
— Why do butterflies die so soon?
— When will granny die?
— Will you die when I am old?
— Do I grow small when I die?

She too will learn that death is causal, universal and inevitable. It exists and it exists for everyone. Though people hold different beliefs as to what happens after death, death itself is a phenomenon which cannot be denied. Even though some of us might describe it as merely a process of gradual transformation, this process makes an absolute difference.

A child is considered to have acquired a mature death-concept when death is perceived as a natural process which is final, irreversible and universal. The ability to perceive death in this way is thought to be reflective of the child's development. Many authors believe that the concept of death is highly abstract and complex (Orbach, 1985). They suggest that in order to grasp the phenomenon of death we need to be able to distinguish between animate and inanimate objects, understand the difference between I and other, know something about constancy and inconstancy, and have discovered that time exists. When we have fully grasped death's implications we are aware that time flows in the direction of growing up and growing old. Then death will follow. Unless of course, we die young.

It is often emphasized that the child's age, their anxiety and their cognition affect the way in which they deal with their understanding of the meaning of death (Orbach, 1985). This is undoubtedly correct. However, it might be prudent to remind ourselves that the child's relationship with death is above all influenced by their temperament, their actual life-experience, cultural background and religious beliefs. The stability in their home-environment matters as well as the health and illnesses of family, friends and the animals with whom they share a home.

The young boy whose father died in a car-crash when he was only four years old, will relate differently to death from the five year old girl whose beloved grandmother died slowly and gradually following a debilitating illness. Equally crucial are the boy's involvement in the preparations for the cremation-ceremony, his drawings, the flowers he gathered, the song he sang, the deeds and omissions of the important adults around him.

As are the girl's dreams about her granny's impending death. The fact that she wanted so very much to go and visit her grandmother. That this could not be arranged. Then she had pleaded to be allowed to see her dead granny. As she said: 'She is still my granny.' She remembers her screaming protest in the night before the funeral, when she heard that she would not be allowed to attend. Then the sudden silence. As if something inside her snapped. The last words she spoke that night were: 'It is not fair. It is not fair. She is my granny. I want to see her and say goodbye.'

Obviously the meaning of death to us is influenced by the meaning of death to the important people in our life, especially when we are young. For whenever someone dies the child needs the adult's encouragement and permission to say good-bye, to attend the funeral or cremation, to express grief and participate in the mourning-ceremonies. Sometimes such permission is granted, sometimes withheld. Whatever the adults decide, their choice has serious implications for the child's and therefore at a later stage, for the adult's relationship with death.

Maybe the adults fear that their child, when discovering the existence of death will respond like Hare, a trickster-figure about whom the Winnebago Indians told the following sacred story.

Hare had been sent by Earthmaker to rescue the two-leggeds (people) from the evil ones. At a crucial moment he did not do as he had been told. Instead he tried to save his aunts and uncles from death, which was against the laws of life. His grandmother Earth had also told him not to look back. But he disobeyed her too. Then he saw what he was not meant to have seen. He saw how the place from which he had started caved in, completely and instantaneously. He heard of Death.

The story then continues:

> When Hare discovered Death, he ran back to the place where he lived. He shouted and cried: 'My people must not die.' Then he suddenly realised: 'Everything will one day die! He imagined the sloping rocks. They just fell away. He imagined the big mountains. They fell apart.

He imagined the place below the earth. Everything that lived in the soil stopped scurrying about; they froze and died. He imagined the skies high above him, and the birds which had been flying stopped flying and fell to earth, dead. He crawled into the place where he lived. He reached for his blanket, and rolled himself into it. He lay there and wept. There will not be enough earth for all that dies, he thought. There is not enough earth for all that dies. He buried himself in his blanket. He made no sound.'[1]

We may fear that our children will, like Hare, be panic-struck when they hear of death. Maybe we are rightly apprehensive of their initial fear and real pain, for when first realising what death means it would be strange if they were not unsettled. Some children, however, relate to death in a matter of fact way, showing merely a near 'surgical' interest. It takes them time to become ready to express their feelings about the reality of death as a permanent possibility. We ourselves might also be reluctant to admit to our feelings about death in general and about the actual death of beloved people or animals in particular. A reluctance which we frequently hide behind our concern about a child's untimely introduction to death and dying.

It might therefore be helpful to remind ourselves of the answers we received, when we were a child, to our question: 'Why do people die?' We probably encountered a variation of one of the following:

— because that it the way it is
— God wanted it so
— then all the pain could stop
— because of what Adam and Eve did
— to begin a new life
— all living things must die
— I don't know
— don't worry. You'll live a while yet.

Given the importance which many children attribute to death, the answers might have felt woefully inadequate, leaving the child in us to wonder whether adults really took this issue seriously. Alternatively, the brevity of the answer might have been oddly reassuring. Maybe death wasn't such an important issue after all.

However comforting or inadequate we found the answer to be, the question was never settled once and for all. From time to time the child we were is likely to have returned to the theme of death and dying, whether we wanted to or not. The author Judith Viorst remembers how night after night, when she was young, she thought about death. At last she resorted to praying: 'Please God. I know you can't take death away. But couldn't you just arrange for me to stop thinking about it.'[2]

We know that the ceaseless preoccupation with death casts a veil over life. A veil of fear, sorrow and paralysis. As such death is numinous and exercises a potentially fatal fascination. This fascination has to be overcome so that questions related to death and dying can be engaged with. Sometimes it may have seemed to us as if the search for answers represented itself with every burst of growth, particularly during those storm- and urgency-ridden years of our adolescence. We may remember the long secretive hours during which we put the world to right, and sorted out the meaning of life as well as death, until we felt that we could search no longer and enquire no further. Until we gave up.

The child's desire to stop thinking and to forget about death neatly mirrors many an adult's desire to give the question a miss. The wish is expressive of the blind longing not to have to take death seriously, for maybe then it will not happen. This is our ultimate game of 'Let's pretend'.

However, it is truly difficult to ignore a once-raised question. It tends to rankle, meet us in the disguise of morbid preoccupations, phobias, aches and pains, as well as in a distinct lack of motivation. The decision 'not to think about death' has serious consequences. To mention a few:

— It is always tiring to try and pretend that we do not have feelings about something, especially when these are feelings of fear or anger.

— Such feelings do not simply go away; they attach themselves to the nearest available experience, become displaced onto other situations or people. This is unlikely to be helpful either to them or to us.

— Ignoring our feelings about death may lead us to take our relationships for granted. We thereby deprive ourselves of a real appreciation of their importance and of a profound celebration of their value, of the full knowledge that all we ever really have, is this actual moment of togetherness.

— The realisation that we are truly alive and that we will surely die can lead to a profound sense of wonder, a deepened awareness of beauty. This in turn may lead to the desire to create, to make something which expresses our relationship with this awe-inspiring creation.

— When we forget about death we might end up postponing life, presuming there is always tomorrow. Tomorrow, which may never come. This can lead to disappointment and bitterness in our old and not so very old age.

— The denial of our thoughts and feelings about death may also lead to inertia or an overwhelming sense of greyness. Thereby we perversely embrace an early death whilst staying alive.

Since time immemorial people have realized that humankind pays a substantial price for not reflecting on issues of life and death from time to time. If we don't, we become curtailed and controlling. If we are prepared to face up to dying as well as living we become ready to explore, open to renewal and change.

Silence on death issues leaves us vulnerable to manipulation, as well as frightened and impoverished. True awareness of death generates the motivation to bring about change. Thus, not surprisingly, death-education and death/life awareness training are also political issues, primarily because consciousness of the circumstances of existence gives us the courage to bring about those changes, which help us to make our dream of life come true.

Therefore the wise old storytellers of yesteryear told the ancient tales about life and death, of adventure and misadventure. Stories which reconciled and those which generated more questions then they answered. Broadly speaking, such stories offered three kinds of explanations:

— *A causal explanation.* In these stories death has a clearly described, explicable cause. The beginning of death thereby becomes logical.

— *A motivational explanation.* In such tales the creator(s) and/or an opponent's motivation to bring death into the world is clarified. Frequently the motive behind the original deed is also explained.

— *A justifying explanation.* In such stories the rules of life are explored. Rules which have to be respected and which are ignored at one's peril. These stories can be said to offer an unquestionable justification. It had to be just so and no different.

Causality, motivation and justification are reassuring. We use these categories of knowing to explain our surrounding reality and to come to terms with the Great Unknown. Our longing for reasonable explanations - such as those provided by motive, justification and cause - springs amongst others from our hope that ultimately all can be connected with all. If such a pattern of connections were convincingly proven to exist, then 'chance' could be ruled out, and all would be for the best in the best of all possible worlds. Life would then demonstrate not only divine inspiration, but also divine guidance. When all is 'meant to be' our anxiety is contained. No longer do we have to face up to an unpredictable existence. Most of us will recognise this desire for such a well-ordered life where all has its place, as well as its seasons. Maybe this desire is uniquely and merely human. Maybe, however, it bears witness to a strongly felt attunement to the actual hymn of the universe.

The questions of life and death, their cause, purpose and presence are important. If life is a mystery, then death surely is a bewildering complication. Maybe we pursue the search for an answer in the hope that in finding an eternal cause of death we shall also find a cure for death, an everlasting remedy. Maybe we continue our enquiry because we perceive that questions about death lead invariably to questions about life. The true questions, such as:

— who are we

— why are we here

— how may we live in accordance with what we know.

The human quest for an answer to these questions has through the centuries generated profound encounters with despair and hope, love and bitterness, disbelief and faith. Encounters which have been recorded in art, literature, music and myth. As such they have yielded a rich harvest.

Fear, yearning, protest and depression are experiences we go through when bereaved. To a minor extent we live through such emotions when contemplating our own death, and in a major way when we face our actual death. The preparation for a time of grief undoubtedly deprives us of our penultimate certainties, which up to then we might have taken for granted. In this sense we become 'dis-illusioned'. However, our gain shall be that less is taken for granted: ourselves, others, life. We also develop a stronger bond with the world. The treasure thus gained is a deep respect for unfathomable life. Such respect and wonder are inexhaustible sources of nourishment. They also lead to the wish to protect and safeguard the ultimate mystery of creation. Our much polluted earth urgently needs our desire in this direction.

Not to educate ourselves and our children about our relationship with death means not educating ourselves and them about life. It is dangerous to do so, and not because of death - sooner or later we all will die - but because it profoundly affects the quality of our life, both before and after we have become bereaved. The best preparation for bereavement is death-education. The best preparation for life is to relate death to our ways and values of living.

References

1. Retold by the author. Contemporary source: Radin, P., (1945) *The Road of Life and Death: a Ritual Drama of the American Indians*, Bollingen Foundation, Pantheon Books, pp. 23-24.
2. Viorst, Judith, (1988) *Necessary Losses*, Simon & Schuster, p.305.

A grief without a pang, void, dark and drear,
A stifled, drowsy, unimpassioned grief,
Which finds no natural outlet, no relief,
In words, or sigh, or tear.

Samuel T. Coleridge

CHAPTER THREE

Some characteristics of the days between the actual death and the burial or cremation

Loss hurts. Talking about loss hurts even more. Immediately after the death there was nothing to say. All words failed. Our feelings were desperately raw, and we knew that something unexpected might happen the moment we opened our mouth to speak about the event. Our voice sounded hoarse, or we feared that we would laugh a peculiar, alien laugh. Our eyes moistened. We felt exposed in so many different ways. Our trust in life had been wounded. The person we loved had just died. They would be with us for a few more hours and days, then their body would be disposed of. We felt the cruel harshness of those words. The final journey to the crematorium, the cemetery or to the hospital dissecting room would soon be made. We were abandoned to mortal existence, expected to consent to continuing our days and nights without the partner, husband, wife, child or friend who mattered greatly to us. Would there ever be enough feelings to express what we were going through?

Immediately after the death there were innumerable arrangements that had to be made, thought about, negotiated even. Who needed to be told. Who invited to the funeral or cremation ceremony? What to say and above all 'what not to say'. How to reconcile the uttered or imagined wishes of the dead with the needs of the living.

Could we cope with meeting under these circumstances our son's first wife with the grandchildren whom we had not seen for years? Should we let her know what happened? Our husband or wife wanted her to be there. Why didn't they contact each other then, when there was time yet. What if she were to come to the funeral without an invitation?

Though our own concerns are likely to have been different, we recognise those deliberations. For we too have relatives and friends who nurture their grudges. Can the grave-side reconcile what the deathbed failed to achieve?

Thus our thoughts rambled and railed, moving from one thing to the next, from one decision to the next: which clothes to wear, which songs to sing, which silence to obey. Meanwhile people came to the door to offer their condolences or help. Some were relatives and friends whose presence we valued. Others came uninvited out of warmhearted concern, or 'because they felt they had to'. The most painful guests were those who sought our company out of misplaced curiosity. We might have been too tired to defend our right to privacy, too shocked to refuse an unwanted visitor. Anyhow it was impossible to predict whom we did or did not want to see, and we have never forgotten the sudden, blessed surge of emotions when someone we cared for stood on our doorstep. They came because they knew they had to be with us, and how very right they were.

Shortly after the death someone probably went to see the Registrar of Births, Deaths and Marriages. The municipal building was entered in bewildered confusion. Was this the door? We may well have encountered crowds with confetti, weddings with wellwishers and bridesmaids. These strangers will have seemed so very alien on this our 'death-announcement' day. How little we know about death, the causes of death. We handed the paper to the clerk. Was this death timely, tragic, a waste? Or did we experience relief, a sense of gratitude for a life and death well lived? The clerk asked us 'what relation'. We spoke and gave all the details that were asked for. As we reported we heard our own voice hesitate. Should we speak in the past or the present. Should we from now on only say about our 'dead' one: 'She was, she lived, she used to like'.

All questions answered satisfactorily, we received the Certificate. 'You give this to your undertaker'. Death had entered into our life and we, unwilling or relieved heroes bore its scars. We hoped with dignity and courage. Maybe we then made our way to the next port of call, the undertaker's shop, wishing that nobody would stop us in our track. Having done our grievous duty we recommenced the journey home. They may have asked us how it was, or maybe they did not dare ask. How could they have wanted

to know when the undertaker would call round to discuss further arrangements? If only the pain and the fear and the worries could be locked away.
We may well have succeeded in our game of 'Don't you worry about me'
amidst the bewildering turmoil of demands and decisions which had to be
made immediately. As long as the one we lost was above the ground the
urgency of 'doing what had to be done' took priority: which cards, which
coffin, which burial ground. We kept going, had a drink; maybe we ate just
a little. Unexpectedly, we found ourselves discussing politics or even holidays with a distant friend, asking our niece how things were at school. Not
feigning but feeling momentary interest. We watched and thought and acted
and sometimes we wept. 'What would become of us?' The chasm of time
closed in. Life crashed into this alien present, a trancelike time capsule. Our
only true companion was our still alien grief, and next to our grief were our
bewilderment and determination. It had to be a worthy farewell.

The time just after the death of someone we love and before their burial
or cremation can be clearly remembered by most of us. We recall our
journeys to the mortuary or the bedroom where the body was laid out. They
are etched in our mind. Years later, our feet know how to retrace our reluctant
steps. We were on full alert, trying to prevent the fall into forgetfulness.
Therefore the images endure, limpid and cold, or passionately alive with love
as well as pain.

When entering the mortuary we may have noticed the awe-inspiring
difference of smell and hushedness. The man at the door greeted us with
restrained professional courtesy. A name was mentioned. Then the walk
through endless-seeming corridors just a few yards long. The room was
found. How intensely we may have hated the background music and the
paintings on the wall, or felt our spirits lifted upon seeing the carefully
arranged small bouquet of fresh flowers. And we can still hear the hesitancy
in the undertaker's voice as he explained about make-up and folded hands.
'Is it all right this way?'

How we may have hoped against hope that the room in which to view
death would bear undeniable witness to the life lived and the life desired,
only to be faced with the neutrality of the communal vault. We possibly
wondered: 'Who will be our parent's or partner's neighbours tonight, when
the body is returned to the cold cell'. Did we dare ask? Dare to know what
would happen to the person we love. How we may have longed to take the
body home. To demand of each person who arrived that they greet both the

dead and the living. We so much needed to rehearse the good and the bad qualities of the one who died. To confirm the reality of death. For here in this no-man's land of the mortuary, life lingered all too hesitantly. Our longing for the sharpness of life meeting death may have helped us to make up our mind. The body had to return home before the funeral.

Either way, the decision was difficult. Chill death lying in our bedroom or front room, hurts. Chill death in the shared mortuary-room also hurts. Outside the vibrant flowers, inside us grief. We tried to see the purpose of it all through the eyes, the thoughts, the longings of the person we lost. Objects carrying hitherto undiscovered meanings in the unsuspected form of his cup, her toys, his poetry. The surprises were manifold. Some of them stung with a vengeance. Some were surprisingly comforting.

If the coffin stayed inside our house we had time to know our loved one beyond the moment of the actual death. Slowly we may have come to terms with the further dying. Though we might have been numbed by shock, our senses registered the continuing changes. If we dared look, we saw the differences. We smelled them too, undeniably so. Thus we noted death's slow progression. The steady advancement confirmed that the death was real; not just a bad dream, but above all a physical reality.

Sitting, waiting and waking, or simply visiting the mortuary, the same questions returned. Where have they gone? Did they go anywhere? Are they at peace?

These questions presented themselves with poignant urgency, especially if we were absent at the moment of dying and the death was sudden and violent. Then we so much wanted to know that our parent, partner or child was at peace at the moment of death. We wanted to see such acceptance in their hands, their face. For it would have hurt us even more to witness the grave evidence of pain and struggle, bitterness. Nurses and mortuary workers did their best to disguise suggestions to the contrary. Aiming to reassure us, who are left behind, that surrender was a real possibility. We too may have heard ourselves say: 'At least he didn't suffer much', or 'She really does look very peaceful.'

We may have listened to inane but vitally important stories by people who survived serious accidents, assuring us that at the moment of impact you just black out. Black out? Did they not even think of their partner, their child? What was the last thought on their mind? Was she feeling awfully lonely? Why weren't we there to accompany our loved one on this, the ultimate journey. Our self-accusation began.

Now they can never again hear how much we loved them. What was the last thing they said to us? What was the last thing we said to them? We searched for profound meaning in the final words exchanged. How little did we know that these words were for ever, never to be added to. 'Enjoy yourself, love', or 'We'll talk about the bathroom-paint tonight', or 'Mum, do think about that bike for my birthday', or 'I don't care what you do with yourself, just get out of my way.' And the next thing we heard was the doorbell.

Those wretched words, they resound again and again, for better - for worse. Did we dare share them with someone we trust? The moment they are uttered the words shall lose their potency, the power they hold over us. Thus we may have carried our secret, in shame or in glory, for years and years to come.

The times of encounter in death feel so much greater than the daily contact. This too may have bewildered us. How come life did not equal the intensity and clarity of feelings we now experience? Why could we not have realised earlier how much the loved one mattered, when he or she was still alive? Then we failed to understand so much. Now we know with unwavering certainty. Why this further cruelty?

As if this was not enough, we also discovered, during those complex in-between days, the strength of our faith, as well as the strength of our disbelief. Maybe we were surprised at the realisation that we believed beyond doubt that the dead one was called away by God to an eternal presence, that our beloved now enjoyed some kind of heavenly peace. Peace we prayed for and anticipated for ourselves. If this happened to us, then we may have found great comfort in the belief or even the knowledge that the current parting was to be no more than a temporary separation, that a re-encounter will be possible, either when we ourselves return to this earth in the company of our cohort of re-incarnate beings, or at a foreseen time of resurrection.

With Isaac Watts we might then say:

> There is a land of pure delight
> Where saints immortal reign;
> Infinite day excludes the night,
> And pleasures banish pain.

There everlasting spring abides,
And never withering flowers;
Death, like a narrow sea, divides
This heavenly land from ours.[1]

If we did indeed believe that our beloved travelled to such a land, our religious knowledge is comforting, for we could nearly be envious of such a state of bliss, given that we have been left to dwell in the earthly world of tears and thankfulness.

But what if we discovered that in this hour of trouble our faith collapsed? A mere whisp of a cloud, which evaporated before our grief? No hope. Nothing to support us. What if all we relied on was scattered by the overwhelming experience of tragic, early death? Bad things do happen to good people. How then to explain the tragedy which entered into our life? Without a faith to support us, how to face inexorable meaninglessness, where to find consolation, the courage to continue? Then we may have felt that we were stuck fast in deep mire without ground anywhere. Such sorrow made us grow old. We dreaded the days; we dreaded the nights, and did not realise that there is an ebb and flow of mourning too. Death created havoc and our bitterness invited surrender. The rage with life tore us apart. Long were the dark avenues. How ashamed we may have felt of our hopelessness, outrage and despair. Ashamed that our good old 'philosophy of life' which we had enthusiastically talked about, was as nothing in the face of the disaster which confronted us. We stood empty handed before our suffering. Such shame touched us to the core. If only we could have admitted how empty and helpless we felt. More often then not we didn't, pretending that old convictions held out amidst this storm. While we knew we went bankrupt, we dared not declare our bankruptcy. It would be one failure too many.

Then the undertaker, rabbi, minister or imam asked us if there was anything we would like to say or to have said during the final ceremony. Words of gratitude for the life of the dead beloved which we wished to speak or hear during the ceremony in the crematorium, the church or meeting hall.

Our whirling mind knew not where to turn. Should we surrender all responsibility to comparative strangers? Maybe Uncle Tom or the children would say something or Mrs Johnson. Maybe they would do justice to the life that was lived. For we ourselves were torn asunder.

No one told us that grief felt so like fear. No one told us that numbness felt so like madness. At this point the doctor may well have been called, a mild tranquiliser or sleeping tablet suggested. We possibly failed to speak our knowledge that we were better off hurting. What would happen the day we had to stop using the tablets? Then all those who surrounded us with their care would have returned home again. Gone will then be the tide of compassion. Alone, and so very much later, we would then need to reconnect with the intensity of our wounds, but maybe a good night's sleep would help a lot, strengthen us now that we feel weak, crazy and inadequate.

We knew that we wanted to say goodbye respectfully. Not to make a show ourselves. To allow everyone's attention to be directed towards the one who died. These in-between days, while the body is still above the ground, are unbelievably complex. Colin Murray Parkes says that

> Goodness is not gone from the world because one good person has died. Meaning has not gone from life because one who meant so much is no longer present. The loss of one trusted person need not undermine trust in all those who remain.'[3]

The trouble was that, for a while, that was just what it felt like. The other trouble was, that during the in-between days we knew that we had the unique opportunity to honour the life of our loved-one by arranging an appropriate funeral or cremation service within or beyond the framework of religion. A lot was demanded of us and we wanted to get it right.

In all likelihood we received advice from the funeral director, friends who had gone through this before and maybe religious leaders. There were also the customs and mores of our community at large, with which we may or may not have been be familiar. Should curtains be drawn and mirrors covered? Did we need to soften the sound of the doorbell? Serve alcoholic spirits, or serve no drinks at all? We may well have wondered what was expected of us. Must there be flowers or no flowers, an advertisement or no advertisement. Should we dress in black for the occasion, in new clothes or in our best-beloved outfit. The confusion was at times sad, at times hilarious.

Death is an experience which has happened to others and it is likely to happen again. How come then, that we are oftentimes caught so utterly unaware? If only we had been better prepared. If only we had discussed life and death with the person who died. We probably realised, even amidst our sorrow, that everything would have been a great deal easier if we had known their wishes and our own desires. If only we had had the courage to face the undeniable reality that sooner or later each one of us will die.

'If only' ... And the burial or cremation still had to take place. Many years later, a woman recalled how she felt on the morning of her husband's funeral.

It was strange, waking up and realising that it was the day of the final journey. It felt like our wedding, or going on a holiday. I was angry that I had to go through this without him. If I had been given a choice, I wouldn't have gone to his funeral that day. Not the next day either. Never in fact.

I felt that I was going crazy. Very confused, and yet also very clear. I wanted it all over and done with. I was so tired. There would be people to meet. Some I had not seen for years. Why did I have to meet them again? Why couldn't they have made an effort before then? I remember wondering who would not turn up. As far as I knew, everyone who needed to know was sent a card. Some might have seen the advertisements. The undertaker had gone through the lists with me. Everyone who had a place in the 'funeral procession' had been asked to be there on time. 'Don't be late for the funeral', I thought. I remember, that the idea that you might be late for a funeral, made me smile. My legs felt very heavy. I never knew they could feel that heavy. I worried that they would give out on me. I looked in the mirror, and saw that I looked absolutely awful.'[3]

During the day of the funeral or cremation, more than during any other day since the actual death, we can feel that we are like actors on the stage of our very own tragedy. A show, which has been created for everyone's sake, in which we are the main performers. During the last few days a ritual has been assembled which now reaches its culmination. The arrangements have been made. Flowers were ordered or not ordered. Candles may or may not be lit. Music is or is not played. Coffee served or not served.

But whatever does or does not happen, one thing is certain, the ritual of parting will take place. It can only be prevented by a court of law. And even then we will still have to go through it sooner or later. The dead and the living must be separated. Made to go to different places. Turn their backs on one another. The whole event, however brief, has been designed to ensure that this occurs. We know as much and though we may not want it to be like this, we also realise that it offers us a way forward. The only way forward.

The movements of the funeral procession were carefully orchestrated. Time was precisely allocated. There was little room for spontaneity or surprise. The very predictability of the ritual saw us through. It had a momentum of its own. We had no choice and maybe that was just as well.

That day we looked at the place where we live with new, grief-wisened eyes. Knowing that later, when we returned home again, further tasks awaited us. The child, partner, parent would then be truly gone. Yet the house would continue to bear witness to their presence in a thousand and one ways. Clothes and toys, books and tools are obvious. But there were also the walls she carefully redecorated last spring, the darned socks, a note casually left in a book. Numerous silent witnesses to a life lived. We knew that we would have to come to terms with this initially pervasive presence. To change, or not to change, would be our question. Some of this we realized as we got ready to leave the house for the last time, the old way.

As we took our place in the car which took us to the church or meeting-hall, or as we walked there, our thoughts did not know what to do with themselves. In whirlwind fashion, yet amidst strange stillness, we relived scenes from yesterday and yesteryear, from here, there and everywhere. The thread which connected this miscellany of images? The life we lived together; the life we shared. That day we made our way separately to the place where our roads were made to part. We followed the car with the dead body. We followed the people who carried the coffin. Maybe we even carried the coffin ourselves. Through our presence we appeared to be consenting to this final reality. But how reluctantly these steps were made and yet how unavoidable they were. No wonder our legs had felt heavy that morning. We wanted to go home, but there too all had changed. We wanted to go back, but there was no road back. Ahead we saw the church, the burial-ground, the crematorium. Others had gathered whom we did or did not recognise. We sensed the air, the trees, the presence or absence of bird-song. If only there was somewhere else to go.

The Ainu-people in Northern Japan used to speak directly to the dead person, saying 'You are a god now, and without hankering after this world, you are to go now to the world of the gods, where your ancestors abide. They will thank you for the presents that you bring. And now go on quickly! Do not pause to look back.'[4]

We too were confronted with the need to find the 'right' words to be spoken or sung during the funeral ceremony. Write our own text, or shall we rely on the ancient words spoken at so many other grave-sides? We probably sensed that the ritual ending served an important function, that it had to offer us protection as well as guidance. That day we discovered whether the ritual we chose, was right. Right for the dead one whom we love, and right for us who had to bid our God-bide-with-ye. Was the farewell-service a poignant expression of everyone's loves and losses?

We had prepared ourselves for the various stages which the ritual led us through, the stages we needed to endure during the seemingly endless time of letting go. These are:

— the acknowledgment of the death
— the settling of outstanding issues
— the thanksgiving
— the actual farewell
— the blessing
— the parting of the ways

We must experience these stages so that the separation becomes real. We cannot easily skip a phase. We knew that we had to come to terms with the good, the bad and the ugly, become aware of forgiveness and gratitude, and the need to be granted permission to continue a separate existence. Sooner or later we too would long to hear words like those spoken in Terence Rattigan's play:

Ross   I will not insult you by trying to tell you that one day you will forget. I know as well as you that you will not. But, at least, in time you will not remember as fiercely as you do now - and I pray that that time may be soon.[5]

We probably dimly sensed that at some time in a strange and alien future we might reconnect with a full yet different life - a life which includes the experience of profound loss, and which nonetheless incorporates love and real attachment. The permission for such an occurrence forms an essential part of the burial or cremation ceremony. However, at this stage in our grief we may not have wished to hear it. We did not want to be reminded of the possibility of life without so much we loved and liked and wanted.

Somewhere we knew it all and endured the full reality: there was nothing we could say; there was nothing you could have said. The dead cannot be called back - that was what hurt us so. We could but hope that in our shared helplessness and our shared sense of uselessness, we did not turn away from one another. Not to have turned away, when our world would never be the same again, neither in its essence nor in its periphery; this much we learned.

Those were the days of the long parting. Presence - wordless, clumsy presence - was temporarily all that was required. Sorrow made us grow old. A life ended. We were not spared our grief. It is to be hoped that we were able to share it.

Once we arrived at the crematorium, church or meeting hall, we mixed and mingled with those who mourned a little, those who felt that they ought to be present, and those whose hearts were also wrenched with pain. Each had their place, each their task: to express grief, to receive condolences, to offer sympathy, to help with the coffee and cakes, or to speak on behalf of the Bridge-Club, the Union, the 'Save the Village Green Campaign' or the School-Choir.

— We have lost ...

— We shall miss ...

— We wish to express ...

— We hope ...

We, who mourned intensely and were close to the 'dear departed', will at times have been shocked to see how much he or she mattered to other people, people we never before met and probably never met again. How his immediate colleagues were obviously grief-stricken. How the members of the Gardening-club, about whom he spoke so fondly, did not seem to be that upset. How her students were hurting, hurting. We did not know that she meant that much to them.

We were bereft because we shared a life, an experience which now ended in a physical way. Our mourning was inspired by our time together and our time apart. We were familiar with the private as well as public faces. Their other sides were encountered by us, sometimes only too often. How we knew about the snide edge of his tongue, the cruel inability to keep a secret, her rigid self-righteousness, the long, bitter sulk which clouded the house for days on end. We listened to her desperate sobs. She who seemed so confident to the outside world. We held him in our arms when he cried about the childless marriage. We cradled the teenager whose despair about her mother's drinking led to a torment of pained understanding and hatred. We also cherished memories of quiet contentment, of profound pleasure with small attentions, the giggles, the tears and laughter. We knew so very much.

How to encapsulate it all? How to do justice to the richness of the lived experience?

As we stood by the graveside or sat in the crematorium, images of this shared life passed our horizon. Tributes were voiced. The trials and tribulations were at best noted. Yet we knew that our loved one wasn't all good. Not all bad either. We probably felt relieved when the rich kaleidoscope of life and actions was allowed to be. Their life too was for better and for worse.

Death, when it is the timely culmination of a full life, is an event which also arouses gratitude, but when the death feels sudden and much too soon, it is so very difficult to accept. Then we are left with the accusing question: 'Why did it have to be this way?' And where to find an answer to this question?

At the end of the ceremony we returned home. The house seemed invariably alien and empty. How could it ever be warm again, a home again? We were abandoned to our grief. We may have tried hard to look after the house, to tend the fire, cook the meals and weed the garden. Going through the gestures of ordinary day-to-day life, but when did we contribute to life again for life's sake and not for death's sake? It all took time. Possibly more than we had anticipated, or others expected of us. We knew that we had to experience and express the emotions and reactions to our loss. We sensed, though dimly, that sooner or later we had to allow our deep attachment to the one who died to change and to let go of the sorrow which bore witness to our bond. Far, far away we also knew that at some point we would make another commitment to life, to a life which includes death. All this we sensed, vaguely, confusedly. But at that stage, we drew the curtains and went to bed, exhausted with meetings and sorrow and the numerous things which had be done. Frightened of all we lost and equally frightened of all that remained. We reached out for comfort and may have found some, or none.

References

1. Joyce, P. (1984), *A Guide to Abney Park Cemetery*, L.B.H., p. 57.
2. Parkes, C.M., in: Whitaker, A., Ed., *All in the End is Harvest*, Darton, Longman and Todd, p. 8.
3. Case-notes, 1980.
4. Campbell, J., (1973), Primitive Mythology, Souvenir Press, p. 343.
5. Rattigan, T., in: Whitaker, A., *op. cit.*, p. 22.

Part II

A Tracery of Connections Through Mourning and Myth

Come! Come! The bells do cry.
I am sick, I must die.
Lord, have mercy on us!

Thomas Nashe

CHAPTER FOUR

How come we all must die?

It is hard to imagine that after all we have done and omitted to do, we shall simply vanish from this world, disappear without an everlasting trace. In less than two hundred years it shall be as if we never existed. We, footprints in the sand, ordinary, mortal people, who should not have tried to compare themselves with an eternal god or gods. Yet, if we are able to grasp the concept of infinity, why should infinite existence be beyond our grasp? Stories and tales bear witness to our engagement with this dilemma.

In many of these stories there is, however, more at stake than immortality. In some tales we discern the disquieting sense that life and death are irreconcilable. Life is so very much *something*, a source which runs through us: changing our cells, empowering our heartbeat, stimulating our breath. Death is so very much *nothing*, a nothing of a very specific kind. Whereas life equals presence, death equals absence, irrevocable absence. Thus we might be tempted to conclude that life or presence, and death or absence, are mutually exclusive processes, processes which do not belong together. This apparent opposition, when combined with the sequentiality of life and death, nourishes our wish to create an explanation whereby life and death are linked together.

Death's impact upon our life compels us to try to understand its presence and function. Most of us feel that we were *not* there when we received the gift of life. Equally we realise that we shall be there when death knocks at our door. If our emergence into this world was a surprise, our death is a predictable occurrence. A relationship between these two events, our beginning and our end, must be found. Therefore stories which explain death's appearance and function were created and shared.

The Bushmen of the Kalahari desert tell the following tale.

> It happened in the days of the people of the early race. Moon had noticed how frightened the people were of dying. Moon therefore called the animal who could run faster than any other animal. This was Hare.

> Moon told Hare to run to earth and to tell the terrified people that they need not be afraid of death and dying. Whenever they felt frightened of death they had only to look at Moon. Then they would know that, like Moon, they too would in dying be renewed again.

> Before he had grasped what he had to tell the early people, Hare was on his way. When he came to the early people's dwelling place, he said, 'When you look at Moon you see that in dying Moon is made anew. But when you die, you will not be made anew.' The early people continued to be terrified of dying and it was not long before Moon discovered that Hare had given them the wrong message. Moon was very angry and hit Hare on the lip.

> To this day, Hare has a split lip, but that was not the only punishment Hare received. Since that time Hare has not been given a home of his own. He has to sleep in the open, where the wind blows and the sun shines.[1]

Hare's inability to wait, as well as his blindness to the importance of the message to mankind, led to death's dominion. As a punishment Hare's lip was split. He was reduced to living in the wind. This may not be the great punishment it at first seems for the Bushman have a relationship of great intimacy and reciprocity with the wind. To them, the wind is the first urge of life, a primordial intimation of the spirit. Their breath is the wind. The Bushman says that 'when his breath leaves him and he dies, it goes to join the wind without, to join in the process of making clouds for new rain to fall.'[2] To become part of the wind is equated with a return to the mysterious process of renewal. As a result of Hare's inadequacy all of us live in close proximity to the wind's eternal calling.

In the imagination of the Bushman the moon itself is also a symbol of revival. It represents intuition and gentle hope, especially because it carries light through the darkness of night. This darkness is so great that it envelops even the moon from time to time. Utter darkness is frightening. Then it may feel as if we have been forgotten, that our night journey is full of unfriendliness. When all is dark and our experience fails us, when neither consciousness nor reason provide support, then the knowledge of the moon's return may see us through, reminding us of the possibility of renewal beyond the darkest hour of the soul.

The Moon in the Bushman story wished to share the experience of physical resurrection with the people of the early days, people who were terrified of death. However, once the original message had been wrongly conveyed, the situation could not be changed. What is done cannot be undone, not even by Moon itself. This lesson, too, some of us are reluctant to learn.

In the Bushman story Hare is given true responsibility to carry out a vital task. Moon depends on Hare to undertake the work with care. When Hare fails, Moon cannot intervene. As such the Bushman's Moon endures the very human experience of being unable to protect the people we love against the terror of death, even though the story also tells us about the way in which we may achieve 'earth-bound' renewal. The tale then speaks about another kind of existence, a life close to 'Ruach', the eternal spirit, a life within the embrace of the wind, the breath of eternal life.

The Eternal Ones are, however, not always as generous as the Bushmen's Moon. This is exemplified in a story, told by the Ngala people of Zaire.

> One day a man called Nkengo saw that people die in swarms. He is determined to try and gain eternal life for everyone. He calls out to the Cloudpeople, who haul him up. First he has to wait a day and a night. Then they say to him: 'You have come here to receive everlasting life and escape from death. You cannot make your request for seven days, and in the meantime you must not go to sleep.' He manages to stay awake for six days but on the seventh he falls asleep. Then the Cloudpeople drive him away angrily, saying: 'You shall not receive everlasting life, for every day there shall be death among you.' Nkengo's friends laugh at him for having tried to gain eternal life.[3]

Ridicule has been the fate of many people who attempt to bring about fundamental change. The dreamers in our midst rarely have an easy time - not with the pursuit of their vision and not with the voices which scorn their fragile but determined attempts to make their dream of life come true. Like the Bhudda, Nkengo sees the prevailing human condition. He is determined to stop the insect-like, blind death 'in swarms'. He tries. He fails and is made to look foolish. Black Elk, the wise Elder of the Oglala Sioux, told us that some people receive a vision when they are very young. When they have grown up, they need to withdraw and 'lament', so that they may better understand their childhood vision. Nkengo experiences the ancient call to rescue humankind, in this case from death. He realises that the gift of immortality can only be granted by the great spirits of the sky, the Cloud-people.

His journey to the Cloudpeople is a familiar one. In all times and places people pray to the god of a thousand names to be lifted to the 'sky-world' for inspiration, guidance and wakefulness. Nnengo knows where to go. He knows whom to ask, and he is prepared to undertake the journey. Thus he ventures into heaven and waits. When the task is set, he does not withdraw. He undertakes the test of wakefulness, but his strength fails him; staying awake for seven days and seven nights was not possible. To stay fully awake for even five minutes might be difficult for most of us.

The Buddhist teacher Ajahn Chah describes how the Buddha encouraged his monks by stating that those who practice diligently will surely be enlightened in seven days, or if not in seven days, then in seven months or seven years. A young American monk hears this and asks if it is still true. Ajahn Chah promises that if the monk is continuously mindful without a break for seven days, he will be enlightened. 'Excitedly the young monk started his seven days, only to be lost in forgetfulness ten minutes later. Coming back to himself, he again started his seven days, only to become lost once more in mindless thought. Again and again he began, and again and again he lost his continuity of mindfulness.'[4]

A week later he was not enlightened, but he knew a great deal more about himself. Some gain. And what is reaped when we arrive at mindfulness? 'A quality of mind which notices what is happening in the present moment, with no clinging, aversion, or delusion.'[5] We gain the eternal present, without either past or future - an immortality of kinds.

Nnengo's story is the story of the unsuccessful hero or heroine who returns home seemingly empty handed. Yet it is also the tale of any traveller in pursuit of wisdom, the tale of those who embark upon the spiritual path. Onlookers might have thought that Nkengo had very little to show for his undertakings. To all intents and purposes he failed, with nothing much else to show for his journey than wisdom gained; but greater self-understanding is not worn on our sleeves. As a result of his journey Nnengo discovered the actual and not the imagined limits of his current capability. His journey to the Skyworld thus generated a fall into reality into more ways than one.

Upon his return Nnengo was predictably exposed to the laughter of those who had stayed at home, those who had not tried. Such taunting derision probably hurt. Yet we also know that our ability to endure the group's mockery of our pursuit of a vision leads to a life hallmarked by integrity.

Of course we may speculate whether the Ngala people attached special significance to the number seven. Did they too know about seven-headed dragons, or the seven steps of the Eternal One which transcend time and space? Had they noticed the seven indestructible stars of the Great Bear, which are seen all year round, or the seven lunar divisions, which divide into six days, plus one quarter day? Of course they did, attaching their own secret and sacred meanings to these phenomena. They too knew that the ability to counteract sleep's oblivion is the ability to overcome darkness, darkness which is often equated with death. Like Christ's disciples in the garden of Gethsemane, Nkengo succumbed to sleep. Sleep which is like and yet so unlike, death.

Whereas the Cloudpeople in the Ngala tale are able to stay awake for more than the required seven days and nights, the Kumis in Eastern India accept, albeit hesitantly, that sleep interferes in heaven as well as on earth. They tell us how:

> God's patient work to make the world with trees and creeping things and people is destroyed every night by a mighty snake. God was at his wit's end. He had to sleep, for he would be no good if he didn't. Then, one morning he got up early to make a fierce dog. That night, when the snake came, the dog barked and frightened the snake away. To this day the dogs will howl when someone is dying. But the Kumis have had to accept that God seems to sleep heavily nowadays, or maybe the snake is less afraid of the dog. For people die in spite of its protection. If God didn't have to sleep, there would be neither sickness nor death, but then God wouldn't be able to do much good during the day either.'[6]

In this tale the reconciliation to life and death is informed by a profound recognition of the balance between opposites. Creation and destruction, composition and decomposition belong together for ever and ever more. A similar, though diluted concept of the eternal dance of opposites can be found in Hesiod's Theogony. His poetry evokes the ancient Greek concept of Virginal Night giving birth. Through this, birth-giving finality is generated. The poet says:

Night bore also hateful Destiny, and black Fate and Death.
She bore Sleep likewise,
she bore the tribe of dreams,
these did the goddess,
gloomy night,
born after union with none.[7]

To this day we experience death, sleep, dreams, destiny and fate as siblings.
The progeny of disillusion and our profound sense of regret at not being able
to live in a state of eternal bliss, where we never need awaken, 'and waking
say Alas!' There dwells within us a stubborn longing for a state of everlasting
bliss, which we believe to have existed and which came to a calamitous end.
This universal longing for paradise contributes to the development of the
numerous myths which attribute the appearance of death to an original
wrong-doer. Hare commits this fateful deed in the Bushmen story. May-imba
the honeybird carries the blame in a Kaonde tale. They recount how:

The creator gave the honeybird, May-imba, three calabashes which he
had to take to the first two human beings without opening. May-imba
was then to tell the human couple that they were allowed to open the
two calabashes, which contained seed. The third calabash had to stay
closed until Leza, the creator, came and told them what to do with it.
When taking the calabashes to the first people May-imba became very
curious. After some time, he was so curious, he had to do something.
He opened all three calabashes. Inside the first two he saw seeds of all
kinds. He had a good look at the seeds, then he sealed the calabashes
again. When he opened the third calabash suddenly all kinds of horrible
things, such as death and disease, all kinds of beasts of prey and
dangerous reptiles, came out. Try as he might, May-imba could not
catch hold of them. Then Leza came to earth. He and May-imba looked
everywhere for the beasts and reptiles. Even though they did find the
lion in its lair and the snake in its hole, they were unable really to catch
them again. Leza then said to May-imba: 'You have broken your word
and you have made this happen.' The bird was petrified and flew into
the forest. It no longer lived amongst the people. Then Leza went to see
the first human beings. He told them what had happened. He spoke of
May-imba's disobedience and how death and disease, and the dangers
of the wild beasts and reptiles, had now come onto the world. May-imba
had brought them much trouble indeed. Leza also said that he had told
May-imba not to open the third calabash, until he himself had come to

visit the people. There was nothing Leza could now do about this, for these things had run away and could no longer be captured. This is why the first human beings had to build themselves huts and shelters, so that they might live in safety.'[8]

The Honey-bird's rejection of the God-given injunction is inspired by his desire to act upon his curiosity. Without the urgency of this longing neither change nor progress would be possible. Many Europeans are familiar with this unwillingness and the actual inability to obey such a limit-setting injunction through the biblical story of Adam and Eve, the biblical first couple who act upon the wonderful and dangerous wish to do what is forbidden. In Genesis it is written that:

> The Lord God took the man and put him in the Garden of Eden to till it and keep it. And the lord God commanded the man, saying, 'You may freely eat of every tree of the garden; but of the tree of the knowledge of good and evil you shall not eat, for in the day that you eat of it you shall die.'[9]

If we wish to broaden our experience and move the frontiers of the known, we have to challenge boundaries and surmount constraining limits. In many stories the punishment for such audacity is death - death of life as it was known.

This is a prudent warning, for we are probably familiar with the experience that our enacted curiosity frequently leads to irrevocable change. How many of us have read letters which were not meant for our eyes only to discover that our peace of mind is profoundly disturbed after we have absorbed their contents? How many have gone against the pleas and demands of parents or partners in pursuing a course of action which we felt we had to follow, knowing in our heart of hearts we had no choice? 'To thine own Self be True', but at substantial cost. Yet a cost which cannot be avoided, the imagined choice being no more than an illusion. For we also intuitively know that we tend to lose what we desperately try to preserve. When the choice is between a living death, or the possibility of life by dying to the old ways, which choice would you make?

Most myths and tales suggest that only the banishment from paradise, the fall from grace and the pain of the removal of protection lead us to a full acceptance of responsibility for the life which is ours to live. These same myths and tales frequently also reflect our protest against this reality. We have always wanted it both ways. We want bliss to continue, never to grow up, never to grow old and have to die. We wanted to stay in paradise, but we also wanted to explore beyond its borders without the return-route being closed off by angels with flaming swords. We must be free to explore, to discover this 'forbidden' unknown, to push against limits, and thereby to accept limits. Of course we do not want the unbearable burden of immortality, but we would like to have had a choice. We did. We did? It is all very complex and therefore someone, somewhere must have made a serious mistake.

Thus we can hear how the Ashanti people ask themselves why the early people had to be so stupid that they eagerly accepted the gift of death from goats. If they had realized what they were letting themselves in for they might have waited for the sheep's present which was the gift of eternal life. When accepting the goats' present, the early people joyfully accepted the gift of death. If only they had known.[10]

Less common are the stories where humankind knowingly and courageously elects to die. Stories in which death is chosen in order to make the sun move, to obtain fire from heaven, or to ensure that life may continue. On the Island of Madagascar the first human couple had a painful choice to make. This happened many, many moons ago.

> In the early days the first human couple lived in heaven. One day God spoke to them and said: 'What kind of a death do you want, the kind of death the moon has or the death of the banana.' The couple did not have a clue and were somewhat panic-struck at having to make a decision. God therefore explained to them what the difference between the two kinds of death was. The banana puts forth shoots. Shoots which eventually take its place, whilst the moon renews herself. The couple pondered their choice for a long time. Then they made up their mind. They thought that if they had chosen to remain childless, that then they would have avoided death, but they would also have been rather lonely. There would not be anybody to work with and to care for. They therefore asked God for the death of the banana. Their wish was granted and since that time people do not live on this earth for a very long time.[11]

Death and children are also interconnected in the following Melanesian tale.

> At first men never died, but when they advanced in life they cast their skins like snakes and crabs, and came out with youth renewed. After a time a woman growing old went to a stream to change her skin. She threw off her old skin in the water, and observed that as it floated down

it caught against a stick. Then she went home, where she had left her child. The child, however, refused to recognize her, crying that its mother was an old woman not like this young stranger; and to pacify the child she went after her cast integument and put it on. From that time mankind ceased to cast their skins and died.'[12]

We can hear the early suffering, imbued with early longing. The wish to do well by one's children. To ensure that life will continue. The urgent dream of the species cannot but live within the potency of the longing for survival. Equally, we hear the faint, far-distant groan at the ultimate sacrifice which is demanded of the old in order to protect the young. The painful weeping must be stopped, tenderness prevail.

Thus people everywhere have sighed and held in balance the shining advantages and dull disadvantages of our time-limited existence against those of life without end, hoping that thereby we may become reconciled to death's undeniable reality and consequently to life's finite possibilities.

Of course our cherished ideas about after-life profoundly influence the way we approach living, dying and death. If death is the threshold to a future existence, which is how death is often regarded in various religious traditions, then personal immortality is within our reach. When secure in such a faith we do not have to take refuge in comforting thoughts about survival in the minds of others. We may hope that though our life is obscure and of no obvious significance, yet sufficiently striking to adorn a tale or two, a degree of influence will be exercised on the lives of other people. We can then imagine that this influence, though diffuse and apparently lost, will be like a ripple on the water borne down the stream of time towards eternity. Thus we might exert a kind of homeopathic posthumous influence. When we are secure in our faith, there is no need to cling with stubborn tenacity to so fragile a hope. For then, afterlife is ours because we believe that we die only to be borne again. Life is ours for ever more, either through a gradual evolution of the soul through the ages, or because we shall waft gently to a heavenly, eternal life. We are like a phoenix rising. Then we shall gain by dying, and be victorious over death itself, not merely by temporarily outwitting death, but because we have been promoted to greater glory well beyond death's reach. During his long life Luther is said to have worn a golden ring with a Death head. The ring was inscribed with the triumphant words 'O Death, I shall be thy Death.'[13] His wearing of the ring suggests that Luther too faced the daily struggle with the undeniable reality that all of us must, sooner or later, die. His belief-system helped him to engage with the issues this awareness raised.

As we come to the end of this chapter we need to remind ourselves that the many stories about death's presence in the world convey humankind's protesting awareness that the circle of being demands that some enter and some leave. When the cause of death is old age and when the circle is replenished with young ones, who will in turn contribute to continuity, we rest at peace. Then we know beyond doubt that bananas do shoot forth from the tree and that likewise birth is generated through death. But when death comes to those who are young, or after a long life with many bitter struggles and traumas, we cannot but wonder 'why' and feel a surge of protest rise within us. A question which we shall explore in later chapters.

Of course we are also aware that in many non-European societies, and amongst the followers of the great world religions, death is neither absurd nor definitive but simply necessary. For death then holds the promise of resurrection. This resurrection is often a presentiment of rebirth into another mode of being, as Mircea Eliade suggests, a continuum as well as a continuity. From the perspective of many primitive societies, the anxiety associated with death in our modern world parallels the anguish of death which their members experienced during a rite of initiation. It was known that such anxiety is not a state in which one can remain. The dangerous journey through darkness must be completed, the crisis with death and life resolved.

Likewise we too are urged to move beyond our blind fear of death. We cannot afford to stay in a permanent state of barely conscious anxiety, which can best be described as 'afraid of death and therefore unloving of life'. For our troubles with living, and consequently our struggles with bereavement, will be then be greatly intensified.

Each of us has to integrate and thereby to transcend, the experience which an anonymous 14th Century poet expressed in the following words:

> 'Loerd, thou clepedest me
> And I not ne answered thee
> But wordes slow and sleepy:
> 'Thole yiet! Thole a little!'
> But 'yiet' and 'yiet' was endeless,
> And 'thole a little' a long way is.'[14]

Many of us hear such a calling to embark upon an adventure of the spirit, to engage seriously which the questions raised by life and death, and most of us try to respond. Oftentimes we are held back by fear, laziness, worries about ridicule and our inability to choose. These are the conditions which constrain our engagement with themes of death and life. But they tell an incomplete story. For we are also moved onwards by curiosity and the courage to make a commitment.

Once a year on Whitsunday in the small town of Echternach in Luxemburg, the people can be seen to move through the streets in a most peculiar fashion. They take two steps forward, then one backward, two forward, one backward. Our mysterious inner pilgrimage may well follow a similar route. Ardently at work, then falling asleep at the eleventh hour. Unbeknownst to ourselves, we trust that the still voice within awakens us before midnight calls.

References

1. Retold by the author. Contemporary source: Van der Post, L., (1962) *Patterns of Renewal*, Pendlehill Pamphlet.

2. Van der Post, L., ibid. p. 23.

3. Retold by the author. Contemporary source: Abrahamsson, K., (1951) *The Origin of Death*, Studies in African Mythology, Alquist & Wiksell.

4. Kornfield, J. and Breitner, P., (1967) *A Still Forest Pool*, Theosophical Publishing House, p.93.

5. Kornfield, J. and Breitner, P., ibid., p. 191.

6. Retold by the author. Contemporary source: Van Over, R., (1980) *Sunsongs*, Mentor Books, p. 303.

7. Van Over, R., ibid., p. 200.

8. Retold by the author. Contemporary source: Abrahamsson, H., *op. cit.*

9. Genesis, verse 15.

10. see: Feldmann, S., (ed.) (1975) *African Myths & Tales*, Dell Publishing Company, 1975, p. 108.

11. Retold by the author. Contemporary source: Feldmann, S. (ed.), *op. cit.*

12. Codrington, R. H., (1891) *The Melanesians*, Oxford, p. 265.

13. Parkes Weber, F., (1910) *Aspects of Death in Arts*, Fisher Unwin, p. 29.

15. Anonymous. Cited in Greene, B. and Gollancz, V., (1962) *God of a Hundred Names*, Hodder & Stoughton, p.37.

O how feeble is man's power
That if good fortune fall
Cannot add another hour,
Nor a lost hour recall

John Donne

CHAPTER FIVE

Why did it have to happen now?

A man in a train. Evening has long since fallen. Lights streak in the distance: streetlights, carlights. Along the rails, a village, a town. In some houses curtains have been drawn. Others allow the travelling stranger to partake of their life in fast-moving glance. People not meeting, yet touching one another's lives. The man leans towards the coolness of the window. He feels the slight draught. A thought wells up. They all, lifted onto this summit of one wave of time, subject to its urgent force, shaping the nascent form. He feels moved beyond words. Knows himself bonded to all who this night breathe the evening air. Again he wonders: 'one wave of time'. This very moment some will enter, some depart. The exit and the entrance change all that was and ever will be. How much longer will he live?

In front of her kitchen window in a small cottage on the Isle of Inishman, face to face with the unbridled ocean, stands Norah. The sky is throwing the light about, and she shares its awesome beauty. She holds quite still. Then she speaks in slow, halting English, unfamiliar to her Gaelic tongue.

Sometimes I look at the waves.
I see them come.
And I think to myself:
There it comes. Look. There it comes
and there it goes.
That's how it is.
There is a wave. Do you see?
There it comes and look,
there it goes.

Her eyes rest on her visitor. 'Bless you child', she says. 'Bless you, don't be frightened.' Again she turns towards the window, where the sky still dances with sun and cloud. 'That's what I think sometimes.' The faintest of sighs curls against the window. A quick movement of her arm. A shadow of sorrowed breath is wiped away. Some days later she talks of her young brother Mehan, buried in the seaside cemetery when he was only three years old. 'Our father was a different man since then.' And she tells of her husband who is also buried there. 'When death visits, you sing a different song,' she says, 'a different song.'

Though they are unlikely ever to meet, the man in the train and Norah of Inishman, they voice a kindred concern with the passage of time. Sooner or later life will reach its conclusion. Before its time or at the right time? It is written in the newspaper that in the Caucasus some people live to be one hundred and forty years old. But what difference would it make if we too were to reach such a venerable age? Would we simply pursue more experience for experience sake? Grow in wisdom and charity? Or might we merely become increasingly lonesome old people?

A woman, eighty-eight years of age, said: 'It makes no difference you know. You get old, and you still don't want to die. You're still frightened to die.' Her lips trembled. She looked painfully young and unprotected. Death's first meeting with her had taken place when her brother died during the Great War. Many more encounters followed. In her own way she had searched for life everlasting. A quest which had failed. She knew her failure and, realising it, gave up all hope that she might be able to face the life which is hers to live, let alone the death which is hers to die. Her words recalled John S. Dunne, who writes:

> The wisdom that knows that all things must pass, is a tempering of the human spirit. To temper, however, can mean to soften or it can mean to harden. It can mean to soften cast iron or hardened steel by reheating it at a lower temperature; it can mean to harden steel by heating it and cooling it in oil. The knowledge that all things must pass can soften or harden the human spirit. It can soften it, taking away its arrogance and its ignorance of human mortality; it can harden it, taking away its hope.[1]

The old lady's hope had expired a long time ago. She had seen no way forward through her fear. Though advanced in the seasons of life, she still struggled with disbelief and faith, hatred and love, despair and hope. Once there was someone to listen, she spoke. There was no real alternative.

When we count the years of our life, and ponder ' another spring, how many more to come', we do so to what purpose? Maybe we wonder what the total arithmetic will amount to. For we know that within less than one hundred years the ups and downs of our life shall be encapsulated in a small, horizontal line. Guarded on each side by four numbers, silent watchmen over our beginning and our end. All the deeds and misdeeds, the longing and regrets represented by this one short, black line. Time passed, measured by the trickle of the sand in the sand-glass or the jumping numbers of our digital clock. Years came and went. How many more, and above all, why one day no more?

An ancient Somali proverb says: 'The wood burns away, but the fire goes on forever.' We experience the temporal and can grasp the eternal, become witness to both wood and fire. Because we are able to relate to both past, present and future, we want to know why it had to be that someone we love, died, this very day and not another one. Why not the day before or some time later? We want to make sense of the hour of death, the time and date of the end of life. Not only because we resent its early arrival, but also because we know that we are capable of hastening death. Therefore we doubly wonder whether natural death occurs at a strictly appointed hour, at a time which is fixed, even before we were born.

Whereas an old Inuit woman, knowing that she is ready to die, may go on her last journey and rest to death in the snow, in our society the attempt to bring forward the day of our death is considered a crime against life. The debate surrounding voluntary euthanasia bears witness to the passions evoked by our reflection on the right to life and the right to death as related to the gift of life and the gift of death. The passions are great because some of us carry enshrined in our memory, the accusing voice of a painfully ill parent, who demanded the right to die, no longer understanding why their adult child would not and could not help to hasten death. Some heard the old woman in the hospital scream for days on end: 'Let me die. I want to die. I want to die.' Others witnessed the grief-stricken man in the wheelchair, eighty-seven years old. He had to bury his fourth son. When the minister offered him a handful of earth, he threw it into the grave and wept: 'Why couldn't I die? Why is it not me who lies there?' To these people death was an anxiously awaited grace.

But we have also endured the helpless rage and impotence at the death of a child, a young man, or a woman in the fullness of life. We call such deaths untimely, premature, a waste. And of course we must then ask: why now?

The answer could be very simple, if only we believed that beneath the great Ash Yggdrasil three Maidens mighty in wisdom dwelled: Urth who makes laws, Skuld who sets our fate, and Verthandi who allots the span of our life. Then we would know that not one more hour shall be ours, unless ordained by the triple goddess. Not one more hour.

This concept of gods or goddesses who spin, measure and cut our fate is found all over the world. In Ancient Greece they were known as Clotho, who spins the bright thread of life, Lachesis who measures and Atropos who wields the terrible shears. The cut threads falling like rain.

In a well known Greek myth, the great Goddess Demeter has lost her beloved child Persephone, who is also known as Core. She has searched every valley, field and mountain-crevice. Nowhere is her daughter to be found. In utter desperation she turns to the three goddesses of fate. In Garfield and Blishen's magical retelling of the tale, Demeter comes at last to the harsh stony mountain in whose deep cleft the three blind sisters crouch.

> The cut threads lay on the stony ground in a mad profusion and the goddess began to pull and pluck at them. Her great search had led her to this, the last place in the universe. But she found no severed strand that was bright enough to have been her daughter's life ... 'Core-Core!' wept mighty Demeter, 'My heart is emptied of everything save you! It is cold, my child; cold and dark as the Kingdom of the Dead. Core-Core!'[2]

Core-Persephone's hour of death had not come, nor would it. She is a Goddess, one of the Olympian immortals. When her mother at last finds her, the events of young Persephone's life are to be marked by eternal repetition, not by temporal uniqueness and limitation. We, ordinary mortals, cannot rely on Olympian immortality to see us through. When we or our loved ones are lost, possible death is an undeniable reality. We hear ourselves say with Siegfried Sassoon:

> Speak to him; rouse him; you may save him yet.
> He's young; he hated war; how should he die
> When cruel old campaigners win safe through ?
> But death replied: 'I choose him'. So he went,

And there was silence in the summer night;
Silence and safety; and the veils of sleep.
Then, far away, the thudding of the guns.[3]

Death's answer sounds triumphant: 'I choose him'. We respond with stunned silence, and the guns continue to thud. Our power fails us. Is there nothing we can do? Nothing to immobilize this arrogant being, who considers neither opposition, nor challenge? Our anger fuses with our despair and leads to blind action, at least in the imagination. Death itself must be rendered impotent. The following Nepalese tale is fueled by this universal urge to end death's might. Variations on its theme, can be heard by many a fireside in Scotland, Kenya, Columbia or Japan. It appears that humankind must protest, and protesting learn to surrender to the inevitable reality that to all things death will come.

Once there lived an old woodcutter. He was very poor and could scarcely make ends meet. One day he went into the forest and gathered a lot more wood than usual. As he bent down to lift the bundle onto his shoulders, he found that he was too frail to raise the heavy weight. He sighed deeply and cursing his age, said: 'If only I were dead.' Suddenly someone stood next to him. A strange voice asked: 'Did you call me?' The woodcutter felt a great fear. 'No, no, I didn't', he lied. Ignoring the old man's clumsy deception, Death made himself known. He explained that he had simply come, because he had been called. The woodcutter became less frightened and looked at Death. He found it very hard to believe that this was really Death himself. Seeing his doubt, Death pointed at an old woman who bathed in a nearby pond. The woman crumpled and died. This immediately brought the woodcutter to his senses. He at once remembered why he had wanted to die, and asked Death, now that he was here, if he could please give him a hand and lift the bundle of wood onto his shoulders. Death gladly obliged. The woodcutter was ready to hurry home, when the thought came to him, that he might ask how much longer he had to live. As he left, Death answered: 'Five years to a day'.

That night the woodcutter did not sleep very well. Strange thoughts haunted him. Early the next morning he returned to the forest. He looked for a big, big tree. And when he found it, he cut a single hole in the bottom of the tree. Then he started carving out the inside of the trunk. He carved for five whole years.

Then Death returned, just as he said he would. The old woodcutter promised to come along, but before he was ready to leave the world, he so much wanted Death to see what he had carved as a gift for posterity. Death climbed into the tree-trunk. Proudly the woodcutter showed him round. When Death was looking round in the top of the tree-trunk house, the woodcutter hastened down, crept outside, jammed a log into the hole and returned home.

Time passed. People and animals were giving birth, but Death came to no one. Hunger and illness resided everywhere, yet nobody died. Even the gods were alarmed. They approached Lord Shiva, the great destroyer who, donning the garb of a human being, came to earth. He went to visit the old woodcutter and asked him if he still wanted to go on living. The poor woodcutter had become even older and weaker, and was by now so ill that he could hardly leave his bed, let alone return to the forest where Death was still locked away in the tree house. The old woodcutter said that he was ready to die. Then the Lord Shiva helped the old man to get up and slowly they walked to the forest, where they released Death. Death was shaken by his ordeal in the tree, and he begged Lord Shiva to make him invisible, so that humans could no longer devise ways to stave him off. 'So be it', Lord Shiva said.

From that day onwards Death has been invisible to mankind, though he sees all of us. And the woodcutter, he died.'[4]

How we too might long to have the choice to lock death away inside the trunk of the tree of our life. Incarcerated, until the day we are willing to surrender to his might. In this benign tale the woodcutter endures no punishment for his attempt to do away with Death. The Greek Sysiphus who likewise attempted to remove Death's power by stealing the pen with which Death writes the names of the dead in a book, must to this very day push a heavy boulder towards the top of a hill. When the top is reached, the rock falls back, and the labour of Sysiphus begins all over again.

Once the woodcutter encountered Death his life was forever changed. He left the village and from that day onwards he worked only inside the tree. We do not know whether he tried to create his 'magnum opus', the greatest of all his works, for those who would come after him, or whether he designed the lockable space with the sole aim of immobilizing Death.

What we do know, though, is that the kind of mortal existence he chose for himself during the last five years of his life was far removed from the fellowship of man. He went into the dark forest, and dwelled alone. Thus he devoted his life to death; his work became an acknowledgment of the temporal character of human contributions. When the tree died, his life's work would die. Thereby the old woodcutter succumbed to the wonderland where death is not only a danger, but above all a lure. Unable to surmount his fascination with Death and dying, he paradoxically entombed himself. Our woodcutter failed to win back a life, a human life, an earthly life. Heidegger says, that 'death is a strange and unhomely thing that banishes us once and for all from everything in which we are at home'.[5]

Though we may be banished, we still have to find a way of returning to a simple human existence and to human relationships.The lure, dread and fascination of death, must be overcome. Sometimes the Creator-God herself tells us why this has to be, as in this Cochiti Indian tale;

> The early people had come into this world from the place of emergence, which is called Shipap. Then one of the children in their midst started to feel unwell. None of them knew what was the matter with him. They did not know what it was to be sick. They went to see a man (who later became chief of the curing society) and said to him: 'Maybe our Mother in Shipap can give us help. Go to her and ask if she can put a stop to this.' He did go to see her and she spoke to him, saying: 'The child has died. All people must die, for otherwise the world would get fuller and fuller, and none of you would have a place to live. After you have died you come back here. You return to Shipap to live with me. Continue your journey and when your people die, do not be troubled.' The man came back to his people. He spoke of all our Mother in Shipap had said. In those early days Indians of the Pueblos treated each other like brothers and sisters. They used their digging-stick to plant corn. They did this together, and the work did not tire them. They also dug small trenches to bring the water to their fields. The corn ripened in one day. They were different those early days. But when the early people came to Freijoles they left one another. Each pueblo went on their own journey.'[6]

Death entered the early people's world; until that time they had lived in harmony and ease. Once the Cochiti people became aware of death, they lost the familiar and the comfortable. Consequently, they separated and left each other.

Like all other people they had to learn that death has a place in life, a life which is ours to live. Our Mother in Shipap, the place of birth and life-after-death, advised the early people that they should not be troubled. For thus is the way of things. She said: 'When grieving, grieve and then let go. Return to life again.'

This is in itself a difficult task, and one which can be made all the more difficult when we believe that the death of our loved one has come about due to our own negligence, the failure of our love.

Such failure is the theme of one of old Peter's Russian tales. In this story a childless old couple is very unhappy. They watch as the children from the other huts play outside. All the time they watch, because they do not have a little one. When winter comes the old man says to the old woman:

> Let us go into the yard behind and make a little snow girl; and perhaps she will come alive, and be a little daughter to us.' They roll the snow so tenderly. Their little snow girl is very beautiful. They beg her to speak, they beg her to run. Then a miracle happens, the snowgirl begins to dance, and run and sing. She warns the old people that she'll gladly stay with them, unless they love her too little, for then she will melt away and return to the land in the sky.

> The old people are beyond themselves with gladness. The little Snow girl laughs and plays and brings great happiness into their life. One day the village children go into the forest. The little snow girl goes with them. She gets terribly lost. Darkness falls and she starts to cry, begging the animals of the forest to help her. They offer to take her home, but she is afraid of the old brown bear, and afraid of the grey wolf. At last the little red fox comes and she accepts his help, for he does not frighten her. Meanwhile the old man and the old woman lament bitterly, for they believe that their little daughter of the snow is lost. They are therefore overjoyed when she comes safely home. They thank the fox, and offer him a crust of bread as reward. But Fox asks for a nice, plump hen saying: 'After all your snow girl is worth a nice plump hen.' The old people grumble. A hen is a big gift and they try to fool the little red fox, even sending a fierce dog after him. As they do this, they hear the little snow girl, sing that because they love her even less than a chicken, she has to leave them and return to the land in the sky. Then the snow girl is gone.[7]

This old Russian tale encapsulates our most painful fears, namely that our selfishness, greed and crudeness have destroyed those dearest to us. That our thoughtlessness hastened their death and brought forward the end of their life. In short: that we are in some way or other responsible for their dying.

This gruesome sense of responsibility contributes to our question: 'Why did they have to die now?' The question helps us to face any self-accusation, which we might otherwise hide behind the frozen stillness of our guilt.

The 'why now' question also helps us to consider the loss of our past, as well as the loss of our future. Because our loved one died now, and not twenty years later, we shall never know them at a later age. They shall be for ever eighteen. We have lost the shared memory of our past. Our story becomes lodged only with us, the one who stayed behind. This is our sorrow. In addition we have lost the possible shared future. A future we had every right to expect. The years and experiences we anticipated. The plans we made. Never again shall we visit together our favourite bench on the hillside, and if we ever do find a seat on a terrace in the sun, drinking a coffee on San Marco square in Venice, the person we love shall not be there with us. But how we had hoped to be there together, imagining ourselves happy in Venice. Those dreams of future delights require their mourning too, and they are difficult to surrender. Why did the person we love, die now, and not so very much later. There is still so much we had wanted to experience with them.

We cannot but commence our search.

References

1. Dunne, J. S., (1973) *Time and Myth*, SCM Press, Ltd., London, p. 12.

2. Garfield, R. and Blishen, E., (1977) *The God Beneath the Sea*, Carousel Books, p. 112.

3. Sassoon, S., in: Allott, K. ed., *Penguin Book of Contemporary Verse*, Penguin Books, p. 89

4. Retold by the author. Contemporary source: Sharma, N., (1971) *Folktales of Nepal*, Sterling Publishers

5. in Dunne, S., *op. cit.*, p. 19.

6. Retold by the author. Contemporary source: Benedict, R., (1931) *Tales of the Cochiti Indians*, USGPO.

7. Retold by the author. Contemporary source: Ransome, A., (1916), *Old Peter's Russian Tales*, Nelson.

> Sad storms, whose tears are vain,
> Bare woods, whose branches strain,
> Deep caves and dreary main,
> Wail, for the world's wrong.
>
> *Percy Bysssche Shelley*

CHAPTER SIX

What did I do that it happened to me?

We are mortal. Sooner or later people we love, die. This much we know, and we know it only too well. As the seventeenth century poet says:

> The wind blows out, the bubble dies;
> The spring entombed in autumn lies;
> The dew dries up, the star is shot;
> The flight is past: and man forgot.[1]

We know that we are like a spark from the fire, a bit of straw or a bubble of water. Easily extinguished, returned to ashes, scattered into nothingness. So very much like, and yet also so utterly unlike.

When we are bereaved we experience the harsh contradictions within these metaphors. For weeks or months we feel severed from our roots. Beyond the reach of friends and family, we oftentimes carefully construct a facade of coping, whilst we quietly surrender to the creeping awareness, that really nothing much matters and may never matter again. We do what we did before the death occurred, but we do it automatically, nearly mechanically. What else can we do, now that all options seem foreclosed? Meanwhile, we probably entertain misguided ideas about courage: the courage not to express our pain, to control our tears, to live in private with our wounds. The poet Edward Thomas conveys how we may then feel:

> I have mislaid the key. I sniff the spray
> And think of nothing; I see and I hear nothing;
> yet seem, too, to be listening, lying in wait

> For what I should, yet never can, remember;
> No garden appears, no path, no hoar-green bush
> of Lad's love, or Old Man, no child beside,
> neither father nor mother, nor any playmate;
> Only an avenue, dark, nameless, without end.'[2]

We feel drained of the capabilities of love, while our unuttered sorrow dims our trust. Thus thoughts and feelings become of little worth. Beyond despair, we try to find the key to the place of return, only to discover that the entry is closed. There is nowhere else to go but forward. Ahead of us lies the dark avenue of the soul.

We may vaguely know that the world's tide continues to bear us along, but our consent is weak and full of fear. Our pain attacks not only the hand which comes to feed us, but also the only thought which might console, namely that this sorrow too will pass. We catch a fleeting glimpse of ourselves in the mirror. Our heart cringes for us alone. We have come to this? We can no longer understand it. Sick and helpless as children, wondering whether we shall ever get well again, we may at last cry: 'WHY ME?'

Amidst our sobs we may then hear others, who say that 'grief is the price we pay for love', reminding us that 'we must all be prepared to pay it. Why should this happen to me, and me, and me? And why not? God never promised you a rose garden. Why should you be exempted from the laws of chance or mischance? Life was never fair.'[3] Undoubtedly it never was, and undoubtedly we were never promised a rose garden, at least not on this earth, but we are nonetheless outraged and bewildered. We feel, rightly or wrongly, that the visitation of misfortune unfairly befell us. The felt sense of injustice demands that we discover our role in the eternal drama which became our personal tragedy. Why has this happened to us? Did we do anything wrong? Do we stand accused or guilty? Inform us of the accusations, the judgment and the punishment and we might be able to make amends ... 'If only! If only!' Until we are sick and so very tired from restless sleeplessness.

People of all times and places have uttered the question 'why me' when pain and sorrow entered their lives. We are no different. We do not presume to live outside time, destiny, history. We are able to anticipate, to clarify and above all to rectify. Therefore we must begin by presuming responsibility. Human life is experienced as generating from us and we know that death can be brought about by us. Are we therefore guilty of the death of our loved one? We cling to our prerogative to demand an explanation. Raising our voice we are answered by whom? Which voice responds to our calling to soothe our fears, our utter sense of abandonment?

Thus we begin our search for an answer. Assuming responsibility where none is ours to carry. Presuming possibilities where none exist. Driven by doubt and by the remote chance that we could have prevented the death. We feel so very powerless in the face of death and dying. Leave us the question 'why me' and we begin to feel better already. The implied assumptions are consoling. Paradoxically, the apprehension that we have been singled out for suffering helps us to find a way through, although the road is treacherous, for we go and arrive not, seek and regain not. When our bonds have been severed by death and we feel cleft asunder, we must protest. Unwind the bitter recrimination that we had to surrender the other to death. No longer willing to meet other people's gaze we avoid eye-contact and stare into empty space.

During the lonesome hours of night and day, we see again the life lived and the life we could merely dream. The possible drowns in the harshness of the actual. We view again. We hear again. As the poet Adrian Henry says:

> remembering
> lying in bed
> in the dark crying listening to my mother and father argue
> wind banging a shutter
> indoors somewhere
> dead eyes looking out from flyblown photographs
> empty mirrors reflecting the silence.'[4]

Out of the weariness, with expectations torn apart and beyond the bitter severance from all we hoped and needed, emerges the only protest worth remembering: 'why me'.

And so it has come to be that in Zimbabwe the following tale is told.

A long time ago there lived an old woman. She came from an ancient family. And because, Leza, the creator, is also called Leza, the besetting one, he pointed his hand at her and her people. Her mother and father died when she was only a child; then all the members of her family died. She married, had children and she said to herself: 'These ones, the ones I cradle in my lap, they shall live.' But Leza being the one who sits on one's back, he made her children die an early death. He also slew her children's children. In her old age, the woman who had lived through all this, looked forward to her own death. But she did not grow any older. She seemed to grow younger. Then a wild desire grew in her heart, as well as a blind determination. She was going to find Leza and ask what all this meant. Why should she grow younger when all around her died. What was the meaning of it all. She thought that Leza lived somewhere in the sky and she started building a ladder towards the sky made out of the best trees which she tied on top of one another. But the lower ones rotted as time passed by. She started again, but again they rotted, and she had to give up on finding Leza who-sits-on-your back by climbing towards heaven. Then she thought that maybe she could get there by going to the place where the sky and the earth meet each other. There had to be another way to meet Leza and to get an explanation. She began her wanderings. She kept going, inspired by her burning desire to ask him why he had afflicted her this way. She walked and walked. People would ask her where she was going and what the purpose of her journey might be. They asked her in what special way she had suffered. When she told them, they were surprised. Her life was no different from anyone else's. Nobody else could shake Leza off their back. Life is like this. She kept on travelling. She never did find Leza. Eventually she died. Her heart broke.[5]

How many of us recognise her journey? Identify with the sorrow over parents' deaths? The tenacious wish to rest secure in the frail knowledge that at least our children may live, and comfort us in our old age. Then to find that life has cut a sharp line through our calculations. Not our will is done. Our deliberations were in vain. Another kind of reckoning is presented. We find ourselves alone. We look around us and perceive togetherness where possibly none exists. Candles are lit in other people's homes. Our aching heart sees pleasure and ease in family-circles which may in reality be torn by strife. We feel unjustly treated, know that the sad events of our life are incommensurate with our goodwill, our prayers and our hard work. The hand we were dealt was unfair. Who expects that we would not protest?

When we believe that the world is created by a supreme being, who ordains all things, including human lives, then this god or these gods become the final court of appeal. They are the administrators of justice, the apportioners of suffering. To such Supreme Beings we direct our plea as well as our accusations. It is hard to suffer greatly and unfairly. It is equally hard to know where our freedom ends and the obedience commanded by the Gods begins. When we have done our best and attempted to live in accordance with divine and human laws, then why should we endure life's unjust treatment. After all, we tried to be good and obedient human beings. We expect a degree of reward for such goodness, not the punishment of misery.

Whether or not we direct our pleas to near or distant gods, we cannot avoid the examination of even the remotest possibility that we brought our troubles upon ourselves through thoughtless action or inaction. If we went wrong we must establish how and where. Our capacity for reparation demands the search; for if indeed the suffering was caused by our own omissions, mistakes or wrongful actions, we must know this. Then we can choose to make amends, by altering our habits and the way we go about things. Thus we enquire, looking for the cause of the troubles and trying to think of constructive changes, which would prevent the re-occurrence of trouble. To make recommendations for change which can actually be implemented, remedies for our felt helplessness.

Whenever great sorrow strikes us down, the urge to avert further collective or personal disaster is overwhelming. We put security-locks on our doors, protect our zebra-crossings and take daily exercise. Curtailing our actual possibilities within the narrow dictates of prudence and fear, until we reach the limit of preventative actions. Only to discover that we are still forced to reconcile ourselves to the undeniable reality that great trouble or great delight may meet us around every corner any time now.

Given this insecurity, it can be deeply comforting to believe that there is an Ultimate Being who decides which sickness or blessing shall be meted out, and who, equally, has the power to prevent this from happening. Some of us may sincerely believe that such are the ways of heaven and earth. A faith which entitles us to ask the Supreme Being, our God or Gods, the question: 'What have I done to you, that you afflict or bless me so.' The answer is received through oracles, during prayer or deep meditation, or through other forms of revelation. The insight thus gained then guides us further along our path through life. We may make a sacrifice, ask for forgiveness, nurture different attitudes, all with the multiple aims of averting further troubles, to make amends for past sins of omission or commission, and ultimately to surrender to the universal will.

Even if we are not secure in such a faith, we may still surreptitiously try to gain influence over life's uncontrollable events. We might say that we do not believe in God, but that we do believe that luck or good fortune exists; that these are dispensed by life itself, or by the great pattern of things. Many who profess to be agnostics or even atheists, have a soft spot for discussing rationally irrational superstitions, synchronicity and life-patterns. Stimulating conversations about the meaning of life contain frequent references to inexplicable coincidences and not quite accidental encounters. Life's meaning then becomes a vehicle through which to explore the road we wander or, more precisely, destiny.

It is hard to conceive of a universe in which we appeared randomly and equally difficult to entertain the thought that our birth might be an accidental event without particular purpose or meaning; that we simply happened to be born into a given set of circumstances. Most of us are driven by a longing for an original purpose, a sense of having been chosen. If we were selected to receive the dual gifts of life and destiny, we could probably conclude that what was meant to be 'is' meant to be. The concept of destiny could thus help us to accept the events of our life; especially if the author of the life-script is no longer consulted or influenced.

With Omar Khayyam we might then say:

> 'tis all a Chequer-board of Nights and Days
> Where Destiny with Men for Pieces plays:
> Hither and thither moves and mates, and slays.
> And one by one back in the Closet lays.'[7]

But before we are laid back in the Closet some of us want to understand a few of the rules of this particular game of chess. Assuming there are some. To unveil the gradualness of life as well as its sudden transitions, to explore the balance between blunders and prudence. At the end of this road some know their faith, others continue to wonder whether divinity does indeed govern our ends, while a few comment that we can we but bear with courage the consequences of destiny. Illuminating these themes the following tale came to be told in Ancient China.

A long time ago a man bought a beautiful, energetic bull. Shortly after he had a dream. In his dream he saw how wings emerged from the bull's shoulders. Then the bull soared into the sky. When the man awoke he felt that his dream foreshadowed misfortune, he felt that soon he would suffer the loss of his bull. He decided to take the bull to the nearest market. Eager to sell, he sold the animal for less than he had paid for it. Then he embarked on his journey home, with the money he had gained safely wrapped inside a scarf which he slung over his shoulder. Then his eye caught sight of a hawk eating a dead little rabbit. He approached them slowly. The hawk did not take flight. He took it in his hands and finding that the bird did not resist his grip, he decided to keep it. The man tied the bird to the scarf he was wearing and with the hawk thus perched on his shoulder, he continued his journey. He had only gone a little way when the hawk became restless and tried to spread its wings. The man tried to grip the bird, but with one mighty spread of its wings the bird took to the sky with the man's scarf still tied to its legs. Forever after, the man reminded people that we cannot avert the fate which awaits us.[7]

People have, since time immemorial, tried to find an explanation for life's events. We ponder and hope to arrive at our own truth of the crucial questions of life and death, knowing that we are alive and that we may die at any time, in any place. We also experience the fact that terrible things do happen, irrespective of the strength of our feelings or actions. This reality demands our attention. Of course it is true that some folk want their luck buttered, and eat their cake. And why not? Unless of course, a voice has whispered into our ears that the gods punish those who demand too much and who in vain search of greater gifts, disdain the ones which were presented. When tragedy has marked our life, we too may say:

> When sorrows come,
> They come not single spies,
> but in batallions.[8]

When exposed to the onslaught of frequent misfortune, our senses become terrified. Consequently, we may have adopted the attitude that industry is Fortune's right hand and frugality her left, clinging to our belief that the fealty life does pay the rightful kings. We may have clung to this attitude, even though we also learned through tough experience that neither frugality nor industry guarantee a joyous, healthy and prosperous existence. We, who may once have found comfort in Dante's assurance that when we follow our star 'thou canst not fail of glorious heaven' have found ourselves wondering where the hell he found the evidence for this conviction. Pondering that when we followed our star, we simply discovered that destiny was no more than the relentless logic of each day we lived.

Thus we construct philosophies and tell a few stories. To while away the time and to search for a way of making sense of all that has and has not happened to us. Therefore, please listen to this tale, it could be useful on our journey.

A long time ago, in a place not so very far from here yet no so very near, there lived a man. His life had not been a happy one. Much had gone amiss. He had suffered greatly. When he looked around he saw people who enjoyed greater health, prosperity and joyfulness than he did. Therefore he decided to go in search of God. He knew where to go. He set out on his journey.

He walked and he walked and he walked and he walked ...

Until he came to meet a very thin, starving wolf. The wolf asked where the man was going, and the man said: 'I'm going to find God. I've been down on my luck and I what to know why.'

The wolf said: 'So have I. I am very hungry and miserable. I too haven't had much luck. When you find God, can you ask him for me too?' 'Certainly', said the man, 'I shall ask him for you too.'

And he walked and he walked and he walked and he walked ...

Until he came to a very sad looking tree. All the branches were drooping. The leaves thin and withered. The tree asked where the man was going, and the man said: 'I'm going to find God. I've been down on my luck and I want to know why.'

The tree said: 'So have I. I'm listless and sad. I too haven't had much luck. Will you ask for me too?' 'Certainly', said the man, 'I shall ask him for you too.'

And he walked and he walked and he walked and he walked ...

Until he came to a half-ruined cottage. Out came a young woman. She had once been beautiful, but now she looked ragged and worn-out. The woman asked where the man was going, and again he said: 'I'm going to find God. I've been down on my luck and I want to know why.'

The woman said: 'So have I. I'm so very tired and I've grown old before my years. I too haven't had much luck. Will you ask him for me too?' 'For sure', said the man, 'I shall ask him for you too.'

And he walked and he walked and he walked and he walked ...

Until he came to the end of the world, where he found God. He said: 'I have come to see you because I have been down on my luck and I want to know why.'

'Well', said God, 'that is not right. For I know that your luck is out there waiting for you until you see it.' The man said: 'My luck is out there waiting for me until I see it? Is that really true? That is wonderful. My luck is out there waiting for until I see it!' He jumped for joy. Then he remembered about the woman, and the tree and the wolf, and having received God's answers for them too he went back to where he had come from.

First he came to the woman's cottage. She saw him from afar and walked towards him. She could see that he had heard good news. She asked and the man said: 'It's wonderful. God said my luck is out there waiting for me until I see it. I'm so excited.'

And the woman said: 'I'm really glad for you. That is good. And did you remember to ask about me?'

'Yes', said the man, 'God said you have been to lonely too long. When you meet a man, ask him to marry you. That will bring you luck.'

The woman looked at him, hesitated, then she said: 'Well, you're a man. Will you marry me?'

He turned away and said:' Oh no. God said, that my luck is out there waiting for me until I see it. I'm in a hurry, trying to find it. No, I can't marry you. I'm looking for my luck.'

She could hardly hear his last words as he was already on his way.

Then he came to the tree. The tree saw him from afar and strained to move the branches, so that he might stop and speak, for the tree could see that the man had heard good news.

The man saw the tree. He halted and said: 'It's so wonderful. God said my luck is out there waiting for me until I see it. I'm so excited.' And the tree said: 'I'm really glad for you. And did you ask about me?'

'Yes', said the man, 'God said that there is something stuck between your roots. A chest or a box or something. It needs to be dug up. That'll help both you and the digger. Then you'll feel a whole lot better and your luck will change.'

'Well', said the tree, 'maybe you could do the digging. That might help both of us.'

'Oh no', said the man. 'Oh no. I can't do that. I'm on my way to find my luck. It's out there waiting for me. I'm in a hurry to see it. Really I cannot stop to help you.'

The tree hardly heard those last words, as the man was running onwards as fast as he could in search of his luck.

Then he came to the wolf. The wolf was even more hungry then before. He saw that the man was very happy. The man saw the wolf, looking really miserable. He stopped and said to the wolf: 'It is wonderful. I found God and he said that my luck is out there waiting for me. I only have to see it. I'm so excited.'

And the wolf said: 'I'm really glad for you. Did you remember to ask about me?'

'Yes', said the man, 'I did. God said, you had to eat the first living being that came your way. That will bring you your luck.' The wolf jumped forward and ate the man.[9]

> This my story which I have told, if it is sweet, if it is not sweet, take some elsewhere, and let some come back to me.

How angry we may feel with all the characters in this tale: the man, God, the woman, the tree and the hungry wolf. We, who must enter similar places, face equal tiredness, emotional hunger and thin sorrow. We, who know that we too have to embark upon the demanding journey of protest, hoping to seek and find, whilst we risk not finding. Our lament may one day be heard in the early hours of the morning or during the still hours of the afternoon. As the pain of loss writhes within us, we may well stifle our moans, until we are at last able to object to the ways of the universe, knowing full well that ultimately we cannot but become reconciled to those ways. In spite of this knowing, or maybe even because of this knowing, we have to learn to lament again.

References

1. Henry King (Francis Beaumont) in: Schelling, F. E., (1903), *A Book of Elizabethan Lyrics*, Ginn & Company.
2. Thomas, E., in: Allott, K., (ed.) (1972) *The Penguin Book of Contemporary Verse*, Penguin Books, p. 62.
3. Parkes, C. M., in: Whitacker, A., (ed.) (1984), *All in the End is Harvest*, Darton Longman and Todd, p. x.
4. Henry, A., (1984) in: *Penguin Modern Poets, The Mersey Sound*, Penguin Books, p. 50.

5. Retold by the author. Contemporary Source: Parrinder, Geoffrey, (1967) *African Mythology*, Hamlyn

6. Khayyam, O., *Rubaiyat*, in the translation of Fitzgerald, E., Quatrain XLIX.

7. Retold by the author. Contemporary source: Moss, R., (1979) *Chinese Fairy Tales and Fantasies*, Pantheon Books.

8. Shakespeare, W., *Hamlet*, Act 4, Scene 5.

9. Oral tradition. Told amongst others by Pomme Clayton, Crick-Crack Club, London 1989.

Ah God! That it were possible
For one short hour to see
The souls we loved, that they might tell us
What and where they be.

Alfred, Lord Tennyson

CHAPTER SEVEN

In search of reparation

It is so very difficult to lose, to have someone we know intimately, taken away from us. No longer to be able to sit by the fire which our friend lit. To eat his bread, to listen to his favourite records. The phone will ring, but it will not be our daughter's voice to tell us that she'll be home late, again. We shall not even have the chance to feel the familiar irritation and disappointment. Death placed a full-stop behind it all, behind the laughter and the small-talk, behind the cups of tea and planned expeditions. The future is foreclosed. The past has truly ended. Our shock, numbness and disbelief mould with our self-reproach and resentment; why did it have to be this way? Our desperate search begins.

During the early stages of our grief we feel in a state of perpetual alarm and we are. Our body is adjusting to the change which has come into our life. Especially when the death was sudden and unexpected, the sense of cruel amputation leaves us feeling that the world went topsy-turvy, and we are moving through it like an inadequately functioning 'Heath-Robinson' invention. A human machine which has told the pituitary gland to produce and release extra hormones into the bloodstream (through CRF and ACTH). In turn these informed the adrenal cortex to generate and release yet more hormones. It all helps the animal within us to fight and to run. But who is there to fight with and whom can we run towards? Even our body feels a strange and alien abode. It, too, has betrayed us.

Restless are our nights and tough our days. Our heart is beating faster. Our blood pressure is raised. The pupils of our eye are dilated. We breathe more quickly and deeper. Our liver has given the okay for the greater release of blood sugar, and thus our muscles can avail themselves of large energy resources. We know we can lift mountains, but we feel wrecked. Everything within us is prepared for action. Everything within us makes digestion and excretion difficult. Whilst feeling empty beyond description, we probably do not feel like eating; our appetite is demolished. Unable to let go, we do not yet cry our helpless tears. That is to say: people call us courageous.

For days or weeks we may live in this peculiar, heightened state of arousal. We want to stop, cannot stop, and wonder when the alarm-bell will ever be switched off. We do not want to get used to this way of being. It is exhausting and feels dangerous. It is. We grow to realize that we are on the verge of a breakdown if the sense of alarm is not overcome. That it will result in actual bodily harm. We must do something, go somewhere, but where?

The only roads we know are the old roads. The only deeds which are engraved within us, are the once familiar deeds. We know that we must act, our body demands it. We long to be relieved of the intolerable tension. Stifling our sobs feels hazardous, but sobbing feels equally hazardous, lest we should become truly aware that the person we love and need has really died. Ancient knowledge tells us that if we want to survive, we too must do what humankind has invariably done, when all contact with the immediate family group was lost. We have to search and attempt to retrieve, respond to the urgent call of the species.

It might be helpful to remind ourselves that during the many lives of humankind, as well as during our own, individual life, we had to react with an immediate, strong and automatic act to the loss through absence of a person who cared for us. For their absence was placing us in peril. Especially when we were very young, our actual survival was at stake. Therefore everything possible had to be done, to try and re-establish contact.

The memories of those days have left their mark upon us. We may even remember how, at the end of one of those searches, when we were lucky enough to have found the beloved person alive, we did all we could to discourage them from ever going away again. We had to express our fear, our anger, our pain. Our behaviour probably evolved in this way, because it safeguards us, and ensures the survival of people who matter to each other, people who need to stay in close contact with their young ones and their kin, offering one another food, shelter and protection.

This impulse to search can be found in an old Akikuyu, African tale, called 'The girl who was sacrificed by her kin.'

In this story we are told how the sun was very hot, and no rain fell. This happened one year, than the second, than a third year. The people gathered and consulted their Medicine-man, who sought guidance. At last he said: 'There is a virgin girl here, who we must buy if we want the rain to fall. Her name is Wanjiru. Everybody must come back here the day after tomorrow, and every single adult and child must bring a goat, which will be used to buy the girl.' The people did just as they had been told. On the said day the girl Wanjiru was put in the centre of a circle of people. She began to sink into the earth. She called out: 'I am lost.' Then her parents cried out: 'We are lost.'

There were a lot of people in that place and as they heard her cries, they hurried near and pushed their goats towards the girl's parents. Meanwhile the girl kept sinking into the ground. The earth covered her up to her waist. She called and called: 'I am lost.' Then she added: 'The rain will fall'. The earth had come up to her neck, and the rain did fall. Great big raindrops fell. Her people immediately wanted to stop her sinking even further, but the onlookers just gave them more goats, so that they did not run towards her. Then the girl called out and said: 'I am finished.' Now and again someone from her family tried to rescue her, but they would get another goat, and they would not even get near her. Then Wanjiru called out: 'It is finished and my family made it happen.' Then she disappeared from view. The earth covered her completely and the rain poured down. It rained and rained, and everyone hurried back to their own villages.

Their was a young man, a warrior, who had really loved Wanjiru, and he wept, saying: 'Wanjiru is finished and her family made it happen.' So he took his spear and his war-shield, and he walked and walked by day and by night, until at last, it was the hour of dusk, he arrived at the place where the girl he loved, had disappeared. He found the place where she had vanished into the earth. He stood there in just the same way as she had stood, and the earth did open up and let him in. When the earth had closed above him, he found himself in a corridor. He walked this corridor until he found the virgin girl, Wanjiru. He felt very sorry for her for she looked awful, all her energy had been shaken out of her. He spoke kindly to her, saying that the people had made an offering of her in order to bring the rains, but that the rains had now come and that he would carry her home. He took the girl on his back for she was now as light as a child and returned to the corridor. They both came to earth. Then the young man told her that she should not go back home for her family had treated her very badly.

At nightfall the warrior took Wanjiru to his mother's home. There she stayed until she grew strong again. At a great dance she mingled amongst the dancers. Her relations saw her, but her lover tried to beat them off, for they had sold her shamefully. Wanjiru returned to his mother's house. But her relations again came to visit on the fourth day. then the warrior relented, saying, 'surely they are her father and her mother and her brothers.' So he paid her relations the purchase price for a bride, and wedded Wanjiru who had been lost.[1]

In our mind's eye we might add 'and they lived happily ever after'. Our hasty conclusion born from our irrepressible desire for permanence. Though the permanence in this tale is likely to reflect the reliable anticipation of the turning of the wheel of time, which gives birth to buoyant seasonal variations, starjourneys and patterns of sun and moon. The story of the maiden's sacrifice may, however, equally evoke images related to various pathways towards psychological development, the process of maturation in a nutshell.

Young Wanjiru is one amongst the many story-women, some of them great goddesses, like Inanna and Persephone, who descend to the nether-world in order to experience death, and who achieve the seemingly impossible return to life again. In Wanjiru's case her death has a painful, additional meaning: she is made to die for an apparently greater good. Because she died, much rain did come, and therefore the land was fertilized. Fecundity was secured. Thus the story obviously suggests the psychological and environmental events which in this part of Africa accompany the yearly rebirth of vegetation.

But it also speaks of reluctant sacrifice. We are made witness to Wanjiru's protest expressed in her pained: 'I am lost'. A young woman, who became the victim of circumstance and of the firmly held beliefs of those who surround her. When she is wholly swallowed by the earth, her life seemingly ends. The story might have finished here, were it not for the young warrior, who loved her greatly, and who therefore failed to silence the question: 'Where has she gone.' He voluntarily enters the great darkness, walking the road she went before him.

When at last he meets her in the grim underworld, she has changed beyond recognition. In many other tales, the male hero, who goes in pursuit of the dead beloved, is seized by panic upon discovering the woman, who was once beautiful, in an advanced state of decomposition. However, our African warrior is stirred to profound compassion. He does not take flight, like the Japanese Izanagi, but pities young Wanjiru sorely. He says: 'You were sacrificed to bring the rain, now the rain has come and I shall bring you back.' Whenever we are in a state of shock and terror, we need to hear such straightforward words which describe to us what has happened. Many a child or adult who survived a serious accident, may recognise what a warmhearted relative, ambulanceman or stranger said: 'You have had an accident. You've been hurt. We'll take you to hospital. Rest as best you can. I'll stay with you.'

In our story, the young warrior takes Wanjiru onto his back and carries her, like a child, back to the upper world. Once there, she is separated from her kin, the people who were unable to safeguard her. This separation matters, for did they not abandon her to her fate? Accepting a goat in exchange for a girl?

Of course we may also think of this tale as a symbolic representation of the young women's separation from their parents when menstruation starts, the return of blood to the earth, a description of a girl's transition between childhood and womanhood. It is also possible to interpret the tale as an image of a woman's struggle with the masculine aspects of herself, or of a man's attempts to integrate those sides of himself which can be described as feminine. Masculinity and feminity which encounter one another in the symbolic belly of the earth, where death and life dwell in intimate embrace. Each stage of the story then calls forth resonances with different stages of human and therefore of spiritual development. As such, the story could also have been retold in another chapter. What matters here is the young warrior's response to the death of his beloved: the impulse to search.

When someone we love dies, we are intuitively and innately compelled to go and look for this person in all the corners of the house, and in the farthest corners of the universe. Inspired by a desperate, excruciating hope: to find them somewhere, alive and well. Of course we know our loved one died. We are fully aware that we shall not see our child's familiar face again. We know this only too well, but search we must, and search we will. Blindly, we perform our duty to the species, the duty to our own survival.

This theme of searching for the person who died can therefore be found in stories from many different countries. In such tales a close link exists between attempts to change the hour of death and the presentation of death as a malevolent character, who has come to take the loved one away, a removal which we try to counteract. Death is then outwitted by being put in a knapsack, stuck to a tree, or as we saw earlier, by being locked up in a tree. Whatever the method, the outcome remains the same. Death is no longer able to perform his duty. He cannot take the person he had come to fetch to the place of no return.

During the middle ages a variation of the following tale was often told:

> A poor man is in search of a godfather. Since he believes that Death is more just than either God or the Devil, he chooses him. As his godfather, Death gives the man the power to see him stand at the head or the foot of every sickbed. Thereby the poor man is able to foretell how someone's sickness will progress. Once he begins to use his godfather's special gift, the man soon becomes famous. However, when the hour of his own death approaches, he is not at all ready to die. Again and again he uses the fact that he can see Death to keep him at bay. At last Death outwits him. The man is taken to the lower world, where all living people are represented by radiant life-lights. Death and his god-son walk and walk, until they reach the man's own light. Then Death takes a deep breath and blows it out.'[2]

In our mind's eye we can see Death and his godson in the mysteriously illumined underworld, halting when they near the man's own light, which shines amidst the others. One breath and the lifelight is extinguished.

Was this the scene imagined by the man in the train, who envisioned the throng of people emerging on one wave of time and did old Norah sigh because she saw this dance of lights reflected in the evening sky, or in the swell and fall of the waves?

Both Norah and the man in the train shared a profound awareness of the temporal. The realization that one day we shall die. None of us can help but wonder, where we shall then go. And the people we leave behind, they too will ask about us, where have they gone?

We realise full well that death's actual home is difficult to locate. It is about as difficult as it is to think of Death's temporal actions. Yet our imagination forces us to consider that death must have a place to dwell. After all, if we are going away, then we must have somewhere to go to, a way of getting there, as well as a means of travel to this strange and alien abode.

We can understand how the belief in other worlds thus had to become a necessary part of the imaginative background of many tales. It was unavoidable. Once death is personified, he is a person who needs a home of his own.

For even though the dead abandon us, it is impossible to abandon them to being a nobody in a no-man's land which exists nowhere. Ashes and bones dissipated by wind, water and earth. So much in us protests against this notion. We want a dwelling-place for the dead to exist, and are supported in our longing because we remember how it was when our husband or wife, our parent, died. Was it not as if we saw a ripplelike movement, and heard a faintly audible sound? And this instilled in us the unshakeable awareness that an actual leavetaking occurred. Something separated from the body. A body which stayed behind. We may not know what to call this something: soul or spirit. But many of us will never forget WHAT we witnessed when the physical body was vacated, which then became a mere husk in a painfully empty room.

This experience has led many of us to the conclusion that the departing spirit, if that is how we call it, went somewhere. But where? It seems logical to think, that it travelled to Death's abode. A dwelling-place which the living must consequently try to visit, so that we may retrieve the dead beloved, and perform the ultimate deed of friendship.

Like Orpheus we want to travel to the Netherworld and negotiate with grim Hades about Euridice's return. When Hades had then given his permission for her resurrection to life, we would certainly obey the imposed injunctions. Stronger than Orpheus we would not look back in wonder, only to loose in one stealthy glance all that we had hoped to achieve. Like the young warrior in the African story, we would succeed where Orpheus failed.

Harsh reality shakes us into asking what possible use such dreams have, when our room is empty, when we absentmindedly lay the table as of old and seeing what we have done, choke away our tears. How very bitterly we then envy Wanjiru and her young warrior. We, who search, but find not, who enter into darkness, and meet ourselves alone. The tale now probably arouses our acute envy. We too want to pull the dead person back from the grave. We want to prove that death did not happen to someone we cared for. Why does it have to be this way? Logically we know that death is a reality. Why then do we feel that emotionally it is unreal. That it must not be true that the bonds which matter to us are severed by death. Why do we feel with such blind and often overwhelming passion that our entire security depends upon the loss not being irrevocable?

A long time ago we discovered the world. It consisted of our cot, of the arms of the person who brought us up, the house, the street, the village or town, the county and country, the earth and the universe. Does not this endless place offer an abode somewhere to our dead parent, child, friend? A shelter to which they have now gone? We remember that only some days ago the dead person was alive, here in this very place. We cannot be expected to understand, let alone to accept, that their last breath moved them beyond the confines of time and place. It is hard to contemplate the possibility that they may not have gone anywhere else than into the grave or urn. Maybe they have now entered timeless time or spaceless space, but we do not understand what this could possibly mean. During the early stages of acute grief, we helplessly cling to the vague sense that death dwells in a place where time continues as usual. For if there were to be such a place, then we too may go there and meet the beloved again. If only ...

Throughout our life we have evolved through crisis. We learned before now that love changes us for better and for worse. That in order to mature we had to let go of the people who bathed us and fed us, encouraged and restricted us. We discovered what it was like to give up, to lose and to share. We cried our eyes out before today, and know only too well that growing up leads us to incur necessary losses. Such is the way of things.

But none of this means that we shall therefore accept the death of someone we love lying down. On the contrary, of course we protest. Waves of distress tighten our throat. Our legs start to feel heavier and heavier. When our grief is acute, our pain is hard to endure, because we feel so impotent. As Emily Dickinson says:

> 'So huge, so hopeless to conceive,
> As these that twice befell.
> Parting is all we know of heaven
> And all we need of hell.'[3]

It is not surprising that, at such times, we have trouble thinking. We feel very confused. Our concentration deserts us. For a while it seems that all we can think about is loss, loss and more loss. We want to recover the person who died. We owe them the debt of attempted retrieval, for otherwise our love may be proven to have been nonexistent. The faint whisper of emerging guilt can be discerned.

Then the nightmare begins. We hear footsteps, and feel startled. Are they returning home again? The sound of the key in the door. A face in the crowd. A voice on the radio. We know that the beloved friend, parent, our child has died, but it feels as if they've come back, hurtling us again and again towards hope, only to cast us contemptuously into the harsh reality of grief. Nobody can expect us to turn to the little things, to look happily on the sun and rain, when all we feel is 'the heart-break in the heart of things'.

We start to behave differently. Skipping meals, possibly drinking or smoking too much. Like old horses we walk or drive blindly to once shared places and awaken to our pain. In our dreams the person we lost lures us into a make-belief world of shared life. Those terrible dreams in which our father, our child, our friend is as alive as ever. We meet, talk, laugh, and then, often without a memory of departure, we reawaken to being alone again.

As the longing to meet them in the 'hollow vale' grows stronger, we may find ourselves desperately trying to resist death's urgent pull. We avoid the street where he used to work, the museum, the school playground. We pine and search and yet avoid. All this inspired by the wish to awaken and find that the death was not true, that the dead person is restored to us. The bitter pain holds us in tight embrace. We fear that we are going crazy, while in fact our experiences are, within the context of our western world, normal, predictable and completely average, provided these occur during the first months or the first year of grief. If they continue for many years after the death, we may have become stuck in our grief, and because we then need to find a way through even more urgently, we may then, it is to be hoped, seek professional help.

During the early stages of mourning most of us, if not all of us, seriously question whether we have the strength to endure this pain and, with equal seriousness, we consider the possibility that we have lost our mind. The urge to 'die-to-life', becomes strong. The urge to search for the dead person, instead of death itself, holds it in balanced check. In a tale of the Cochiti Indians we are told how:

> A woman had given birth to a young baby boy. The boy was looked after by his elder sister, for the mother was busy making baskets. She did this every day in the kiva with all the other men and women. When the boy cried, his sister took him to their mother, so that she might nurse the child. But the mother always said: 'Oh, I'll do it later.' The baby kept on crying though, and the girl took him four times to see his mother. Again her mother said: 'Oh, go away, I'll nurse him later.' The girl got really upset and she went off taking the baby-boy with her. She walked towards the north. She met a woman and the woman asked where she was going and she just said: 'We are going.' She cried as she said that.

The woman therefore asked her again and she said the same thing. This time she added that the little baby boy was tired of crying and hungry because their mother did not feed him. The woman asked her not to go to the dead's place, but she would not listen and just asked the woman to tell their mother what she had done. This the woman did and the mother went after them straightaway. She got there in time to see her children go down into the Whirlpool place. They were sitting on a cedar-tree which grows in the centre of that place, and which helps people to get down into the other world. The mother heard a voice which told her that she could try four times to get her children back. She had to take a stick with which she had to strike the water four times. She did hit the water and opened it, but it only showed her the children as they sat in the cedar tree which took them to the other world. Every time she tried to rush towards them, the water closed and she got out. When she had tried four times, she just stood there in that place, crying and crying. She cried for her daughter and her little son. She died whilst she was there.[4]

We can see the image of the weeping woman, who lost two children. These days the photographs in our newspapers confront us only too frequently with intimate close-ups of such overwhelming grief. Overwhelmed by her grief she died. We understand that she had to die, actually or symbolically. For such grief changes us beyond recognition. If only we can allow the change to occur, and to trust that another kind of life will emerge from this experience. Such trust is, however, still a long way away.

The Cochiti woman stands and she weeps. 'She wept for her children', the story says. In angry bewilderment we may wonder why the older sister had to leave with the little boy.

Maybe the tale wanted to tell us about the importance of early bonding. Maybe it is a startling example of the oppression of women, or a vivid illustration of a child's rage against the 'bad' breast. The girl's inability to negotiate a depressive position, namely that life is 'just one damn difficulty after another and promises to remain so.' The story offers us a myriad possible interpretations, like all good stories do. And one of these interpretations undoubtedly reflects the fact that we are alive today, because built into our organism is an automatic response to establish and maintain proximity to important people. When we are very young, this is the person who feeds us, comforts and cleans us and keeps us warm. It is therefore likely that, as Bowlby suggests, the urge to recover and scold the lost person will come into action 'in response to any and every loss and without discriminating between those that are really retrievable and those, statistically rare, that are not.'[5]

It may also be helpful to remind ourselves that our early attachment depends on the ways in which our parents related to us, and how they did what they might be expected to do. When our childhood has been characterized by our parent rejecting us, threatening to leave the family, or actually leaving from time to time, worst of all by committing suicide, then it is difficult not to become anxious and insecure in our later bonds with people who are important to us. We lose confidence in our belief that the one who really matters will indeed stay around and be available. Though we may learn to compensate for such early pain and confusion, or even to grow beyond it, when someone we came to trust and love during our adult years dies, the earlier pain about our troubled childhood will be evoked, especially if this pain had remained unacknowledged. Then we hurt again, and our grief may well be very prolonged. We are filled with self-reproach, tense and restless. The general sense of feeling awful then contributes to the overwhelming desire to 'freeze-frame' our life. In such cases we retain everything exactly as it was. Nothing is moved or allowed to be moved. None of the objects in the house are changed. For change would indicate that we accept death's existence, and thereby acknowledge the reality that our beloved has gone away for good. Then we may become strongly identified with the person who died, to the extent that we may even start to suffer with the symptoms of the terminally ill spouse, parent or child.

When this happens we could say that our grief has become chronic, as if we are forever fixed in the place and position where we might retrieve the dead beloved. Though frozen in tormented pain, we are desperately searching. Hoping against hope that, if only we keep still long enough, stay exactly where we are long enough, eventually the person we loved will return and unfreeze us.

Whenever the pain about the death of someone important evokes potent memories of early life abandonments, please be very gentle with yourself. For such pain is initially beyond description. It emerges from the petrified child within us, whose actual survival was once-upon-a-time at stake, and is then combined with the pain of the wounded adult who has lost a much loved person.

This double task of mourning is difficult to cope with, for we feel so small and vulnerable, oscillating between great helplessness and enormous rage. And when our pain is such, who would not wish to stop the world, in order to make time stand still, or because the fear of even more pain is unmanageable? Therefore, take care. Our symbolic search for the dead beloved may lead us dangerously close to our own encounter with death, through illness, recklessness or actually through suicide attempts. When we are hurting badly, we deserve to be listened to and to tell the story of our losses. If, for whatever reason, your pain is severe, consider whether you have a friend or relative who may be willing to listen to your tale. If not, seek professional help. Many of us have sought and found relief from sharing what has happened in life with a 'professional' listener. Thus actual healing can be found.

But, let us return to our journey, for there may be other reasons why we need to embark upon our search. Reasons which we need to discover.

Our attachment explains the urge to retrieve, as well as the vague sense of ongoing presence and the anger about having been deserted. We need to search because the search itself and the strength of the felt presence convince us that we were and are 'people who loved'. This too is important. For whilst we may dread the pain of loving and losing, we can fear with equal intensity the bitter disenchantment of indifference. The drive to be attached also nourishes our hope, that we may think of ourselves as someone who loves, and as someone who is loved.

A long time ago in China, Yang T'ing-yi told the following story:

> Two mice went into a field. A snake came and ate one of them. The other mouse kept away from the snake and glared at him. The snake, well satisfied with one mouse, made his way towards his hole. Then the second mouse launched forward and bit the snake in his tail. Furious, the snake latched out. But the mouse got away. After a while the snake gave up his pursuit and slithered back towards the hole. Again the mouse attacked his tail, just like he had done before. This happened several times. Until at last the snake spat the dead mouse onto the ground. Immediately the second mouse rushed forward. He wept over his friend. Then, squeaking dolefully, he picked up the dead mouse with his mouth and crept away.[6]

Who would not want to be as faithful as the mouse in this story. Not to desert our friends or to abandon them in times of danger. And likewise we hope neither to be deserted nor abandoned by those who declare to love us during our hour of greatest need. And yet ... Oftentimes during our life we wonder about the meagre quality of our love. Whilst longing to be faithful and true, we so often miserably fail. Our shortcomings stare us in the face more blatantly and fiercely then ever, when the amendment of our failures is beyond the bounds of the possible. When there is still so much that needed to be repaired, and no more time for repairs. When all further opportunities to heal the wounds of intimate love and war, have been foreclosed. When all that remains are the deceased person's estate, a bunch of mixed memories and the execution of the last will.

Then we are compelled to search not only in order to retrieve, but also because we want to repair. Hoping against bitter hope that thereby we can achieve a state of forgiveness, and of being forgiven. After all, where was Wanjiru's young warrior, when she was sinking down into the earth, crying helplessly: 'I am lost'? Maybe therefore he journeyed to the other world in order to redeem his impotent absence at the time of her dying.

If ever we find ourselves searching with great intensity for the dead beloved, dreaming and tossing and turning and avoiding, then it might be helpful to ask ourselves what we feel so very guilty about, where and how we failed our love.

Then we can knowingly consent to enter the dark crevices of self-reproach and hopelessness. Consent to the work of grief, which begins with an acceptance of the reality of the loss. An acceptance from which we are still so maddeningly far removed.

References

1. Retold by the author. Contemporary source: Henderson, L. and Oakes, M., (1963) *The Wisdom of the Serpent*, Collier Books.
2. Retold by the author. Contemporary source: Thompson, S., (1977) *The Folktale*, London, University of California Press.
3. Dickenson, E., in: Urch, E., (1981) (ed.), *Sorrow-Poems*, Evesham, Arthur James, p. 27.
4. Retold by the author. Contemporary source: Benedict, R., (1931) *Tales of the Cochiti Indians*, University of New Mexico Press, repr. edition.
5. Bowlby, J., (1979) *The Making and Breaking of Affectional Bonds*, London, Tavistock Publications, p.53.

6. Retold by the author. Contemporary source: Roberts, R., (1979) *Chinese Fairy Tales and Fantasies*, New York, Pantheon Books.

Seas at my feet were flowing,
Waves on the shingle pouring,
Old year roaring and blowing,
And New Year blowing and roaring.

Alfred, Lord Tennyson

CHAPTER EIGHT

How lazily time creeps about to one that mourns

It is normal to experience sorrow when someone we love dies. We may expect it. Our sighing, lack of strength and digestive problems are part and parcel of the distress which is called bereavement. Though the preoccupation with the person who died is painful, we know that we cannot do without the recurring thoughts. They help us to remember the life we shared together and, equally, help us to acknowledge over and over again that the death and grief are real. There is no need to pretend away our sorrow, to hide from the stressful consequences of the death of someone we love. Sooner or later we must acknowledge that our routine has been irrevocably altered, a bond severed.

All this is difficult and we might therefore well be sorely tempted to put a brave face on things and make-believe that the loss really does not make that much difference. Of course we know that we betray ourselves and our relationship with the person we loved if we succeed in this awful game, but who can blame us for trying, when 'death is all we need to know of hell'. However, we cannot magic our pain away. We know that we do not get used to someone's death just overnight. And when we've been hurt, 'a while' is a very long time.

As the weeks pass, we grow to accept the fact of our loss - reluctantly, often angrily. The despair and depression are tough. The loneliness is nearly unbearable. Our heart is not going to break, it has been broken. We know that when it is put together again, at some point in the future, it will show a different pattern.

With the anonymous Irish poet, we might then say:

You have taken the east from me; you have taken the west from me;
you have taken what is before me and what is behind me;
you have taken the moon, you have taken the sun from me;
and my fear is great that you have taken God from me![1]

We are overwhelmed by the sense that we cannot offer our friends and relatives anything other than anger, self-accusation, and hopelessness. We feel distinctly sorry for ourselves, unreasonably but passionately annoyed with those who remain dear to us. Guilty about all that was left undone.

The everyday-ness of daily life weighs heavily. We fear that people avoid our company because we smell of disappointment and emanate an odour of galling awkwardness. Suspicion becomes a dangerous friend. Why are we so thoroughly shaken up? Does it really have to be this way?

We have been left. We loved the one who died dearly and at times hated their guts. Our failures and everyone else's failures are now written in capital letters upon the grey slate of our mournful soul. Grief stinks and we know it.

During those weeks and months, when our wounds open up more often than we wish to admit and when misunderstandings emerge from nowhere, it might be helpful to remind ourselves of *Trickster*.

In a tale told by the Winnebago Indians this bewildering, yet wonderfully complex figure has accepted the challenge to eat a bulb, which will make him defecate. Truly defecate. Trickster finds it hard to believe that a little bulb could do this to him. He is utterly determined not to defecate. He shall only let go of his excrement when he really feels like it: no sooner, no later. He eats the bulb and after a little while he starts to break wind. Immediately he reassures himself that he shall still be a great man, if all he does is to expel a little gas. However, he is passing so much wind that it really hurts. He is thrown sideways, upwards, forwards by the force of the wind that blows out of him. Then, he starts to defecate. At first only a little. Then more and more. He sits down upon a log, but the excrement soon touches him. He climbs into a tree, and still his excrement rises to touch him. It just pours out of him and rises and rises. Soon the branch on which he sits sinks into it. It becomes slippery. Trickster tries to hold on, but he falls down into the dung. It is very difficult to find a way out of it all. He is covered from top to toe in dirt and muck. Everything he carries is covered in muck, his blanket as well as the box in which he keeps his penis. He has to clean the box out, and then put the penis back inside it, the filth is everywhere. Even though the box is now cleaned out a little, Trickster is still blinded by his own dirt. He becomes really frightened and starts to run blindly here and there and everywhere. Because he cannot see anything, his eyes being stuck together with his own excrement, he falls against a tree, shouting: 'Tree, who are you. Speak to me. Tell me where you are, who you are.' The tree says: 'Well, who do you think I am. I'm in the middle of the valley. I'm the tree that has forked branches. That's who I am.' Trickster says immediately: 'Any chance of water near here?' The answer is 'Keep on going.' On Trickster goes. He bumps into one tree after another. The red oak tree and the slippery elm also tell him to keep going along. At last he comes to the basswood tree. This one tells Trickster that he stands by the water's edge. 'Well, that's it', says filth-ridden Trickster. He jumps into the water, splashes about, drifts about and washes himself inside out. The storyteller says that that time Trickster very nearly died. It was really difficult to find the water. If the trees had not told him where to go he would have died. It took him a long time to get really clean, for the excrement had got stuck to him. He also had to clean his blanket thoroughly and the box with the penis. He had to wash everything, remember that.[2]

At first glance, it may seem an odd story to have included. After all, this Trickster figure does not appear to be grieving over the end of a relationship, the loss of an important bond. He simply responded to the challenge to eat a bulb, which will make him excrete. How can one parallel this deed, with having to accept that someone we love, died. We did not choose to encounter death. Nor did we want to fight with death and life for a renewed existence, for the permission to return to other commitments, new delights. We invited none of this. We were simply lumbered with it.

But how we recognise the sense of being violently thrown about. The panic-struck clinging to control and reassurance of both ourselves and others. We have heard ourselves say, 'Difficult, but I'm managing', whilst we know that the floods are rising, and our hold on life as we knew it is loosening. We tighten our grip, but slip deeper into identification with our hopelessness. At this stage of the mourning process the tolerance of ambiguity and ambivalence is still far beyond our reach. Any 'maybe' calls forth strained agonies of misunderstanding and rage. We cannot cope with half-promises and uncommitted suggestions. Our hellish pain seems to demand single-mindedness: life or death, filth or purity.

Unavoidably, the moment comes when we can no longer maintain control. We slip into despair, we plead for death, wishing that we had never been born, and like Job, curse ourselves. In so doing, we disavow responsibility for our life and plead 'not guilty' to the death of the one we love. Willing as we are to make the ultimate sacrifice, we prove ourselves innocent. Thus covered in soulless muck and with foul despair seeping through every pore, we move through sullen day and comfortless night. Who knows how long this struggle lasts. An actual hour, a calendar day or week, or even several months; it seems irrelevant. For when we sink into our swamp, we enter timeless time and die a certain kind of death. In this place beyond all hope, hope is born. In this lowly, mucky stable, surrounded by dust and dirt, a new kind of love is born. A change takes place, when the desire to be cleansed emerges. Only when we know the full measure of our sorrow and have encountered the depth of our outrage, helplessness, guilt and need, only then is the impulse to run towards the healing waters freed.

Then, at last, we start bumping into people. Literally and metaphorically, we are shocked into the presence of others. We stop to ask them how they are. Enquire truly what is happening to them. Again and again we shall become encapsulated within the narrow confines of preoccupation with our own pain and the need for healing, but equally again and again, we shall collide with the otherness of others, until we come to the place where we may rest and bathe and be cleansed of months of tears, and stifled protests and blinding rage.

For many of us, this cleansing is manifested in a trip to the hairdressers, early morning-swims, or a massage. 'Defoliage' in the best sense of the word. Very tentatively we start to expose a new and vulnerable skin to the world beyond ourselves. Believing that we are through the worst of it, we discover that unexpectedly and without warning the same old grief slices through our fragile strength. It seems as if we have gained nothing, retrieved nothing.

That very day we may feel like Hare. This tale is told about him in Abyssinia:

> Hare was taking a walk in the sunshine. Suddenly he saw something move in the grass beside. It had two big horns. They were the shadows of his own two ears, but Hare didn't know that. He was sure that these frightful horns belonged to a dangerous beast. He ran away, and - help

- the great monster could run as fast he could. Hare twisted and turned, ran backwards and sideways and forwards. But wherever he went and whatever he did, the horned beast never once left him. Hare was beyond himself with fright. His heart beat as fast as it could. His breath got stuck in his throat. He trembled all over, and finally his legs gave up on him. He knew he would now die. The great horned beast would pounce on him, and that would be the end of Hare. In the shade of some bushes, he collapsed, panted and waited. Nothing happened. He looked around. The great horned beast had gone.[3]

At such times we are at war with ourselves. Pursued by the shadow of the past, unable to tread upon new ground. Though previously we might have had a memory like a sieve, now we suddenly recall the smallest details about the last months we spent together. The omissions of friends, relatives, doctors. The many ways in which we disappointed the dying person, and the myriad ways in which we were disappointed by other people. Their lack of understanding, the absences and thoughtless statements, their insensitivity to our plight. Such recollections haunt us, and become magnified beyond all proportion. We know this, but like Hare we cannot help but be intimidated. Our anguish makes us run, and meanwhile the beast stays by our side. In the shadow of the bushes he disappears. Once in a while when we have a rest, we hear ourselves laugh again, make plans, reminisce with pleasure, only to be caught unawares by our grief, which confronts us with the reality of our loss. The gaping hole is an actual hole. We become lonely and need companionship, but as the ancient Chinese proverb says: 'To dream of happiness is in itself a grief.' We are isolated and fearful. True, we may begin to get accustomed to the dead person's absence, but it takes time, many months or years. Making a new start then becomes a possibility we consider. But at this stage our sorrow still demands our attention, for even though the acute phases of grief are now behind us, we still need to come to grips with the final remnants of our longing that the death should not have happened. We hear the final whispers of our protest that the way of the universe should have been different.

When our days and nights reflect such withheld mourning, it might be helpful to listen to the story of Coyote in the Land of the Dead.

When the world was still very young, Coyote visited the Eagle's lodge. He had known the Eagle-people since the beginning of time, and had not seen them for a while. He was therefore upset when he saw that

Eagle's fire had been left untended, and that the entire lodge was badly neglected. Eagle-man barely returned Coyote's greeting, and whispered that he had to tell him sad news. Eagle-woman had died. And life without her was too difficult. Coyote had heard such words before from other grieving people. They hurt him sorely. And because Coyote was Coyote he decided, there and then, that the way of things had to be altered. He reminded himself of the new leaves and flowers of springtime and could not see why it should not be like this for people too. Therefore he suggested to Eagle-man that they would travel to the land of the dead to bring back the people, so that they too might be renewed.

Thus Coyote and Eagle-man set out on their journey. They travelled a long, long time. At last they came to a grey, sombre land, where the sun was rarely seen. When darkness was about to fall they reached the wide river which flows between the land of the living and the land of the dead. On the far-distant shore they saw a village, much like other villages.

Coyote and Eagle-man lifted their voices, calling into the darkening night that someone might send a boat to fetch them. Nothing stirred and no one came. Then Coyote thought. His thought travelled deep inside himself, and he lifted to his throat an ancient song, unknown to him, and as he sang this song of power, a canoe set forth from the faraway shore, and made its way towards them.

Four men held the oars, and four sorrow wisened faces greeted them with a friendly, silent smile. No questions were asked, no words spoken.

When they arrived in the village of the dead Coyote and Eagle-man were greeted by a strong, tall woman. Her face shone with the same wisened smile they had seen on the face of the oarsmen. Assuring her that they had come on no harmful business, they begged for hospitality. This they were offered in a small lodge, tightly woven of tule and other rushes. A heap of antelope hides and a warm fire was all they found inside their dwelling.

Soon Eagle-man became hungry, wondering whether he should go outside and look for food. But, as they looked around for the doorway, they saw that the lodge had become completely closed off. They searched for an opening, a possible way out, but found none. They tried to scratch a hole in the walls, but each time they made a hole, it closed over. The walls which imprisoned them were strong and smooth and nothing could make them break. Eagle-man was fear-struck. Would they be left to dwell here and starve to death? Coyote thought a moment, a brief eternal moment. Then he knew. He said: 'Only what belongs to the land of the Dead will create an opening in the lodge of the Dead.'

No sooner had he thought these thoughts than the lodge opened and a person came in to bring them food. When he left the lodge again, it closed over as before. Coyote and Eagle-man ate the food of yonder world, for they were very hungry. Coyote took all care to eat both the meat and the bones. But when he was chewing the last bone, he kept a little bit in his mouth. Everything else he swallowed.

Eagle-man's longing for his wife hurt greatly and when the person came to take away their empty bowl, he asked when he might see her. A wise smile was all he saw. Again the doorway disappeared, and the walls of the lodge were smoother and more solid than ever. Eagle-man knew that the dead would keep them here until they died. He would never be able to see his wife. His hurt was great indeed.

Then Coyote took the bone-splinter out of his mouth and started to scratch the wall. This time it did not smooth over. The hole was made bigger and bigger, until it was so large that they could see through it. In the early moonlight they saw how the dead gathered in a circle to sway and move most gently and beautifully in a mysterious dance. They were dressed in rich ceremonial robes. Some carried musical instruments. The decorations with shells and feathers were as splendid as any they had seen in the Land of the Living. Coyote saw many of the people he knew in that moonlight gathering, and also lovely Eagle-woman. When Eagle-man saw her, he gasped and wanted to run towards her. But Coyote held him tightly, and helped him silence his cry.

Eagle-man watched how Coyote went over to the Antelope hides. He took them one by one, and laid them out for sewing. Then he made the bone-splinter which he had first used to make a hole in the wall of the lodge, into a needle. Using his own hair, Coyote began to stitch the hides together. One after the other. Until he had made a very big hide-bag. Meanwhile the dead danced their ceremonial dance. Coyote looked upon them in awed silence. Then, as if from nowhere, he started to sing a song of his own. It was like the Canoe-song, because it too came from the place of old-knowing deep within him. It seemed as if the whole world shrunk. The dead stood still, held by the embracing song, while all around them darkness dwelled.

Now Coyote and Eagle-man moved towards their still circle, dragging the hide-bag behind them. And one by one, light as feathers, they took the dead people into the cup of their hands. Each one found a place inside the bag. When all the people of the Land of the Dead had thus been gathered Coyote and Eagle-man made their way towards the canoe.

Suddenly Coyote was in a hurry. His ancient knowing told him that he had to reach the shore of the Land of the Living before sunrise. Thus Coyote and Eagle-man took their place in the canoe, the hide-bag between them, and began the arduous journey across the wide river which flows between the Land of the Living and the Land of the Dead.

Fear struck as a faint light shimmered on the horizon. Slight groans and shudders could be heard inside the hide-bag. Eagle-man trembled. Coyote told him once more to paddle as fast he could. When the light grew stronger, the dead people would awaken, and there wasn't enough room in the bag for all of them. Their pain would be agony and besides they would be too heavy for the canoe, which would then capsize.

They hastened across the river. But soon it happened. The people inside the bag twisted and turned and screamed in blind pain. The canoe capsized, and the hide-bag and Coyote and Eagle-man, they all fell into the river.

But still Coyote did not give up. Fast as he could, he swam towards the bag. Dragging it with the last of his strength and holding it tightly, he brought his sorrowful load to shore. Then he opened the hide-bag, smiling gladly as the dead people who returned to life, stood before him on the shores of the Land of the Living, which shone in the early morning light.

Then Coyote spoke. He told them that he and Eagle-man had brought the people back to the Land of the Living, so that there would be no more death. All living beings would now come back to life, like the trees and flowers return. Eagle-man and Eagle-woman could go back to their village. They need mourn no more.

Coyote looked around. His gaze was greeted with the same sorrow-wisened smile he had seen before. Then the old woman, who had greeted him and Eagle-man on the shore of the village of the dead, stepped forward. She spoke thus:

> 'It is good to be remembered Coyote, and we know that you meant well. But we do not long to return and live amongst you again. Our time here in the Land of the Living came and went. Now another time has come and it is good. We find much knowledge and wonder in the Land of the Dead. We wish to return to it.'

She looked away, and turned and went to the canoe which was lying on the shore, silent witness to the journey. All of her people followed her. The last to go was Eagle-woman. As she was about to step into the canoe, she looked at Eagle-man and spoke:

> 'Do not grieve for me. We are not like the leaves on the tree, but like its heart. When it dies, the tree dies and it returns to the still heart-beat of the earth. One day you too shall cross this river, and we shall both be there, dancing the endless dance of the Dead. Do not grieve for me.'

They stood, silent Coyote and silent Eagle-man, as they watched the canoe glide towards the land of the dead.

Then they turned and made their way towards the Land of the Living.[4]

In our mind's eye, we can see Coyote and Eagle-man, as they stand on the shore of the river of separation, and listen to the sorrow-wisened woman's words. To witness the silent procession as it makes its way back towards the Land of the Dead. Maybe they felt the aching harshness of the thought that their journey had been truly in vain. After all, the original intention to create a world without death had been defeated. Though they accomplished the hopeless-seeming task of bringing the dead back to life, their gift of life renewed had not been not accepted. Therefore, what could possibly have been gained in the process?

Eagle-man would probably not find it any easier to live in his lodge and to tend to his fire alone. And Coyote, would he be any less burdened by the grief of the people of the early times? The tale speaks to us in so many different ways. The Yakima people, who first told this story, brought to its recitation their own understanding of life's changing patterns. But amidst all the possible interpretations, one cannot help but feel that Coyote and Eagle-man's journey to the land of the dead is also a moving description of our passage through bereavement. Let us look at this in somewhat greater detail.

When we suffer great loss, we become painfully aware of our childlike fears. The fear of sleeping alone, of floorboards that creak in the night and footsteps outside the window. On the occasion that we go out by ourselves in the evening the dark house seems terribly empty when we return. We are often frightened to go inside. The experience of profound fear might even upset us so much that for a while we may, like Eagle-man, choose to stay indoors, so that we need not pass the threshold into darkness, alone. Whilst our yearning changes slowly and gradually into depression, we retrench. Our overwrought emotions are exhausted with the trouble and turmoil of the earlier stages of our grief. We too may then become spellbound; an experience which is hauntingly conveyed in Emily Bronte's poem:

> The night is darkening round me,
> The wild winds coldly blow;
> But a tyrant spell has bound me
> And I cannot, cannot go.
> The giant trees are bending
> Their bare boughs weighed with snow.
> And the storm is fast descending,
> and yet I cannot go.
> Clouds beyond clouds above me,
> Wastes beyond wastes below;
> But nothing drear can move me;
> I will not, cannot go.[5]

In those times we feel wanting in everything that might make us feel better. Our self-esteem is at its lowest ebb and our self-respect is diminishing fast, whilst any traces of self-interest disappeared with the last person who came to offer their condolances. We eat without pleasure, sleep without enjoyment, and find it hard to remember when we last felt truly rested. If 'bleak' conveys the utter sense of impotent, cold poverty, then it will describe more or less what we feel like. Maybe out of such greyness hope can be born, but currently that seems impossible. When at last we do lie down in the foul rag and bone shop of the heart our fire is no longer tended. We dwell with loneliness, feeling that our identity has been lost, and our social status diminished.

If our partner has died, we are not only deprived of companionship during daylight ours, we also reach out to the pillow beside us, to find nobody there.

The pillowtalk has ceased, and how we can long for the glorious intimacy of trivialities, the small and seemingly unimportant facets of life, which lent our existence colour and depth and resonance! If we enjoyed sex together, then the sexual deprivation can be difficult to bear. The absence of these passions may weigh heavily upon us, and contribute to a growing sense of being unattractive and useless. In addition we miss the hugs, an arm around our shoulders, the kisses given out of routine and habit, and those which held the promise of exciting embraces. All gone. If our partner had been ill for quite some time, we might have grown used to the withdrawal of sexual encounters from the relationship, and had probably come to enjoy different forms of intimacy. We may then be surprised to find that we again fiercely miss the sexuality of the relationship, which in reality had been non-physical for a long period of time. These desires can then be experienced as doubly painful, for not only is our partner no longer alive to enjoy with us the consummation of our longings, but we now also endure the sorrow of feeling unfaithful. Maybe the fire which Eagle-man no longer tended, parallels our own inability and reluctance to keep ourselves warm, in more ways than one.

When Coyote sees Eagleman's sorrowful state, he is reminded of earlier grief. In the same way we witness the return of such memories, both our own and of those close to us. Echoes of former wounds, which throw the current one in sharp relief. Old hurts ache afresh, as if they had never healed, thus adding to the unwillingness to accept death's undeniable irrevocability. Coyote resonates with former pains and ancient grief which strengthen his determination not to accept the end of Eaglewoman's life, and, denying that death is irremediable, he suggests to Eagleman that they both set out on a journey.

Our journeys and actions may aim to cover similar tracks. The neighbour, who means well, takes us on a shopping-trip into town, or asks us to show her some old photographs, and torn asunder between hope and despair, we go along with the suggestions, our will too fragile to exercise choice. We attempt to retrieve the life we lived, even though we know that the old ways are forever closed. Thus it may be as if we move ever closer to the dead beloved, abandoning 'who we were' to emptiness, and thereby becoming more and more identified with the life of the dead. Daylight is darkened and dusk embraced. We dwell in the hall of past shadows. We pull out the telephone and hide our tear-stained face in the hollow of our pillow. Then we enter the lodge without exit, without windows: the dark night of the soul.

We eat what is needed to stay alive, but it is a sombre feeding. Once in a while we may wonder whether it will always be like this. Meanwhile, we wait and wait, longing for the re-encounter with the dead beloved. As the 16th Century poet sang:

> Thus wedded to my woes,
> and bedded to my tomb,
> oh, let me living, living die,
> till death do come.'

During those days and nights it may seem as if only those who have been scarred in similar ways can bring us food. Volunteers from bereavement-befriending services, counsellors and friends or relatives who also encountered the sorrow of loss offer us morsels of sustenance, images of a possible life, as we sit and wait and cry.

Our inner Coyote meanwhile contemplates a possible way out. And the first way out is to undo what has been done. We hopelessly attempt to retrieve the dead beloved. We search and find nothing but memories. We try to evoke the face of the one-we-loved, and encounter either blankness or an image so startling in its vivacity that we recoil in horror. Meanwhile, the mundane continuity of day-to-day existence places an ever greater wedge of time between the then and the now.

While we dwell in this darkness, we sow our own 'bag of hides' with splinters from the past and hairs from our own body, strands of alive, dead matter. We often stubbornly continue this 'mournful labour of love' until we are sure that the task we designed can be undertaken, namely: to gather the past neatly and bring it back to life.

This we do when we believe we have safely contained our grief, granted it an appropriate place which will enable us to embark upon the re-entry into the daily world as if nothing much has happened. Thus having sorted through our robes of mourning, we foolhardily venture forth into ordinary life as if nothing changed at all. Then strange anxieties overtake us.

The twisting and turning inside Coyote's bag of hides as daylight dawns upon the fugitive canoe reminds us of the unfreezing of pain, panic and whirling agonies. How come that we could ever have thought that we were getting stronger? Nothing like it. Our boat is more rocky then ever. We do our best to reach safer shores. But we will not yet reach land as long as the whirling torment of anxious pretense continues to haunt our days and night. And this happens now that we least expected it?

We try harder and harder to move beyond our grief. After all, months or years have passed; people even say that they are expecting us to return to normal. Normal? If only they knew that it all feels so much worse these days. Infinitely much worse then in the beginning. How to make sense of it all? True, we may find comfort in the thought that it always gets worse before it gets better, and that one needs a certain strength in order to be able to face the depth of despair and powerlessness. But no one ever said it would hurt this much, and especially so much more fiercely now than during those early weeks and months of grief. A different kind of tiredness sets in. The exhaustion of pretending to have recovered, of being brave, of having succeeded in salvaging the past as best we knew how.

Then we fall over, literally or metaphorically. We are thrown into the swirling waters of life, and we either sink or swim. And, tragically, some of us sink. Too exhausted and too wounded by all that has happened, death is embraced as a welcome relief. Not waving but drowning, all hope was surrendered. Unless someone came to the rescue quick and immediately, some of us had to forego the gift of life. But at the height of such inner turmoil, when the struggle with the dark night of the soul is fierce, gladly most of us take the 'bag of deadness' between our teeth and drawing upon unknown reserves, we make the worn-out way back to the land of the living, still stubbornly hoping with blind hope that the resurrection of the old is possible.

As the story says: the dead were brought back to life, and the gift which was won after so harsh a journey, was refused. As the sorrow-wisened woman reminds us, even the heart of the tree must die and join the earth's heart-beat.

We too may have tried to outwit death by weaving our experience of grief and mourning neatly into the fabric of an unaltered existence, to give the dead the place of honour which we prepared. We seem compelled to anticipate the emergence of a new lease of life within the secure framework of well known, threadbare routines, always wanting to rekindle the old fires. To make space by our self-same hearthside for all that has been and was. Always to remember. Never to forget. The one we love died and is so very sorely missed. How can we expect to do anything else but try to safeguard continuity, to create the fullest possible restoration of all that has been? We do not wish to become thankful for all that was, including death, only to let it all go.

It is true, we realise, that the sun rises with or without our consent. The sea swells in tidal flow. We greet the rain and snow and thunder too. But we have now encountered the ancient knowledge that our loneliness may be more lonely before it will be less.

Having attended to our own desert-spaces and having experienced this aspect of the awesome reality of our soul, must we then accept the bankruptcy of our attempts to retrieve all that was so, that all might be as it had been? Do we really have to witness the dead as they return to their own land, leaving us to turn to the land of the living? Coyote and Eagle-man stood and witnessed the going. Then they turned and went their way, and we too must turn and go our way.

That is all there is to it. Either we choose a living death or with reluctant or relieved consent we turn towards the land of the living, thereby surmounting our fascination with death and overcoming the lure of eternal mourning. We turn, and then?

The land which greets us is not a land of milk and honey. We know full well that new joys await us as well as new sorrows. Of course we still have to deal with sudden, unwelcome news, frustrations, satisfactions and the whole blessed mishmash which is life.

It is to be hoped that we gained glimmers of wisdom from our journey through grief, becoming able to say with Dag Hammerskold, the former secretary general of the United Nations:

> For all that has been: thanks.
> To all that shall be: yes.

On good days we will remember our thankfulness, on bad days we will accusingly forget, and anyhow, we might not even aspire to such equanimity. Is not our sense of humour born out of shared muddles and unshared knots? Would laughter still exist if we were to accept all the events of our life with such gracious balance?

Chances are that we do not even have that much choice in the matter. We simply turn to face life, and unexpectedly find that we are really enjoying ourselves. Or we are once more deeply and delightfully surprised. We discover that the small giggles which tremble behind our lips, moisten our eyes, and we shall not know which feeling inspires the moistening. Is it sorrow or joy or relief that at last forgiveness and consent have come? Who knows, and who can really tell? We embarked upon our very own journey into darkness, then we turned to walk the road which is ours to travel in the land of the living. The renewed consent to our life was born. It was born out of the hope which was buried and the love which we believed forever lost. Such is the mystery of life.

We remember that at times during those still, lonesome hours of the morning, when great grief came over us, a small voice deep within consoled our sorrow. At times its whisper may have been too soft to have been heard, because our silent screams drowned its quiet comfort. Screams, which arose from our heartfelt protest that the world which was ours was ours no more. We also remember the experience that, whenever we surrendered all hope, the possibility of renewal came within our reach. A possibility which inspired us with the courage to continue again and again despite it all and thanks to it all.

Then, towards the end of our long journey through bereavement, an inner meeting occurred between our sorrow-wisened knowing, which had become a potent inner source of renewal and our awareness of life's ultimate uncertainty. When our experience and awareness met we discovered a different kind of security, one which is rooted in the felt knowledge that light and dark, dusk and dawn contain our life. From then onwards this gift is ours. Then we may cradle our pain as well as our joy, whilst we remember that:

> In the morning the day is born,
> in the afternoon it fades,
> then it disappears all at once.
> When this happens
> don't think we took it back,
> don't think that.
> The day appears,
> Then comes the night.
> It will always be this way.
> Don't think it will always stay
> dark when night comes.
> That we stole the day from you.
> Don't be afraid.
> It will always come back.'[6]

Thus a new thought about life is born, a new thought about the remainder of our life. A thought which becomes a new vision of a possible future; one which is based on the firm foundation of memories and experiences, which embraces tears and gratitude, regrets as well as laughter and above all our awareness that such is the way of life. We step out of the void, into another space, from which comes the power of growth.

References

1. Anon. cited in: Heaney, S. and Hughes, T., (1985) *The Rattlebag*, Faber and Faber Ltd., p. 462.

2. Radin, P., (1956) *The Trickster*, tales no. 24 and 25, Schocken Books.

3. Retold by the author. Contemporary source: Manning-Sanders, R., (1972) *Tortoise Tales*, London, Methuen.

4. Retold by the author. Contemporary source: Robinson, G. and Hill, D., (1975) *Coyote the Trickster, Chatto and Windus.*

5. Bronte, Emily, 1818-1848.

6. Quoted amongst others in Van Over, R., (1980) *Sunsongs*, New York, Mentor Books, p. 111.

And now the sun had stretched out all the
hills
And now was dropped into the western bay;
At last he rose, and twitched his mantle blue:
Tomorrow to fresh woods, and pastures new.

John Milton

CHAPTER NINE

Acceptance, more often than not

We loved a man, a woman, a child. He or she died, slowly or suddenly, and because of love being love and life being life we entered the complexity of grief. There was little else we could do. To deny our feelings would have meant a greater loss. If, in human terms, the death felt terribly wrong, our struggle with grief was probably difficult and frightening. If, however, death came gently and at the end of a long and rich life, our grief may have been nourished by profound gratitude, inspired by awareness of the privilege of having been able to share our life with someone we love.

During the months and years which followed our bereavement, each of us, if we were lucky, encountered at least one warmhearted person who accompanied us on our road and who, like Ninshubur in the Inanna myth, waited in alarmed concern at the gate, while we entered into the dark night of the soul, someone who cared sufficiently about us to call us 'back to life', who held onto the strengths and satisfactions of existence, while we dwelled with sorrow.

We will probably remember the occasions when a friend, relative or child encouraged us to turn towards life again. Maybe their timing was very wrong and we responded angrily, saying, 'What for...?'. Then they may have told us about their need for our care and attention, or about the scent of freshly-brewed coffee and the pattern the rain creates on the windows of a cafe in France; and we couldn't have cared less for the pattern which the rain creates on windows anywhere, let alone in France, but maybe we were bemused and wondered, 'Yes, what about France ...'

Maybe they simply said: 'Join us for supper', and they were not bothered by our withdrawn state. Possibly the girls had wanted to play a game of football. They asked: 'Will you play?' We wondered whether we could so soon? Then the young son, struggling to write a story and get his spelling right, said: 'How do you spell happiness?' Just as we were about to be overwhelmed with envy, our friends spoke about other sorrow and kindred grief and we thought: 'Maybe it is possible, maybe the simple pleasures of life can be retrieved'. With the first 'maybe' the heavy door, which had kept all thoughts of benign possibility locked away, opened just enough to allow a glimpse of a renewed consent to life. Cringing with the fierce awareness of loss, which this opening created, we held back again, but the sight could not be forgotten, and the pull not begin to be undone.

We are told about this process of being tempted back into life in a Cherokee-Indian myth, which describes how the sun and the early people struggled with each other.

> In the days of the beginning of the world, the Sun had a daughter who lived in the middle of the sky, directly above the earth. Consequently, the earth was always too hot and many people died. As it was causing so many deaths, the people consulted their wise men and women. Then they tried to kill the Sun's daughter. At last they succeeded. The Sun's daughter was killed. When this happened, the Sun went into her house and grieved. She would not come out any more. The world was dark all the time. Again the people suffered. Their wise men and women said that if they wanted the sun to shine again they had to journey to the Darkening Land of the West and retrieve the Sun's daughter. They travelled seven days until they came to the Darkening Land, the Ghostcountry. Here they did precisely as they had been told. They retrieved the Sun's daughter, put her into a box and closed the lid tightly. Then they started their journey home. After a while the girl came to life again. She pleaded to be let out of the box. The people tried to ignore her and continued the journey. Again and again she spoke, saying how hungry and thirsty she was. They were nearly home when she begged for air, saying she was suffocating. The people were afraid that she was really dying, so they lifted the lid of the box to give her some air. They heard a fluttering and a redbird cried. They travelled onwards, but when they came home, the box was empty.

> The story teller then continued and said:

The Sun had been glad when they started to the Ghostcountry, but when they came back without her daughter she grieved and cried and cried, 'My daughter, my daughter,' and wept until her tears made a flood upon the earth, and the people were afraid the world would be drowned. They held another council, and sent their handsomest young men and women to amuse her so that she would stop crying. They danced before the Sun and sang their best songs, but for a long time she kept her face covered and paid no attention, until at last the drummer suddenly changed the song, when she lifted up her face, and was so pleased at the sight that she forgot her grief and smiled.[1]

The drummer within each of us will play us many a song in order to comfort those aspects of ourselves which keep our grief in tight embrace, to help us temporarily to forget. For life's healing wisdom can work only through such momentary forgetting. When we consent to the great gifts of curiosity and involvement, through participation in existence, we not only allow a new bond with life to be made, we also allow our grief some rest. This resting of our grief leads to transformation and healing.

When the going gets tough, and it always does 'from time to time', we should be gentle with ourselves. Rest, and cry and protest and walk and talk, seeking out those friends and activities or non-activities which nurture us.

In those days when we feel once again deprived of courage and overwhelmed by fear, the memory of this brief Chinese tale may be of some use:

In China, a very long time ago, there lived a giant Serpent, seventy or eighty feet long and wider than the span of ten hands. It dwelt in a cave on the side of Yung-Ling mountain. The Serpent was always hungry and ate anything it could find. The villagers lived in constant terror, as the beast had killed so many people. They tried offering oxen and sheep, but none of these could satisfy the serpent's ferocious appetite. In their dreams the villagers discovered what to do. Once a year, one day during the eighth month, a thirteen year old maiden had to be delivered to the Serpent's cave on Yung-Ling mountain. The magistrates helplessly accepted the dreamers' knowledge. Each year they choose a girl from the poorest families and took her into the hills. Thus nine maidens were killed.

When the tenth year came, the officials started to look early for the Serpent's maiden. They wished to hold her in readiness for the chosen day.

In Chianglo county lived a man, whose name was Ti Lan. There were six daughters in his family, but no sons. Chi, the youngest child, knew that the officials were looking for the Serpent's maiden. She decided that she wanted to go freely. Her parents were distraught, but she said: 'Dear parents, you have given birth to six daughters, but alas, you do not have a son. You might as well be childless. I shall not be able to take care of you when you are old. Now I may gain some money for you which will be a great help.' Her father and her mother loved her greatly however and would not give their consent. She therefore went in secret.

Li Chi approached the authorities, saying that she was willing to travel to the Serpent's cave, provided they gave her a sharp sword, a snake-hunting dog, some food and a piece of flint.

The appointed day arrived, and Li Chi travelled to the Serpent's cave on the side of Yung-Ling mountain. She knew where to go, and having arrived she seated herself, clutched the sword in her hand, and kept the dog on a tight leash. She made a small fire. Having done this, she placed some riceballs near the entrance of the Serpent's cave. Smelling the riceballs, the Serpent appeared, reared forward, and opened its ghastly mouth. Just at that moment Li-Chi unleashed her dog. The dog leapt at the serpent and savaged it. With all her might, Li-Chi plunged her sword again and again deep into the Serpent's body. Thus the girl and the dog afflicted the most terrible wounds and soon the Serpent died.

Then Li Chi ventured into the Serpent's cave. She knew what she was looking for and after some time she found the skulls of the nine girls, who went to this mountain before her. As she returned to the light of day, she sighed, saying: 'You were killed because you were timid. How terrible'. She carried the nine skulls back to the village, so that they might be given a proper burial. Slowly, very slowly, she made her way home.

When the king of Yueh heard of Li Chi's deeds, he asked her to be his queen. Her father became magistrate of Chianglo county and her mother and elder sisters too were richly rewarded. The district had been freed of monsters, and ballads which honour Li Chi the serpent slayer, are sung in the region to this very day.[2]

The story of Li Chi may well be the story of each of us. Poor in the poor land, feeling useless and superfluous, we too may prepare to travel to

Yung-Ling mountain, hoping to struggle, knowing the risk we run, yet also knowing what will be lost if we do not willingly face the dragon. When we have succeeded in fighting things out with ourselves, we too need to honour our earlier more intimidated ways of living, our more cowardly deeds, and enter into a relationship with the sacrifices we made; for the omissions of the 'timid heart' need acknowledgment and burial. When at last we are ready to return to our own homelands, our scars can be seen more clearly; meanwhile though, unknown rewards also await us.

During our lifetime we may feel again and again that we are back on Yung-Ling mountain, for such is the way of things. There will be days when we can truly see the roses in the garden, hear the bird-song, and feel the warm hand of a friend on our shoulder; and there will be also be days when all these are within the reach of our heart, but we can neither see nor hear nor feel, because we are tired, searching too intently or clinging to our hope too fiercely. When we wrongly think ourselves a lone fish in the water, and have forgotten about the freshness which follows a thunderstorm, the majesty of the sea and the numerous unnamed pleasures which are also ours, we may wish to recall the following Mexican tale:

> Some time ago Mr Wolf was walking about when he got chased by a pack of fierce dogs. The chase was a close one, but just in time Mr Wolf spotted a small hole in the mountainside. He jumped in and found himself inside a cave just big enough for him, but far too small for the big dogs. When he had rested a while, he felt really chuffed with himself for having been able to escape from those bad dogs. He started talking to himself, saying:
>
> 'Feet ... listen to me. Answer this one. What did you do to help me to get into this cave?'
>
> 'That's easy, Mr Wolf', said the feet: 'Remember how we jumped and rushed ...'
>
> 'Too right...', said Mr Wolf. 'Fine feet.'
>
> Speaking to his ears, he said: 'And now, tell me ears. Tell me. What did you do to help me get in here?'
>
> 'You ask us?', said the ears. 'You ask us? Well. We listened for you on the left, on the right, behind you, before you. What? Even above and below you. We told you where those big dogs were coming from, didn't we?'

'Well, yes, so you did', said Mr Wolf, 'So you did. Fine ears. And what did you two do for me, eyes. What did you do?'

'Easy, Mr Wolf, easy now...', said the eyes. 'We did spot this cave for you, didn't we?'

'You did', said Mr Wolf. 'I must say, I'm a fine Mr Wolf, having such good eyes, and ears and feet.'

He stretched and thought he would give himself a pat on the back. Just as he did this, he spotted his tail.

He said: 'Oooh, tail. Useless tail, I want to bet that you didn't do a thing for me. You never have. You just hang there. Flopping about and it's probably you that made those dogs come after me. They must have seen how useless you are.'

The tail was very angry when it was spoken to in this way. It said: 'Listen to me Mr Wolf. I sure did wave about and said to those dogs, 'Come here. Come here and get that terrible Mr Wolf.'

Then Mr Wolf started shouting. He shouted really loud, saying: 'You bad tail. You bad, bad tail.' He turned and twisted and tried to bite the tail as hard as he could. 'Get out, tail. Get out of here', he screamed. He pushed his tail outside the cave and of course, he went out with it. Outside the big dogs were. They caught him.[3]

The story says it all. We can feel miserably chased by ourselves. We can equally feel pretty much at odds with the world, the car and the milk which went off. Though feeling good about some aspects of our life, we may well be fiercely at war within. It is relatively easy to see where Mr Wolf went amiss. It may therefore be helpful to tell ourselves his story from time to time. Then it will ease its way into our bloodstream and pop up just when we are about to bite our own tail once again.

Acceptance of life's ups and downs does not come easy, and even though time's passage may not heal our wounds, it gives us a chance to recognise the light and dark days. Whilst the coming and going of these days may in turn help us to learn to take them in our stride. Thus our loss is slowly integrated into the colourful pattern of our existence. From time to time, along with the revolving cycle of the seasons, we will re-experience a scintillating new freshness, a vivid appreciation of the wilds and the wet. We discover a different sense of belonging.

Death and birth and the life which we grant ourselves and which we are granted, invite us into a relationship. A relationship which has its inevitable ups and downs, twists and turns. We have choices and commitments to make, promises to keep or break, initiatives to develop.

Every decision about the way in which we choose to relate to the circumstances of our days and nights is truly and uniquely ours. Of course our relationship with the life which is ours to live is influenced by the experiences which came our way, but it need not be determined by those experiences. We need not remain victims or victors, even though we may at times have been victims or victors. Because our power is limited, we must not conclude that we are powerless. Of this reality too, the stories speak. To help us to ponder such themes the people of Cambodia tell the following tale about two friends who tried to empty the sea.

> Once upon a time there were two friends. They helped one another when times were good and when times were bad. Both men married. One night one of the couples talked about ways in which they might earn a living. The man said: 'Did you know that a long time ago many ships laden with gold and silver sailed these seas. A lot of ships sank and they are still there at the bottom of the sea with all their riches. Let us go and empty the sea. We'll then find gold and silver and lots of fish too. We'll cook some rice in the morning and then we'll be off.' The next day they went to the sea and set about emptying it. It was hard work. They carried basket after basket away from the sea, hardly pausing to eat. Thus they worked for five days. The man looked out across the sea and he saw that it was lower already. He encouraged his wife by saying: 'It'll only take a few more days. I bet you, within a fortnight the sea will be empty and then we'll have the gold and the silver, and even the fish.'

> When the fish heard this, they did not like it. They spoke with each other and the King of the fish. He advised them to carry some gold and silver to the man and the woman. They had to ask them both if they would please stop taking the water out of the sea, and if they agreed to do so, that then they would receive some gold and silver. The fish did this. The man and woman were very glad to receive the gold and the silver, and they immediately stopped taking the water from the sea.

> Some time later the couple's friend visited them. He saw that they were as warmhearted as before, and that they were now rich. He asked how that had come about, and they told him the whole story. Their friend

went home and told his wife what he had heard. They too decided to try to empty the sea, and to get up early the next morning.

But they overslept, in their hurry they burnt the rice, and by the time they were ready to leave home, midday had come. Day after day they struggled on. They got tired and became angry which each other, but meanwhile they worked so hard that they too frightened the fish.

When the fifth day came they wanted to throw down their baskets, first the one then the other. But whenever one of them was about to give up, saying: 'I'm no fool. I'm tired, tired, tired. We're never going to get any gold from this sea', the other one got angry. They started to quarrel fiercely. They shouted at each other. They fought and pulled at each other's clothes. They pulled so hard that the sarongs they were wearing, fell off. They stood there, naked on the beach. They were tired, frightened and ashamed.

'We were always poor', they said. 'We will always be poor. We won't become rich by emptying the sea. Let's stop.' The fish laughed when they saw the people standing there. Now they would not have to give away any of their gold and silver. Some fishes were so pleased and laughed so loud, that their mouths became very big. These days their mouths are still big and when we look at them we know.[4]

We can ponder for quite a while what exactly we know when we see the fishes' mouths and remember their laughter. We note the story's apparently crude stereo-types, the simply sketched opposites between optimists and pessimists, the differences of perception between the ones who see the glass of wine or water as half full or half empty, noting too the thinly disguised encouragement of cooperation versus conflict. We may even sigh at the 'goodness' of getting-up in time, of pursuing intentions and making sure that the food we eat is nourishing. Does it matter that the second couple overslept, had to hurry and that their rice was burned? Maybe it does. Maybe the quiet care devoted to preparation for life's tasks frees our entrance into belief and therefore into hope.

It is very tempting to smile benignly at the first man's perception that the sea was lower already and that it wouldn't be long until they would reach their goal. The story poignantly raises the question of the value of 'uplifting spirits'. We may well perceive that the second couple's struggle is a precise description of an encounter with the underlying reality of life. After all we know that the sea could never have been emptied. It was foolhardy even to have tried. Of course its level was no lower; the tide had probably run out and anyhow, in our experience, fishes do not grasp human language. Who has ever heard of fish discussing with people if they would please leave the sea alone and be content with the gold and silver which they bring their way? Who has ever heard of people accepting the fishes' justified concerns? Many are the objections of the rational mind to the surface content of the tale, and yet ...

Is not this story also a description of the human cry for a vision, the desire for a different life? Could we not understand the couple's search for betterment, as one which is inspired by this ancient, ever-present longing, the fulfilment of which may take so many forms? Some of us enter into our cry for a vision because we deeply desire to understand better, to become braver in the face of life's events, or to learn to ask for help and favours, to discover the spirit of thanksgiving, to realise our oneness with all beyond time and place, or to reconnect with knowledge, in the sacred sense of the word. So many reasons why we travel to a lonely mountaintop, to the seaside or why we retire into ourselves amidst the turmoil of daily life in busy homes and workplaces.

Many of us are accustomed to sending our voice to our friends and loved ones, or to the sacred, to God or the gods of a thousand and one names, uttering our desires and intentions in human terms at so many different times and in so many different places; for we know that without a vision it is difficult to imagine the future constructively.

Some of us may have experienced the value of devoting special times and places to our 'prayer'. Maybe because we found roots within organised religion. In addition, or alternatively, we may have created deeply personal time and space to give form to our own encounters with the sacred.

Given the desire for a better life, we can also think of this story as relating to the cry for a vision, as an active way of praying, through which many good things may be received. The journey to the sea is apparently undertaken in search of greater material good, the easiest and most obvious way in which humankind recognises prosperous well-being. The rewards of gold and silver may, however, also be thought of as symbols for advanced states of heart and mind. We may consider the possibility that the first couple's willingness to suspend disbelief enables them to encounter the fishes, to listen to their concern about ill-considered human greed, to accept limits, and then to accept and enjoy the fishes' rewards. Their willingness to suspend disbelief opened the eternal gateway to possibility.

Through and beyond life's pitfalls, challenges and offerings, we may then experience the gift of generativity, whereby we become able to recognise one another mutually and wholeheartedly, to achieve a gentle solidarity of benign conviction. The urgency of our desire is then rooted in our willingness to explore darkness as well as light and is nourished by our knowing experience of absence and presence. In turn, these inspire our preparedness to long, our ability to perceive newness, as well as our willingness to act or to refrain from acting.

When death enters our life, most of us go through a time of great grief. We experience the pain of transforming the bonds which matter to us. This process of transformation is movingly conveyed in the words of a man whose closest male friend, a writer, died of cancer some twelve years ago. This is what he says:

> The memory of John is like the view across a channel. On a clear day it seems almost possible to pick up the phone and arrange a meeting. At other times the line goes dead and the separation is almost absolute. It is then difficult to trace the old patterns of our friendship, when I have moved on and we have not shared in this further separation.

> He has not met my wife or our children. How strange it is to make contact with the voice he left behind in his writings - open to so much interpretation without recourse to any answers. True, he anticipated some of this sense of loss by creating footholes in the future; like the book inscribed to my second grandchild. But am I still angry at his abandonment? Why was I unable to say that I wanted to be at his bedside when he died?

> I take comfort in the recollection of our friendship. That these thoughts and feelings continue to assume such importance for me is a testament to his continuing presence in my life.'[5]

We will recognise some of his regrets, the self-blame and equally the profound gratitude, derived from the continuing experience of presence amidst a wide range of new commitments and further joys as well as complexities.

Life, birth and death are about significance. Ideally, we shall grieve for the goldfish we cherished, for our cat, for the beautiful vase which broke, and above all for the people we love who died. Each of us needs to learn to cope with transitoriness, in the full knowledge that though our experiences of bonding and therefore of love and of grief, are shared with other people, they are at the same time unique. Following bereavement, we are invited to bond anew with life in its rich, sometimes bewildering and sometimes exquisitely wondrous complexity. It is true that this deepened sense of wonder deprives our mind of many certainties which had earlier been cherished. Wonder is indeed a form of disillusionment, but let us not forget that the mysterious is also the fairest thing we can experience, for it is the fundamental emotion which stands at the cradle of our commitment to life.

Though we may passionately grow to embrace the innocent brightness of newborn days, at times our courage and love of life will again hang like a wet rag around our knees. Maybe because desire has once again sent us on to a somewhat perilous journey or because we just happen to feel grotty and at odds with the world. At such times when my connection with the fair mysterious is at a low ebb, I tell myself, and anyone who wants to hear it, a story. This tale is inspired by the adventures of a man who, shortly after his wife's death, went in search of the Snow Leopard, one of the world's endangered animal species. This is the story:

> Some time ago a man went in search of the Snow Leopard. It was his heart's desire to see one of these rare animals, who dwell in the high mountains, far away from the lives of humankind. It is Autumn. The snows lie deep and the narrow mountain-paths are treacherous. Weeks pass and still the heart's desire is not fulfilled. Then the weary traveller comes across a Tibetan monk. The man is crippled. He had to flee his home country. Now he lives in this fierce mountainland far from the companionship of people. They meet, our traveller and the Lama. They talk and the traveller asks the monk whether he his happy where he is. 'Yes', laughs the monk, 'Especially as I have no choice'. Then the Lama asks the traveller about the purpose of his journey. He is told about the Snow Leopard and the snow and the treacherous mountains. At last the Lama enquires: 'Have you seen the Snow Leopard yet?' And the man says: 'No.' Then the Lama says: 'Isn't that wonderful.'[6]

I invariably laugh. It reminds me of the fishes.

References

1. Retold by the author. Excerpt from: Thompson, S., (1966) *Tales of the North American Indians*, Indiana University Press, p. 147-148.
2. Retold by the author. Contemporary source: Roberts, R., (1979) Chinese Fairy Tales and Fantasies, Pantheon Books.
3. Retold by the author. Contemporary source: Berg, L., (1977) *Folk Tales*, Pan Books.
4. Retold by the author: Contemporary source: Chandler, D., (1978) *Favourite Stories from Cambodia*, Heinemann Asia.
5. Markson, S., Unpublished manuscript, entitled *Biographies*.
6. Retold by the author. Inspired by incidents mentioned in: Matthiesen, P., (1980) *The Snow Leopard*, Picador.

Part III

Focused Attention on Intimate Loss

This silence frightens me:
like a wave of grass eating the world, first
death of a parent
is all the deaths. All
the bodies that will not stay down.

Lorrie Goldensohn

CHAPTER TEN

The death of a parent

It was indeed late autumn when the old man called his sons to his bedside. 'My sons', he said, 'the time has come for me to leave this world, and you must give me your faithful promise that you will bury me beneath the lime tree. You must promise also, that for three nights you will keep watch beside the tree. Then I know that my spirit will find rest.' Staszek said: 'I'll see to it, that a watch is kept'. Wladek said: 'I'll see to it, that a watch is kept, and Janek he will do as he is told'. 'That I know', said the old man, 'for Janek has already given his promise to carry out my wishes.'[1]

We can see the scene in our mind's eye. The old man gathering his three sons and speaking to them about imminent death. Wishes are uttered, requests made and blessings given. Then, with everything sorted out, the old farmer is free to die. The sons will perform their duty to the dead and the mourning may begin. Mourning which will be marked by the seeds of family-struggle which are sown in the little scene described above. We can already predict that the three sons' mourning will not be simple, but infinitely complex. Though Janek and his father might have liked one another, the relationship between the old man and his two elder sons was trouble laden.

The death of every parent takes a great deal of getting used to. After all, our parent was there when we were born, we lived with them, if only for a little while, and now our mother or our father has gone away for good. We realise very early on that we shall be reminded of their death for the rest of our life. We are affected not only in an immediate sense because new arrangements have to be made as regards house-keeping, and holidays or

Saturday afternoons, which for years have been used to visit Mother, but also because we shall experience what it is like to be parentless on the many occasions which, in our society, include the presence of a parent: Christmas, birthdays, mother's day and father's day. At weddings and funerals, our mother or father will not be there to keep us company, to irritate us or to console. This 'missing' will never end. It is the way of things.

Now that our parent is gone, we shall encounter our gratitude for all that was, as well as the full strength of our longing that all might have been different in our life. It may at first seem bewildering that we can so fiercely miss a parent with whom we had in reality a painfully ambivalent relationship. It does not seem to make sense that we feel such pain over the death of someone who, over the last few years, we did not even see that often, and then only reluctantly, or with whom our relationship was always problematic.

Yet this is many a person's experience. The more difficult the parent-child relationship, the harder it is to cope with their death. This is probably due to the fact that most of us are tenacious creatures, filled with media-images and private dreams regarding healthy parent-child interactions. Our reality may well have been sharply at odds with what we were led to believe was possible. The dream of more than good enough parenting was not surrendered simply because we experienced a less than good enough parent-child relationship. On the contrary, in all likelihood our dreams grew proportionately. It seems to be the case that the depth of our longings is commensurate with the depth of our disappointments. The fiercer our childhood loneliness, the more poignant our conviction that another kind of intimacy could have existed. If only. . .

If we do not address these childhood disappointments, our dreams will quietly continue to do their own dreaming, until our parent dies. Then we shall be caught unawares by the consuming strength of our sense that everything could have been so different and that therefore all might have been redeemed. If only our parent were still alive and if only we had realised in time how much needed to be said, how much had to be repaired. When this happens, the death of our parent initially seems to foreclose all chances of reparation.

Then we feel that the process, which might have been a mutual engagement with the complexities of the parent/child experience, can now only be a one-person journey, in which we have to come to grips not only with the death of our parent but also with the reality of our pained childhood. Once more abandoned to sorting out everything by ourselves, we may, with a sigh of 'what else is new', refuse to engage with the task at hand, and instead add to our set of depressive assumptions.

It might be helpful briefly to list three of these:

— *motivational*:   decreased initiative-taking

— *cognitive*:   decreasing belief that reactions will lead to results

— *emotional*:   anxiety as a result of a lack of control, which leads to an assumed certainty about uncontrollability.

When combined, these three basic assumptions result in the heartfelt conviction that all action is and was useless. We support our case by our evidence that many undesirable situations occurred independent of our reactions. This is the 'Whatever I did, it did not make the slightest bit of difference' syndrome. It is a dangerous syndrome, for it leads to the belief that action and reaction are of little value and the belief that one cannot control those elements or aspects in life which could alleviate suffering, which offer satisfaction and make us feel cherished. This is a grim outlook. One which we may be wise to try to alleviate. To seek help.

It is in so many respects easier to mourn the death of someone with whom our relationship was comparatively straightforward and warm, a relationship where we were able to enjoy knowing one another. Then the inevitable complexities of intimate encounters could be straightened out, resulting in a stronger bond, which provided both the parent and the child with a sense of nurturing intimacy. Though we will miss our mother or our father sorely when they have died, the chances are that we shall more readily grow through our grief. This will be thanks to our own strength, which is at least in part derived from our parents' love, and which had at its heart a commitment to enable us to grow independently from them.

Whether there was ease or dis-ease in our relationship with our dead parent, what often continues to hurt us, years after their death, is that our maturation results in a changing relationship with our parent's deed and misdeeds. We grow to understand them differently, often with greater compassion. When they have died, we can no longer convey this to them. There also continues to be so much that we would like to say, and so much that we wish we had said. Oftentimes it hurts fiercely that such words can no longer be heard by the very people who would have loved to hear them. When we are forever deprived of the possibility to add newness to a relationship, we mourn deeply.

Then the reparation which needs to happen has to take a different course. We have to search for a method of reconciliation and forgiveness beyond the grave. It can be done. Of course, it can be done. But how one might have wished that our mother or father had known about our changed outlook on life's events, about our understanding and forgiveness. How we may long for their appreciation and blessing. None of this can now be achieved externally, be demonstrated in the reality of the relationship. The healing hand of acceptance can merely be felt internally. But still, what a difference it may make. A difference which is movingly conveyed in the Japanese folktale *The Maiden with the Wooden Bowl*.

> A long time ago there lived an old couple. They had only one child, a most beautiful young girl. Then the husband died. Time passed and the old woman too knew that she would not live much longer. One day she spoke to her daughter and said: 'My child. I am old, and know that soon I will die. You are very beautiful. Men will look at you and see your beauty. I do not want you to be loved for your beauty alone.' When she had finished speaking the old woman placed a lacquered wooden bowl over her daughter's head. Now only the lower half of her face could be seen, the rest was veiled by the black bowl. The mother then said: 'Wear it always, for the bowl will protect you when I am gone.' Shortly after the woman died.
>
> Having neither relatives nor friends, the girl went to work in the rice-fields. The other young people working there, tried to remove the wooden bowl, but failed to do so. They tried to lift her spirits, but the maiden knew no laughter and instead she bent down to gather the rice. She worked diligently whilst her heart was heavy.
>
> One day a rich farmer noticed the maiden with the black wooden bowl. He watched her as she worked quietly. After a while he invited her to come and work in his rice-fields. When the harvest was done, the farmer, who was impressed by the girl's bearing, invited her to stay in the farmhouse and to take care of his wife, who was ill. As time passed, the farmer and his wife grew fond of the maiden. They treated her as if she were their own daughter.

Then the eldest son returned home from studying in a faraway town. He was a wise young man, who had grown tired of a life of merry-making and foolishness. Soon after he met the maiden with the wooden bowl, he asked his father who she was and why she wore an ugly bowl upon her head. His father told him the girl's sad story. As the days passed by, the young man grew very fond of her, and he decided that he would ask her to marry him. When he told his friends about his plans, they tried all they could to dissuade him, warning him that she might turn out to be very ugly indeed. But the young man grew to love her greatly, and at length he asked her to marry him. The maiden refused. She said: 'I am but a servant's in your father's house.' However much he pleaded with her, she would not change her mind. That night she cried herself to sleep, for she too loved him with all her heart.

Then she dreamt. In her dream her mother stood before her, smiling most warmly. She said: ' My child. Don't be troubled any longer. It is good to marry the farmer's son. All shall be well.' In the morning, when the young man asked her again to marry him, the maiden accepted him.

As the day of the wedding approached, the girl tried to remove the wooden bowl from her head. It remained firmly fixed. Some relations offered their help, but the bowl merely seemed to utter strange groans. No matter who tried, the bowl stayed fast. Finally the young man said: 'Do not be troubled about it. With or without bowl, you are dear to me.'

The farmer's son ordered the wedding feast to proceed. Into the crowded halls, the wine-cups were brought. The bride and bride groom, were about to lift the ceremonial glass to their lips, when the wooden bowl fell off with a great noise. From it fell silver and gold and all manner of precious stones. The maiden who was once little more than a beggar, was now rich. The wedding-guests were greatly surprised as they saw such shining wealth. Yet even greater was their pleasure when they looked at her for the first time, and saw that she was a most beautiful woman.[2]

Those of us who have experienced the death of a parent, will undoubtedly identify with aspects of the maiden's journey. The helpless decision to work as best one knows how, quietly and diligently. Financial pressures often mean that there is little choice. Bare survival demands that we bend low and work in the rice-fields, simply to make ends meet. As we plod along, we may well feel that a veil has come before our eyes, casting a shadow over all we see and do.

Thus time passes. In our story the maiden is invited into another home, where she takes it upon herself to 'take care', to look after someone who is unwell. We may also recognise this stage in the recovery process. We too may have found that we gained comfort and reassurance from involvement with a caring organisation. Some of us may have become bereavement counsellors, some started work in a nursery, or visiting patients in a local hospital or hospice. When we reach out towards other people who also suffer, we experience relief, the relief of being able to give again. Of being able to make things better for someone else and thereby also for ourselves. Of course each healer also needs to heal him- or herself, and of course we need to take care of ourselves as well as others. But there is no doubt that for many of us, the first steps on the road towards recovery were taken when we reached out to help lift someone else's spirits.

Once the maiden with the wooden bowl has settled into the farmer's house, the young man grows to love her. He asks her to marry him. She refuses.

When we reconstruct our own road towards recovery from bereavement, we too may have found that after some time had passed, new opportunities opened up. We will have wondered whether or not to pursue the chances we were offered: another home, a different job, new friendships. At first we may well have felt unable to make a positive choice. Not daring to embark upon any of these ventures unless we felt that we had an inner sense of permission, the permission to go on living. In this story this process is beautifully conveyed in the maiden's dream about her mother. When she has received her mother's blessed reassurance that it is well to say 'yes' to life and agree to the relationship, she accepts the marriage proposal.

Having thus moved forward, she becomes all the more painfully aware of her sorrow. Until this moment the storyteller has not described the girl's struggle with the bowl. So far we have not yet been told about any earlier attempts to remove it. Now we are. She tries and fails. In spite of the fact that she decided to get married and thereby to consent to newness, the bowl will not be shifted.

Our own experience may well be similar. Having bought another home, having accepted a different job, our expectations may be disappointed. We are still depressed and burdened by the pain of our loss. The new job or partner or hobbies have not performed the trick we had imagined. Our pains have not gone away. We now simply have a new partner and we are still sorrowed. We have another job, which offers us satisfactions, and we are also pained. One does not cancel the other, and how could we even have thought that this might be the case.

Thus the maiden and her young lover again and again come up against the 'bowl', until they acknowledge that it will probably be there for ever and ever more. The marks left by the experience of bereavement will not entirely go away. A scar is a scar, however beautifully it has healed. Likewise the experience of the bowl will be there. The young man in our story then tells the maiden that he loves her with or without a bowl. So, let it be.

It is then and only then, that change can happen. The story tells us that the wedding proceeds. It has been recognised that the past will always be there. When this is accepted, a transformation may occur. Of course our maiden then becomes a woman of substantial wealth, who is also very beautiful. Which one of us is not a person of great personal riches when we achieve surrender to life's limits and possibilities, when we can praise a life which includes death and toast to its complex wonder. Then we too shine with stunning beauty.

Ah. . .but how to reach this place of consenting love?

The pathway will be a special one for each of us, and we shall travel it many a time and oft, each new arrival marking a further beginning. As such, each of us designs our own *via positiva*. In our design we may learn by example from one another, guided by successes, warnings and failures. It is therefore equally helpful to listen to a tale which did not lead to a consent to the events and experiences of life and which resulted in curtailment and everlasting sorrow. The contemplation of the intricacies of such a journey enables us to recognise some of the pitfalls which greet us too on our journey through grief. The following African tale may thereby become a guide.

> Bat lived with his old mother. Suddenly his mother became very ill. Bat called the antelope and said to him: 'Make my mother some medicine.' The antelope looked carefully at Bat's mother to see what ailed her. Then he said: 'Only the sun can help your mother', and the antelope went away. Early in the morning, Bat went to see the sun, but it was already eleven o'clock in the morning when they met. Bat said: 'I'm on my way to see you.' The sun answered: 'If you have something to say, speak.' Then bat asked: 'Come with me, my mother is sick, make

her some medicine.' The sun answered and said that he could not make any medicine on the road and that Bat had to meet him in his own house. Therefore Bat had to come and see him early the next day.

Bat returned home. The day passed, night fell and everyone slept. Bat left home even earlier, but now it was nine o'clock when he met sun, and again sun said: 'Once I've left home, I do not go back. Come another day.' Bat went back home, and so it happened that Bat travelled five more times to see sun, and every day he was late.

On the seventh day Bat's mother died. Bat was grief-stricken and said: 'If the sun had made some medicine, my mother would have recovered. The sun has killed her.'

Many people came to share Bat's mourning. They mourned the whole day.

Then Bat ordered that his mother's body be carried to her grave. This happened. When they came to the grave, the beasts said that they always looked at a person's face before burial. They wanted to look upon Bat's mother too.

When they saw her, they said: 'No, we cannot bury her. She is not one of us. She is not a beast. She has a head like us, but she also has wings. Therefore she looks like a bird. Call upon the birds to bury her.' Thus they left.

Bat called the birds, and they came, all of them, and they too asked to see Bat's mother. Bat let her be seen. They looked very attentively. Then they spoke and said: 'Yes, she looks like us, for she has wings as we do. But we do not have teeth. None of us have teeth. She is not one of us, because she has teeth. She is not one of us.' The birds flew away.

Much time had passed as they talked. Meanwhile the ants had come. They had entered the body of Bat's mother. There was nothing he could do, to drive them away. To make matters worse, one of the birds said: 'You should not have postponed the burial. I warned you, that such a thing might happen.'

Then all the birds and the beasts had gone.

Bat was all alone. He spoke to himself and said: 'I blame the sun for all my trouble. My mother would still be alive, if only he had made her some medicine. I shall never look upon the sun again. We shall never be friends. I shall hide myself, when the sun shines forth. I shall neither greet him nor ever look at him.' Then Bat spoke and said: 'I shall grieve for my mother for all time. I shall visit nobody. I shall always walk in darkness, lest I meet anyone.'[3]

Here the story ends, with Bat having made a commitment to dwell in everlasting, lonesome darkness. What sorrowful pain and what a pitiful state to dwell in. How many of us have unwittingly made kindred commitments? Have devoted ourselves to carrying the burden of sorrow for the rest of our life, out of a mistaken sense of duty, out of unremedied guilt or the hopeless despair that life could ever be any different? If only we then could find an alternative route, some way of achieving reconciliation, relief from the burden of guilt-ridden, angry sorrow.

In a moving autobiography, Toby, a Bristol tramp, describes how he overcame some poignant difficulties which were not unlike Bat's problems, but which were resolved in a very different way. Toby tells us how he and his brothers and sisters were sent to an orphanage after his mother died. He was eleven years old. His mother had been overworked and overtired. A small kind of woman, who had too many children, eight plus two who died when they were babies. Toby had been in the orphanage for three months when his father called him home. He needed his son to care of him for he had been paralysed in an accident. Thus Toby had to leave his brothers and sisters, who stayed in the orphanage. They lost all contact with each other. This eleven-year-old boy then had to wash his father, feed him, dress him and do everything about the house. When Toby was twenty-four his father went into a nursing home and Toby ended up loosing his home. He therefore took to the road.

Here he has lived, on and off, for the last fifty years, ending up in a caravan, a bit rough, as he says, but not too bad. This is what he then writes in his autobiography:

> My privations, hardships and humiliations have given me a full understanding of life. To help one another, man's bond of friendship from man to man, a returned love of a man for his wife, patience, tolerance, forbearance and understanding, above all compassion, these things are the fulfillment of life. If you have these, hold firm. All I ask is kindness, to take with me along the highway of life and to extend it to all I may meet. To share the little I have, to console and comfort the sad, to expound my knowledge to all those who have ears. With these things in mind I feel a deep sense of invigoration, a pure evocation of

the mind, an elevation to higher thoughts. If these words can be of consolation to anyone, I shall be well rewarded.'[4]

Who would not wish to arrive at such a state of mind? To dwell at ease with solitude and people, to be able to picture the world as it is and as it might be, a world where we live with each other, as well as for each other, not having to hide in darkness, like Bat, who refuses ever to meet the sun again, but instead to be able to welcome our days in a spirit of forgiveness and discovery?

This can only be achieved if it is recognised that the loss of a parent through death is always a serious event, whether we are six, sixteen, or sixty years of age. If our parent died when we were young we were, of course, differently affected from when we are old, if only because the adults around us made decisions on our behalf. They also selected bits of information, which they considered right for our ears, and others which were knowingly withheld. This may have added to our confusion. We also had to face teachers and classmates, who may have felt distinctly uncomfortably with death, not knowing how to talk about death in the classroom situation or on the school playground. When a child is bereaved, there are always problems with concentration. The schoolwork is nonetheless marked, and it is very difficult to accept what feels like criticism when the child is simply thinking about a mother or father who died. It takes trust to believe that the concentration and therefore the grades will improve after a while. Such trust is precisely what is lacking during the first months of bereavement.

Meanwhile it will seem, to every child and adult, that friends very quickly forget what has happened. This may be helpful, but it can also be hurtful. Of course, some people only appear to forget out of clumsiness. Not knowing how to convey their care and support, they pretend that nothing much is the matter any more. Whereas the adult may grow to understand this 'clumsiness', it is hard to reach such sympathetic understanding for a child who is not yet wise in the ways of the world. In addition, as the poet J. B. Yeats reminds us: 'We should not make light of the troubles of children. They are worse than ours, because we can see the end of our trouble and they can never see any end.'[5]

As has been said before most of us experience substantial pain when seeing other people with their parents. At times the bereaved 'child' in us will feel set apart, different from everyone. This is best acknowledged by creating as many chances as possible to bring such differences to the surface, to speak about our experience.

Furthermore every bereaved child, whether four or forty years old, has to cope with the reality that follows our parent's death. It seems that change happens at an alarming rate. If one of our parents is still alive, their life-style is likely to alter a great deal; especially if the parent is still young, new friends will be made. Some of these friends may come to stay, and some may intend to stay for a very long time. Lack of clarity about a mother's or father's relationship with these 'friends' can cause both young and old 'children' to feel deeply perturbed. What is going to happen? Does this new person want to usurp the dead parent's place? Will there be enough room in the house for new love and old love?

When the new parental couple is serious about commitments, another phase is entered during which we may feel once more at the mercy of parental decisions. The extent to which the young or the adult child is consulted about the developments will also be the extent to which they are empowered to agree to the changes which are brought about.

The first years of bereavement are marked by change, as adaptations have to be made to life in different circumstances. As Susan Wallbank writes: 'At times you may feel that there is conflict between the changes you need to make in your life and the needs of your family.'[6] Such conflict of interest will almost certainly occur. Then talking and sharing offer us, who are involved in the intimate tragedy of bereavement, a way through. Sometimes it will be hard to believe that anything good might come out of this sad experience. We feel washed together, thrown apart, and once more ship-wrecked upon the shore of each other's understanding. With a lot of help from our friends we grow through the experience, knowing more about ourselves and the people close to us. Good memories return, and a different kind of balance is achieved.

We might have wanted it differently, now that we are left with the memory of our last encounter. An encounter which may resemble the one vividly evoked in the following poem, titled *Father*.

> You speak my name, Ask if I know your daughter -
> My eyes fight the mounting pain
> And watch yours water,
> 'Must be a draught', you mutter
> While my rage and grief

Rise from my stomach
Spewing silent fury at the foolish death
Of once so fierce a brain.
I drive home, weeping that in your mind
I have a name
That does not fit the stranger that you see,
Weeping that you do not know
That you shed tears for me.'[7]

We may struggle bitterly with the memories of such final meetings, searching to retrieve another kind of love, a gentler clarity. When at last we shall become reconciled to the way of things, we know that no one can ever take away the experience of our journey through grief, a journey which helped us to encounter the heart-break as well as the heart's joy in the heart of things.

References

1. Crown, A. C., (1971) *Tales from Poland*, Oxford: Pergamon Press, p. 15
2. Retold by the author. Contemporary source: Gersie, A. and King, N., (1990) *Storymaking in Education and Therapy*, London: Jessica Kingsley Publishers.
3. Retold by the author. Contemporary source: Van Over, R., *Sunsongs, op. cit.*
4. (1976) Toby, The story of a Bristol Tramp, *Bristol Broadsheets*, p. 25.
5. Yeats, W. B., (1955) *Reveries over Childhood and Youth*, London: Macmillan, p. 5
6. Wallbank, S., (1990) *My Mother Died, Richmond: Cruse-Bereavement Care.*
7. Jenkyns, M., *Father*, unpublished manuscript.

'O little did my mother ken,
The day she cradled me
The lands I was to travel in
Or the death I was to die!'

Anon.

CHAPTER ELEVEN

The death of our child

When our child dies a great sorrow enters our life. We know that the experience changes us. Our days and nights will not be the same again. In this sense and in this sense alone, we might say that we shall never get over it. Many parents want it heard that the death of their child is the greatest tragedy which could have befallen them, whilst simultaneously there dwells within a deep gratitude for having been able to share the child's bitterly brief existence. During the days of profound grief we not only need to remind ourselves that we loved and lost, we also need to stay aware of the reality that we shall continue to be a parent to our dead child until our own dying day. This, too, must be remembered by all those who come to counsel or console.

They say that age shall not weary the child who died. Nor the years condemn. But who said that we had wanted it to be this way? When we know that the score of memories of the three weeks, three years or thirty years of our child's life shall never be expanded, we ache bitterly.

In a Maori lament Makere grieves the death of his son Taramoana. He says:

> O my son,
> Only your name remains;
> Now you are gone, alone.
> Love has no power to restore the heart,
> So slow to live, so swift to die. . .
> I will destroy the house of speech
> And drink at the source of rage.[1]

How we may recognise his feeling of awe-inspiring fury now that his son has been cast from the world of light, has gone to a place where he knows 'neither sorrow nor delight'. We may dread our own journey to this place and how can we therefore possibly endure the thought that our child has entered such anticipated nothingness? Has travelled to where we have not yet gone and where we may be so very frightened to go? Thus our protective urges are twice wounded; not only might we feel that we were unable to protect our child's life, we were also unable to accompany our child on the journey into death which we may dread. Unless, of course, we have made our peace with a 'sensed' reality beyond death. Then we may find comfort in the belief that our child has simply returned to a greater spiritual reality, and support ourselves with the thought that our child is progressing towards God ahead of us. If we believe this with conviction then we will also feel responsible for the maintenance of a continuing spiritual relationship with our child, even though we are separated from each other by death. This will be of great help in our mourning process.

If we live securely with such awareness of divine presence we are probably able to recognise the words used by Jane Davies to describe her experiences of the last days of her daughter Sarah's life.

> In the days shortly before her death, she would lie curled up in a chair, half-dozing, half-watching us as we lived out our lives around her. Smiling, she would say; 'I'm so happy, I feel I've got arms tight round me.' Her death was the most exciting moment of my life. Deep in the almost overwhelming pain and grief of her going I was still conscious of a great joy and triumph; joy that she had not been destroyed by her suffering, that she was still confident and reassured; joy that we were able to hand her back into and on to the greatest Love of all; joy that this was not really the end. I felt a very real sense of a new birth - more painful but as exciting as her first one seven years earlier. There was an inexplicable but unshakable knowledge that all was well indeed.[2]

Perhaps we too found great joy in the process of letting go, but for many of us this is not what the experience of losing a child feels like. To the contrary, there is a profound sense of having been thrown into the dangerous depths of grief when we have to bury our child.

> With smeared mascara and a dripping nose
> her mother follows an aunt around the city
> searching, searching, and more remote

than ever her father is just another echo
in the abandoned house, and the rabbi
chided us as willfully blind
who, when called, slid our spadefuls of dirt
down the side of the grave and did not
dump them on that still resonating box.[3]

How can we feel more than an abandoned echo, we, who have been left little other than our memories, photographs and videos, a few note books maybe, some toys and drawings? We search for the evidence of this young life, evidence which we will eventually find in our continuing, changing relationship with the child who lived with us. But how to safeguard such presence in this world? We know that it must be safeguarded, if only for our sake, but how can we possibly be expected to find a form for the unacceptable?

Yet, we sense that it would help if we could find a way of honouring our child's life, and therefore the relationship which we have with our dead son or daughter. After much time has passed, we may decide to honour this relationship on specific days and times during the year, times when we will honour and remember the child we lost in so many different ways. Maybe we will choose the day of birth, maybe we will also choose the day of death. Two anniversaries which enshrine the time we shared, anniversaries which will forever more greet us in the revolving cycle of the seasons.

In most ancient stories the death of a child is described as the great original sorrow, the ultimate pain which occurred at the beginning of time, either due to some original disobedience, or because it had to be this way and no other, or for no special reason at all. The death of children occurs simply because this is also the way of things.

In a moving myth told by Ma'afu, Chief of Tonga, we hear that since the beginning of time the gods live on the island Bulotu. It cannot be told where this island is, though some say that the words, which came down from our fathers, declare Bulotu to be where the sun meets the waters in the climbing path of the sun. On this island dwelt the gods, Maui, the greatest of them all, with his two sons and many brothers. They dwelt in a beautiful land for on this island could be found the Water of Life from which the gods drink every day. Near the edge of this Fountain of life stands Akau-Lea, the wondrous Tree of Speech, and beneath the tree the gods sit.

At one point in the recitation of the feats of Maui, we encounter a fierce quarrel between Maui and his son Ata-longa. Maui tells his son to hold his tongue. Ata-longa refuses to hold his tongue any longer. Father and Son fight bitterly, but then Ata-longa reaches out in reconciliation. At least it so appears that he seeks his father's forgiveness. Secretly Ata-longa is making plans to leave the island of the gods. When the gods are fast asleep, he sneaks away in his father's canoe, taking with him the best of the brave and the young. They want to start life anew on the islands which Maui has just made.

After some time the gods on Bulotu realise what has happened for the great god's canoe is no longer there - the young gods used it in their escape. In frightened perplexity the gods sit and wait.

Chief Ma'afu, the ancient storyteller, continued the tale, saying:

> Then a deep groan from the Tree of Speech broke in upon the silence, and a wailing sound was heard from among its branches, whence a sprinkling, as of rain, fell down upon the surface of the Water of Life, like the falling of many tears ...

> 'They are gone!' said the Tree with a groan. 'Ata-longa has taken them away to the new land. They are gone, never to return. Alas! alas! For the folly of the disobedient ones. Evil is now their lot - hunger and thirst - trouble and sorrow - sickness and DEATH!' At this dreadful word the voice of the Tree ceased, and an awful silence fell upon the host - a silence of dread - broken only by the low moan of wailing among the branches, and by the falling as of teardrops into the Water of Life. And a shudder ran round the circle of gods with the sound of a deep drawn breath; nor did any one ask the meaning, for they felt its meaning within their hearts, though they had never heard it before.

> Then a chill blast came sweeping through the branches, mingling a sound of sobbing and sighing with the wailing moan; and many of the leaves, evergreen heretofore, faded and withered, and fell, scattered hither and thither by the sudden blast. And the gods, looking up in awestruck wonder - for never before had such a thing been known - saw that the branch, from which the leaves had fallen, was sapless and dead.[4]

Groaning, sighing, wailing and weeping, and all the other 'feeling' words in Chief Ma'afu's myth, do not suffice to describe what our child's death feels like. For most of us words fail to convey the depth of our anguish and outrage. Yet we feel that we must find words, for we want other people to hear that part of us shall continue to protest long after our child has died. Anniversaries will hurt. Weddings will hurt, because the little person who we helped to enter this world and whom we looked after is no longer here. A child we had wanted to get to know much better. Life lay ahead of us. Now it feels as if it all lies behind us. In this respect too we sense that our child's death has killed our future. Can it ever be reclaimed and if we do regain a future, will this be a further betrayal, another violence? It is difficult to wish to go on living, after the death has happened, to take an interest in people again.

Many people whose child has died initially feel that they too want to die, or at least that they no longer want to live. The danger of this situation is described in many stories. In an ancient Australian Aboriginal tale we are told how the struggle to survive a child's death, was too much. The mother surrendered her life, and she too died. This is what happened:

> A spirit baby once spoke to the husband of Bunyil, asking him where she might be, for it wished to become her earth-child. Bunyil had always wanted to have a child, and she was therefore very happy when she found she was pregnant. When the baby was born she tried to do all she could to look after the one she loved so much. Her husband, too, rejoiced that his wife and child were happy together, and did all he could to look after them. Whenever the other women came to see them, they too brought fruit and vegetables into the shelter. Thus there was food in abundance for Bunyil and her baby.

> Then suddenly, the baby stopped growing. Its eyes grew larger and larger. The little body wearied with thinness. The child who once played and smiled, now lay quietly, without looking, without moving. As time passed by the baby became thinner and thinner. Young mother Bunyil went from medicine-man to grandmother to plead for a cure for her child. They did all they could, but knew that it was to no avail. They could not safe her baby's life. Then the child died. And sorrowing, weeping Bunyil held in her arms a tiny, dead baby.

> It was her grandfather who took the baby's body and buried it where the rocks have a small hole. Then the entrance was closed and the path towards it swept clean of leaves and grass and stones. Thereby making it easy for the baby's spirit to travel on the path to the aboriginal heaven.

> Young Bunyil returned to the camp with everyone else. Her eyes let go of tears like mournful skies the rain. When she knew that everyone else was fast asleep, she crept back towards the grave. She had taken with her a branch of the Christmas bush, the bush which is the dear home of the spirit children. She placed it carefully by the entrance to the grave.

She stayed there a while and then returned home, convinced that her baby's spirit had found a nestling place in the branch.

Time past, but day and night Bunyil mourned. She kept the branch always within reach. Then her eyes too grew large. She lost weight and became very weak. She felt that her child wanted her to be near. She died then. And her people buried her near the baby's grave.[5]

We must ask ourselves what could have helped Young Bunyil to stay alive. What could have bonded her so strongly to her people that she might have been able to live through the ordeal of the loss of her beloved baby? Old stories are as interesting for what they do not say, as for the events which are described.

In this tale the grandmothers and the medicine-man are no longer mentioned once the baby has died. Bunyil's husband too has disappeared from the scene. It is as if we witness the group's helpless acceptance of the fact that Bunyil's response to the loss is such that the community cannot prevent her death. By acting when everyone is fast asleep, she bypasses whatever care her people might have offered her. This power and choice are truly hers. They are also truly ours. When our child dies, many of us feel that the choice to end our life seems to present itself with inviting clarity. How then not to succumb to the lure to attempt to kill ourselves or to condemn ourselves to a living-death by dwelling with unredeemed grief.

How may we learn to consent to life again?

Some people say that friendship helped. It gave them something to fight for apart from themselves. Visitors too, who listened and stayed around whilst we tore our hair out. Visitors who were there long enough for us:

— to learn to accept that we do not get used to the death for a very long time,

— to realise that we did all we could,

— to acknowledge that whatever we now do or do not do, we cannot get our child back,

— to allow ourselves to hold the child in our mind,

— to give ourselves permission not to forget, and thereby to learn to accept the death as a reality,

— to accept always that we miss the child sorely.[6]

For truly the pain and the crying and the silences we experience when our child dies, are almost greater then we can endure. Years later, the memory of the pain of those early days may hurt us again with surprising intensity. During the early months and years our outrage will tear us apart. We often feel with blind and overwhelming fury that our child's death should not have happened, that it was wrong, utterly wrong for our child to die before we did. We hear the consolations about better countries, happier inheritances, and greater glory. But how meaningless those words seem, now that we face the awesome reality of the grave or the urn in which our child rests.

This is what a woman whose daughter died of a brain-tumor at the age of eight and whose twenty-year old son became severely handicapped following a motor-bike accident, said:

Do not show us the road to recovery. Whatever recovery might mean. Allow us to find our own way through. To find comfort in your compassion, not in your consolation. To find strength in your helplessness, now that we feel so utterly helpless. Let us know that you too are speechless, wounded and outraged because the universe has done this to us and therefore to the human community. Listen to our guilt, when we think in spite of ourselves, that our child's death, was some kind of divine punishment for our shortcomings. Hear the reality of these shortcomings. Do not diminish them in our own eyes, but help us also to see the strength of our love, and the solidity of our care. We have discovered that life can no longer be relied upon to safeguard us. Understand that therefore we feel in so many respects lost and lonesome. Try to comprehend our fear, and hear it. Do not try to remedy it, or to protect us against it. We need the full measure of our fear, so that we may discover the full strength of our courage. We also need the full measure of our self-accusation, so that we may experience the depth of our forgiveness.

Trust us to encounter the profundity of our despair. Have faith that such desolation is survivable. We must meet our own darkness, for only then may we find another kind of ground into which to plant the tree of our life. Never forget that we feel betrayed by the order of the universe, which seems to suggest that children are born, then they grow up and grow old. Until our child died, we too trusted this order, for it implied that it was right for parents to die before their children. This was hard enough as it stood. And if the order of the universe is meant to be such, then why did it have to make an exception for us. Why did it betray us so. Let us struggle with this question. Do not stop our questioning. We need to engage with it again and again, until we grow to see that it simply happened to be this way.[7]

In our mind's eye, we shall replay again and again the last months or moments of our child's life, asking ourselves repetitively whether there really was nothing we could have done to prevent the death from occurring. What if we had taken greater care, paid more attention to the first signs of unwellbeing, acted more swiftly. Thus self-reproach may haunt our days and nights for months or years to come. Unreasonably so, but it does, until there is someone out there who is truly willing to hear it. Until such time we may stand accused in our own eyes of having failed our child and therefore of having failed as a parent. How can we ever find forgiveness for a deed we did or did not commit, for a failure which was or wasn't ours, unless we are able to admit to it? Our shortcomings were undoubtedly the same as those of any other parents, whose parenting is basically 'good enough'. We must, however, be allowed to admit to our sense of failure.

At such times our only comfort may well be found in the simple fact that we are actually surviving. In the friends who stand by, clumsily and lovingly and are able to share with us these hellish days and nights.

For in addition to the pain of our loss, many of us endure a sense of separation from our partner, who too seems lost in a lonesome universe. We cannot reach each other, even though we now need one another bitterly. At this awful time they too seem to have deserted us. How passionately we may hate the man or the woman we once loved. They are tainted by the stain of death. They are not responsible. We know this. But they are responsible with us for giving birth to this child. Therefore they are responsible for the pain we now endure. Logic suggests that this is right. How can we then be expected to forgive them for contributing to our pain? We wonder whether they could have prevented the death. Unreasonably so, but we think these thoughts. In spite of ourselves we do hold our wife, our husband, our partner responsible for much that took place during those fateful days. When they grieve, we scold them for their lack of support with day-to-day tasks. When they carry on with life, we are angry with them for not grieving enough. If before we felt that we were competing in love, we now nurture our reproach that this love was insufficiently shown. We feel so raw and vulnerable.

Then we realise that something has to change, or all will be lost. Once more we start to build bridges, or we are helped to build bridges, to find a place where we may share our grief and let go of our accusations. In order to do so, we need to surmount our fear, the fear that all has been lost.

The following South American story addresses the process which we then go through:

> In the old days the Boa Constrictor was an enormous snake. It would attack and eat everything that crossed its path. Though the Boa enjoyed eating animals, it loved to devour human flesh. No one was safe from its monstrous hunger.
>
> One day, a woman whose two children had been killed by the Boa Constrictor, called out and cried: 'Is there nobody who will fight this snake? Must this go on for ever more? How many more people must die? How many more children get killed?'
>
> Then one man, the man who played the flute most beautifully, said: 'It is not good for people to be this frightened.' He took his bundle filled with roasted maize and a knife. Then, whilst he played his flute, he left the village.
>
> Soon the Boa Constrictor heard the man's playing. It was very beautiful. The man knew the Boa was near him, but he played as if nothing was happening. The Boa pounced and gulped the flute-player down.
>
> Once inside the snake's dark belly, the man made himself as comfortable as he could. He knew that he might have to stay there a long, long time. He opened his bundle with the roasted maize and the knife. Then he cut off a little bit of the snake's flesh. This caused the snake a lot of pain. The Boa tried to make himself as big as he could, which only gave the flute-player more space inside the belly. Whenever the flute-player was hungry, he cut away a little piece of the snake's belly. The Boa was in terrible pain, and he told all the other giant snakes never again to eat a human being. Then at last, the flute-player came to the Boa's heart. He cut this too and the Boa fell dead. Only then did the man creep out of the snake. When he came back to the village, he was playing his flute.
>
> All the people came rushing up to him, and asked: 'Where were you?'. The man said: 'I've lived inside the Boa Constrictor for a while. Here is a piece of its heart.' Then the people knew that the boa had been killed.'[8]

Each one of us needs to find the melody which enables us to encounter the darkness which dwells within. We will need straightforward sustenance for the sombre days, and by absorbing our pain bit by bit, we too may arrive at the heart of the matter, eat it and then be able to leave the sorrowful darkness behind. The tune we play when we return to the village will probably be different from the one we played when we left, but who says that it isn't even more beautiful?

References

1. Finnegan, R., *The Penguin Book of Oral Poetry*, *op. cit.*, p. 306.

2. Whitaker, A., *All in the End is Harvest*, *op. cit.*, p. 54.

3. Goldensohn, Barry, (1978) *Uncarving the Block*, Vermont Crossroads Press, p. 45.

4. Lee, F. H., (1931) *Folktales of all Nations*, London: Harrap, p. 451.

5. Retold by the author. Contemporary source: Mountford, C. P., (1976) *Before Time Began*, Melbourne: Nelson.

6. Gorer, G., (1977) *Death, Grief and Mourning*, New York: Arno Press, p. 121-126.

7. Client case-recording, 1982.

8. Retold by the author. Contemporary source: Baumann, H., (1972) *Hero Legends of the World*, Wurzburg: Arena Verlag, 1972.

> And all that Memory loves the most
> Was once our only Hope to be,
> And all that Hope adored and lost
> Hath melted into memory.
>
> *George Gordon, Lord Byron*

CHAPTER TWELVE

The death of the man or woman we love

When we lose our life-partner, the person with whom we shared the intimacy of day and night, we face temporary desolation. The house feels lonesome. The windows are like dark holes, pictures seem to stare at us, and even the chairs display mere emptiness. How can it be that the place which once felt welcoming now breathes indifference? It has become a strange and alien abode.

Not only are we deprived of our loved one's companionship and care, we may also face a wide variety of other problems, ranging from financial worries to a change in social status. If we have children, we encounter the harsh reality of becoming mother as well as father, experiencing time and again that it is not the same. It cannot be done. The demands placed on our adaptive ability are enormous, while we have lost the one person with whom we probably shared most of our concerns. Now we may talk about our worries with friends and relatives, knowing full well that their interest in us is qualitatively different. Emptiness dwells within as well as without.

We endure the absence of unguarded conversation, which is one of our greatest deprivations. Soon we discover that our children cannot be talked to in the same way as our partner. Wherever we turn we face the blank left by death; it cannot be ignored. We feel the odd one out, therefore at odds too with ourselves, the world, the others.

Unless, of course, the role of husband, or wife, or partner, was always submerged in the joy or pride we took in our work, the children, the garden. Then thankfulness about all that is left may be a source of comfort. Such thankfulness may also be the dominant emotion if our partner died at the end of a long and fruitful life. But the chances are that we shall miss them nonetheless, fiercely and achingly. Meanwhile many of us feel that we must not surrender to our grief. With great determination we keep busy.

We hold on tightly, because we imagine that the alternatives are a dreary existence in a house which has outgrown us, lethargy and a prevailing sense of purposelessness. A life which will consist of little other than waiting for death. We hang on and try not to stop cooking because 'we can't be bothered'. We fear that, if we do let go, we shall be unable to take care of our appearance, unwilling to look after house and hearth. Amidst such dapper lonesomeness we reach out for our cat or dog, praying that with them we shall find a bit of warmth - warmth which we need but often dare not request. After all, we have lost the protection of marriage or steady partnership. We are frightened that we shall be experienced as the third wheel on the wagon. People who are butting in.

Though we may receive a lot of help from our friends, and even though we ourselves may try our best to be gladdened by the love we receive, sooner or later we become tired of this daily struggle, and tired of living with the pain of sorrow. Without any real intent to harm ourselves, and even though we are not actually planning suicide, our exhaustion may be such that we consider death a preferably option. When this happens, it is crucial to recognise the danger we are in. For we may indeed attempt to end our life, not realising that, although all options seems foreclosed, our depression can be alleviated, the pain in our soul relieved. If only we would trust someone enough to offer us a helping hand. Friends and relatives, the Samaritans, Cruse, or our GP are there to hear our desperation. When there is time yet, we need to seek contact, or our friends and relatives need to seek contact on our behalf.

Whereas during the early stages of bereavement we probably experienced a wide range of incompatible feelings, months later it often seems that all we feel is greyness. We have recognised the permanence and irrevocability of the loss. There is no further need to search. There is no need to retrieve. Mistrusting that anything worthwhile will ever be salvaged from this experience, depression sets in. This period may last months or even a year or two. Our disinterest can no longer be hidden. Our concentration goes. We have trouble sleeping and experience the loss of appetite and weight. Oftentimes we look like we feel: hollow.

The sense of loss of identity adds to our confusion. If once we were known as our partner's 'other half', then how could be possibly survive the halfness. Who are we? Shall we from now on only be defined by our loss, someone who was, rather than someone who is? Forever a widow or widower, never again a single man or woman? Independent status is anyhow hard to achieve in a society which is geared towards couples, and presents us relentlessly with images of 'joyous' togetherness. Thus we experience not only the pain of our loss, but discover at the same time some harsh societal realities, now that we have re-entered the world of single people. Our eyes may be opened in some surprisingly pleasant ways, making us aware of earlier prejudices. But the chances also are that we knew little of the difficulties of the single life when we were still ensconced in coupledom. At first we shall miss many of the freedoms created by travelling in twos, by dining out in twos, accepting invitations in twos. Suddenly it will seem as if everywhere we see pairs, pairs and more pairs, wondering how come we did not notice this before. As Charles Stewart says: 'You were a wife or husband, which is a socially accepted position in a family and in the community. Others looked on you as John's wife or Mary's husband, and that role does not exist anymore.'[1] Not only has our daily life been changed because we lost the person we love, we often also lose the basis upon which many of our friendships were conducted, namely 'couple to couple'.

Consequently, we experience substantial changes both at home and in our social relationships. This contributes to the stress we experience.

Our way of coping with the stress may well be expressed in frantic attempts to alter the circumstances of our life. Feeling that life has foreclosed many options, we now frequently limit our own choices to three predominant response-sets:

— The desperate search for permanent companionship, either by avoiding time alone, or by looking for a new partner before too long

— Burying ourselves in busy-ness through extra studies and voluntary work

— Changing jobs or moving home. Older bereaved men or women, may well return to a once familiar home-town. This is often a disappointment.

The attempt to bring about such change is the attempt to consent to life again, and indeed sooner or later fresh starts need to be made. However, the timing

of these new starts matters. As a young woman who had tried most avenues
of avoidance of pain said, when she finally found the courage to face her
own sorrow, 'No one can cry your tears for you'. And indeed nobody else
can. We each have to work through the full measure of our losses, but what
a difference friendly companionship on our journey makes. The following
Shakespeare sonnet encapsulates this experience:

> When to the sessions of sweet silent thought
> I summon up remembrance of things past
> I sigh the lack of many a thing I sought
> And with old woes new wail my dear time's waste.
> Then can I drown an eye, unus'd to flow,
> For precious friends hid in death's dateless night,
> And weep afresh love's long since cancell'd woe,
> And moan th'expense of many a vanishe'd sight.
> Then can I grieve at grievances foregone,
> And heavily from woe to woe tell o'er
> The sad account of fore-bemoaned moan,
> Which I new pay as if not paid before.
> But if the while I think on thee, dear friend,
> All losses are restor'd, and sorrows end.[2]

When the person whom we love has died, 'thinking on thee' at first hurts
grievously. As time passes we may find that another process occurs, char-
acterised by the comfort of a sweet presence; an awareness that the other
continues to dwell within us. This experience is aptly conveyed in a tale of
the Tlingit people of North America. Although actual life rarely mirrors
story-life, the story may provide us with mirror-like reflections of aspects of
ways of being. The Tlingit tale contains several such aspects of the journey
through bereavement. A journey through which the search for the dead
beloved develops into a growing awareness of the presence of the loved one
in a vital, life-enhancing way. A 'tonic' as Lily Pincus says, when describing
her experiences after her husband's death. This tonic is our partner's ongoing
presence, which happens for many of us most of all upon waking up, or when
going to sleep. The presence is experienced as a 'reassuring, gratifying
experience which feels absolutely realistic.' Many generations of North
American Indians have told their children how this process became reality
for a young chief.

Shortly after their marriage the young wife of a chief on the Queen Charlotte Islands became ill. The chief approached all the shamans, those near and far. He sent his best canoes to ease and hasten their journey. Their help and healing was to no avail. The young woman became more and more sick and then she died. The young chief was mourning deeply over the death of his wife. He went to all the villages and asked their best woodcarvers to carve a statue of his wife. None of them succeeded at making one that resembled her. Meanwhile there lived a woodcarver in his own village, who was a very good carver. On a certain day, this carver met the Young Chief and he said to him: 'You wander from here to there asking strangers to carve your wife's image, and nobody makes anything that looks like her. I have seen your wife. I never thought I might carve her face one day, but if you were to let me do it, I will try'. The woodcarver found a block of red-cedar wood, and began his work.

When the statue was finished he dressed it in clothes like the ones he had been used to see the Chief's wife wear. Then he invited the Young Chief to come and see his work. Upon seeing the statue, sitting there just like his wife used to, the Chief felt profoundly happy. He took the carving home with him, but not until he had richly rewarded the carver, even though the carver had asked not to be given too much, as he had done the work because the chief's sorrow had saddened him.

As soon as the statue was home, the chief dressed it in his dead wife's real clothes and her robe. He really felt that she had returned to him, and he treated the image just like he used to treat his wife. But he still grieved greatly. One day, when he sat by her, feeling very sorrowed, he felt the statue move. He thought that he had only imagined it, but he could not help checking the image every day; he felt strongly that sooner or later it would come to life. Even when he was eating he had the image very near to him. After some time everybody in the village knew that he had this statue, and people came to look at it. They too could not believe that this was not the chief's young wife, who had died. They too had to look closely. When a great deal of time had passed the Chief carefully touched the statue's body and it was just like a human body. Although it was a real body, the image could neither move nor speak. A while later though the image seemed to groan from its chest, like wood groaning, and the Chief realised that the statue was unwell. He asked someone to help him move the statue from where it had customarily stood, and there in the house, beneath the statue and on top of the floor, grew a small red-cedar tree. It was left there and grew to be very tall. To this day the red cedars on the Queen Charlotte Islands look beautiful. When the people see a beautiful cedar, they still say: 'This one looks like a baby of the Chief's wife.' As time passed the image of the young woman became more and more like a human being, and people came to look at it from far and near. The woman did not move much and she never spoke. But the Chief knew what the image-woman had to say. It was through his dreams that he knew she was talking to him.[3]

In our dreams we too may well endure the strange pain of being with the person we love, but who is dead. Some of these dreams may be infuriating or comforting in their aliveness, others focus on the replay of complex aspects of our relationship. Such dreams do not only occur when we are sleeping. Some people feel their partner's life-like presence most when slumbering, relaxing or even whilst at work. It is as if we hear again the voice of our mother, grandfather, child or partner. As if we are even able to have a little conversation with him or her 'up there' or 'out there'.

As Elizabeth Collick says, 'grief is the pain of not having. Through the suffering of grief - the yearning, fears, anger, guilt, depression and loneliness - we gradually learn to live without the one we have lost. We win through to an acceptance of our loss, to a freedom from not having. Then, and only then, we find healing, which is not only freedom from the pain of our loss, but a positive recovery of having'.[4] This recovery frequently involves 'internalisation', the clear sense of the ongoing nearness of the person we lost. Such benign 'ongoing' company is a great comfort to many.

At times we may feel that we have grown more at ease with our partner's death, only to lose our acceptance when we are buffeted once more by one of life's surprises. During such a period of feeling low, we may well find ourselves tired beyond description, exhausted by the very process of recovery from grief. Then our weariness may become such that we experience the despair of the incontinent spirit, of becoming a person who craves without, however, being able to act. The image of the doomed and fated man or woman looms large. The embrace of a life of exhausted indolence due to the impoverishment of our days is a dominant characteristic of this fate. Because we have encountered death we foresee a trouble-laden future, one where we have to wait for change to occur. This paralysis of will is insidiously destructive. Yet, when we feel terribly low, we may feel that we can merely accept our sense that life is done. Nothing much is to be expected other than mere repetition. No change, no development to be aspired to, either inwardly or outwardly. A tale about such a situation is told in Japan.

In the days of arranged marriages, it was unusual for a man to remain a bachelor all his life, unless he had taken the Buddhist vows of celibacy. There was, however, such a man, and he died when he was seventy years old. He had lived alone for a long time, but during the last few years of his life he had invited the widow of his only brother with her son to share his home with him.

One day, when his uncle was very ill, the young boy sat with him. He saw how a large white butterfly flew into the room. It hovered above the old man's pillow. The nephew tried to brush it away, but the butterfly could not easily be moved away from the man's pillow. The boy feared that it might disturb the already sick man, and kept on trying to move the butterfly out of the room. The butterfly behaved so unusually, weaving close circles above his uncle's head, that the boy wondered whether this might not be an evil spirit. Then the butterfly suddenly flew away. As his uncle was now fast asleep, the boy hurried out of the house, for he was deeply curious and he followed the butterfly. Across the road from the house was the local cemetery. The butterfly went straight there and vanished into one of the tombs. The boy looked at the tomb and saw that the name 'Akiko' had been inscribed, what seemed a long time ago.

Though the boy had only been gone for a little while, when he returned to the house he found that his uncle had died. Some time later he told his mother about the butterfly; how he had felt compelled to follow it and how he saw it disappear inside the tomb.

Then his mother told him that when his uncle was a young man, he and a girl named Akiko had loved one another deeply. She had died just before the wedding-day and was buried in the cemetery. His uncle had bought this house in order to be near his beloved Akiko. He tended her grave daily, but never spoke about her to anyone. She herself had known about the reasons behind his solitude, but had never talked about these either. She did not doubt that the butterfly was Akiko's spirit who had come to fetch her beloved man at last.[5]

When the only future we can hope for is the moment when we will be released for earthly bonds and be able to join the dead partner, life is tough and woefully curtailed. Of this dangerous curtailment numerous folk tales and poems speak. One of these can be found in the ancient Finnish Folk-legend *The Kalevala*, which tells us in one part of this long beautiful tale how Smith Ilmarinen has lost his wife. He mourns for her day and night, weeps in the sleepless hours. He can no longer work, weeks after weeks pass by and he has no desire to do anything. Ilmarinen speaks to us about his experience, saying:

> And the nights indeed are dismal,
> Worst of all when I am waking ...
> Grieve for her, the dark-browed beauty.
> 'Sometimes in these times so dismal,
> Often in my time of trouble,
> Often in my dreams at midnight,
> has my hand felt out at nothing,
> And my hand seized only trouble,
> As it strayed about in strangeness.'[6]

We too may have been this lonesome, felt this sad. Consequently, some of us might see ourselves reflected in this ancient folk-poem. But dare we recite our woes, and do we have the will to invite others to listen to our tale? Yet we too need to speak about the dismal nights and sorrow-laden mornings, for if we do not speak and therefore do not let go of the pain of grief, we may follow the path of the Breton Loik Guern, who lost his sweetheart Marahit to the land of the dead. Like a latter-day Orpheus, Loik tried to rescue his fair maid, and like Orpheus, he forgot the crucial injunction. Thereby he lost his beloved woman for ever more. Upon realising the finality of her death, Loik was sorely tempted to throw himself into the sea, but some hidden power held him back. The story then says: 'But for many years afterward, the Pardons of the neighbourhood were attended by an idiot man carrying a holly branch, disheveled and pale and dressed in tatters, who cried piteously, 'Take me to the Shore of the Dead. Give me back my Marahit'.[7]

Those of us who lost our life-partner at a comparatively early age often have serious difficulties in recovering from our bereavement. The chances are that if our partner died when still quite young, the felt 'unfairness' of early death may be hard to come to grips with. We too may know Loik's temptation to embrace the madness of everlasting sorrow, the overwhelming wish to cover ourselves in rags and tatters. We desire to embrace such relentless sorrowing not only because we experience great pain, but also because our re-entry into an average life is, amongst other reasons, not made easy due to the fact that many married friends experience the 'bewidowed' person as a threat to the stability of their marriage. If we became a couple at an early age, it will be extra hard to discover that 'being bereaved' affects our social status. An effect which is felt by most bereaved people, (unless we are very old, and considered by those nearest and dearest to be 'far too old' ever to get remarried). Even though, as far as many a bereaved person goes, this may be 'never'. If, however, we moved from adolescence into courtship and family-life, it is hard to be thirty, forty or fifty, and for the first time in adulthood 'single'.

Thus there are numerous pressures which reinforce the temptation to remain devoted to the memory of what was, for many are the complexities we encounter when embarking upon a new way of life. An embarkation which is particularly difficult for shy people. At a time when we are already feeling particularly sensitive, it is not easy to develop new interests in order to make new friends who either live through similar circumstances, or have similar interests. Elizabeth Collick writes: 'After the early months of bere-avement the widowed who feel able to play a part in the community have many opportunities in voluntary social and charitable work, or in organisa-tions in which their particular experience may be specially appreciated. There is real need and wide scope for those who are anxious to be of service.'[8] Indeed there is and it is undoubtedly helpful to aid others. However, we must also not forget that we ourselves need and deserve attention and care. It is to be hoped that some will come our way, given generously and wholeheartedly by friends, strangers and relatives who care about us.

Even though we might be surrounded by people who are only too willing to listen to us, one of the frequently mentioned reasons why we do not speak about our pain is that we are frightened to drive away the friends we need. That we shall be too much of a burden. We wonder how often we can say that we are feeling low. After all, we feel that it cannot be much fun to be with us. Our mistaken ideas about the nature of friendship may lead us to withholding silence, not quite knowing that this in turn nourishes the fear that the expression of sorrow will lead to uncontainable situations. This fear is described in numerous folk tales. A typically British example can be found in the story of Titty Mouse and Tatty Mouse.

Titty and Tatty were a couple who used to do absolutely everything together. He went a leasing. She went a leasing. She made a pudding. He made a pudding. Then suddenly Titty died, upon which:

> Tatty sat down and wept; then a three-legged stool said: 'Tatty, why do you weep?' 'Titty's dead,' said Tatty, 'and so I weep.' 'Then,' said the stool, 'I'll hop,' so the stool hopped. Then a broom in the corner of the room said, 'Stool, why do you hop?' 'Oh!' said the stool, 'Titty's dead, and Tatty weeps, and so I hop.' 'Then,' said the broom, 'I'll sweep,' so the broom began to sweep. 'Then,' said the door, 'Broom, why do you sweep?' 'Oh!' said the broom, 'Titty's dead, and Tatty weeps, and the stool hops, and so I sweep.' 'Then,' said the door, 'I'll jar', so the door jarred. 'Then' said the window, 'Door, why do you jar?'. 'Oh!' said the door, 'Titty's dead, and Tatty weeps, and the stool hops, and the broom sweeps, and so I jar.[9]

Well, on it went. The window creaked. The old form ran around the house. The walnut-tree shed its leaves. The bird moulded all its feathers. A little girl spilt her milk, and an old man on top of a ladder decided to fall off the ladder and to break his neck: all because Titty was dead and Tatty was weeping. When the old man had killed himself because Tatty wept, the great walnut-tree fell, upsetting the old form, the house, the door and the window, the broom and the stool and finally, poor little Tatty Mouse was buried beneath the ruins.

Our worst fears become story-reality. From the moment Tatty started to cry, everyone else acted out. No one offered comfort. Nobody contained his feelings. With such an internalised fantasy, who would dare let go of even one tear in public? Thus we may withhold our pain because of the frightened determination to safeguard the world that's left to us. Not to drive away our friends, not to set into motion an uncontainable cycle of events, during which nobody will stop to ask what is really happening, and 'where nobody offers consolation'. Thus we may choose to cry ourselves asleep, to seek companionship with our dog or cat, a cup of tea, or a book.

How long can we live this estranged from the world? How lonesome do we need to be 'ere we reach out and let it be known that our heart is sore beyond words? 'Ere we seek comfort and find the courage to acknowledge that:

> Had we never lov'd sae kindly,
> Had we never lov'd sae blinly!

> Never met - or never parted,
> We had ne'er been broken-hearted.[10]

For if only we were to be able to give voice to the depth of our sorrow, then we could also hear the depth of our feelings, the kind and blind and mixed-up love which was ours and is still ours.

With this quiet knowing we may then indeed descend into the darkness of our sorrow. A journey to a new inner place, which is beyond indifference, guilt and malignant doubt. So that we may at last come to accept the blessing:

> Fare-thee-weel, thou first and fairest!
> Fare-thee-weel, thou best and dearest!
> Thine be ilka joy and treasure,
> Peace, Enjoyment, Love and Pleasure.[11]

References

1. Stewart, C. W., (1988) *Calming the Storm, Abindon Press, p. 39.*

2. Shakespeare, W., Sonnet XXX.

3. Retold by the author. Source: Swanton, J. R., (1909) 'Tlingit Myths and Texts', Bureau of American Ethnology, *Bulletin 39*, Washington.

4. Collick, E., (1986) *Through Grief*, Darton, Longman & Todd, p.66.

5. Retold by the author. Contemporary source: Piggott, Juliet, (1969) *Japanese Mythology*, Hamlyn.

6. Van Over, R., (1980) *Sungsongs*, Mentor Books, p. 147/148.

7. Lee, A. H., (1931) *Folktales of All Nations*, Harrap, p. 196.

8. Collick, E., *op. cit.*, p.66.

9. Lee, A. H., *op. cit.*, p. 249.

10. Burns, Robert, in Stallworthy, J., (1973) *The Penguin Book of Love Poetry*, Allan Lane, p. 246.

11. Burns, Robert, *op. cit.*, p.246.

Part IV

When A Tyrant Spell Has Bound Us

'Late, late yestreen I saw the new Moon,
with the old Moon in her arms,
And I fear, I fear, my Master dear!
We shall have a deadly storm.'

Sir Patric Spence

CHAPTER THIRTEEN
The descent into darkness

Because we cannot shut the gate against our thoughts and keep out sorrow, nor cancel memory and unthink all that we did or did not do, we are able to reach a place of reckoning with ourselves. Able, but rarely willing, unless compelled by the circumstances and events of our life to seek a different kind of existence, not necessarily out of curiosity but probably inspired by sheer necessity. As things are, we can endure them no longer.

Once the initial response to our bereavement has faded away, many of us experience a time of profound depression. Our heart feels dressed in sorrow. We know to the full that life has irrevocably changed, and the imagined lonesomeness of the years which stretch ahead feels unbearable. This stage of depression may last a month or a year, until we ask ourselves how much longer we must cope with dwelling amongst such grey constraints.

In a moving North American Indian myth of creation the early people lived in a bleak underground world. After a long time in this great darkness they began to get restless. Some of them said to one another: 'Is this all the world there is? Will there never be another world? There must be more of world somewhere.'[1] These are the crucial questions and vital assumptions for the very thought of the possible existence of another world was new. The early people's ability to conceive of an alternative heralded the possibility of change. Only when our experienced reality is questioned can processes of change be set into motion. As such the painful utterance 'Will it always be like this', is also reassuring, for it signals the possibility of the beginning of newness.

However, the waiting for the emergence of the quest for another world and therefore another kind of life demands that we begin by recognising the sojourn in darkness.

In myths and stories the world over, we meet heroes and heroines, victims and seekers, who live for a period of time in a state of bleak isolation. Separated from the communion of fellowship, they sojourn in the belly of whale, wolf or snake, inside a cave, at the bottom of a well or in prison.[2] Many are the places which represent being cut off. Each and every one of these surroundings suggests through its imagery: darkness, the absence of human companionship, an uncertain supply of food, a sense of loss of time, as well as total lack of stimulation and diversion. This is a very uncomfortable womblike dwelling place where we are alone with ourselves, deprived of the opportunities offered by distraction and communication. As such we meet at the bottom of the well, in this dark prison, the other side of paradise. Whereas we encounter in heavenly realms of abundance limitless supplies of food and love, as well as effortless communication and eternal life without either sickness, pain or death, in the well of isolation we discover the reverse qualities of this same set of images. Eternal life is now experienced as never-ending misery, not as never-ending bliss. Harsh pains are endured. Death, including our own, is a reality. Starvation of the body and the heart are actual experiences. It is stagnation of an altogether different kind. Due to the lack of external stimuli our thoughts are in danger of becoming entirely self-referential. We turn out to be the sole subject and object of our thinking, devoted to ourselves alone. Though we may also use this opportunity to rest and reflect and dream, most of us spend a great deal of energy resisting the constriction, fighting the darkness. But as the Eskimo shaman says, 'All wisdom is only found far from men, in the great solitude, and it can be acquired only through sufferings. Privations and suffering are the only things that can open a person's mind to that which is hidden.'[3]

During our life all of us are likely to experience most aspects of both sets of imagery. Times of deep pleasure and times of utter sorrow. Times of clarity and times of a chaotic muddle of thoughts. Grey days and nights intertwine with others of deeper hue and brighter colours. Do we grow in wisdom?

Let us however return to the Tewa myth of creation, when some people ask 'Will there ever be another world?' Many animal people had until then believed that the world they experienced was the entire world. They accepted that their felt reality was the same as the available reality. Then some of the old men remembered to ask Mole, and Mole said:

'Sometimes I go up, and sometimes I go down. When I go up, the world feels different. I think there is a new kind of air there, when I go up. I cannot see the difference because I am blind and my eyes cannot see the daylight as yours could. Maybe if some of you went up there and looked around, you could see whether there is another world above or whether all there is is here below.' Having heard Mole's tentative vision, the early people began their journey. Though they had little more to go by than a mere glimmer of a sensed alternative, they formed themselves into a line behind Mole as he dug his way upward. As Mole clawed away the earth, the clay was passed back along the line. The ancient storyteller says: 'This is why the tunnel that Mole dug upward for the people was closed behind them. That is why they could never find their way back to their old dark world.'

The apparent journey forward resulted in entry into the worst darkness and tightness the people had ever known. In their search for greater ease, they were deprived of the relative comfort of house and hearth, being squeezed in a narrow tunnel. Heaven alone knew where they were going, if they were going anywhere. Mole had gleaned a slight possibility. He knew not what would happen, or where they might arrive. These were great uncertainties. The journey had been embarked on in a spirit of discovery, which was also born out of a spirit of despair. We are left wondering whether the early people had taken any special precautions, safeguarding themselves against mishaps, or whether they simply set out in the full knowledge that the first step away from the comparative light of the known changes all, irrevocably.

Whether they arrived in a better world, and what happened along the way, are questions which will not yet be answered, for we shall temporarily leave the early people as they tunnel their way towards newness, in order to concentrate on a similar journey which was undertaken centuries ago in ancient Sumeria by the great goddess Inanna, who later came to be known as the Babylonian Goddess, Ishtar. Inanna is a goddess who travelled towards the great below, experienced death, and achieved the seemingly impossible return to life again.[4] This is the basic story, but there is also an important later variation of the myth. In this version Inanna seems to be in quest of herself, and emerges as one reborn from a symbolic sacrifice and death. In a later Babylonian variant of the myth Inanna enters the land of No Return in order to procure the return to life of her Son-Lover, Tammuz, a young god who emerges into life each spring-time, dies and is then renewed again. Repetition myths, like the Babylonian version, are common the world over. At an external level the myths obviously refer to the yearly birth, flowering and death of vegetation. Internally they bear witness to the human experience of love-death, and our profound wish to experience somehow a moment of truth beyond good and evil, a moment we need all the more urgently when someone we love has died, so that we may achieve a reconciliation not merely with our consciousness of shortcomings and aspirations, but above all a reconciliation with the universal will. We shall therefore look at this three-fold myth in somewhat greater detail.

Each journey, and consequently also the one undertaken by the goddess Inanna, is a journey away from as well as a journey towards. The travel is towards the unknown future, which is nonetheless anticipated, and away from the experienced past, which continues to be surprising. Inanna travels in the direction of the land of No Return, her place of embarkation is in the land of the living. Her destination becomes her destiny; in this sense too her journey is exemplary.

When Christopher Marlowe's Faustus cries out a few minutes before twelve o'clock, at which hour the devil shall return to claim his soul, 'Let time stand still, and midnight never come,' he expresses his great reluctance to accept the unavoidability of a self-chosen fate. However, Faustus also gives voice to our deeper longing, namely the wish to make time stand still. To return to the once upon a time before time, to move from the profane to the sacred, from time into duration. Although he probably wanted to freeze time primarily in order to postpone death, our goddess Inanna entered timeless time, the eternal darkness of a womblike embrace, in order to challenge death, to meet death in the place of darkness, which is also the place where the urge to life dwells. Here life begins. Conception and growth which are the result of sex, of passion, and an original meeting.

Who is this ancient goddess? She, the goddess, Inanna, is queen of heaven, spouse of An, god of heaven. She is the power in the rain, goddess of love and war, the power of both storehouse and gatepost. She is the morning and the evening star, and is called by some 'the ultimate bitch-goddess'. An ancient hymn addressed her in these words:

> 'O harlot, you set out for the alehouse,
> O Inanna, you are bent on going into your (usual) window

(namely to solicit) for a lover -
O Inanna, mistress of myriad office,
No god rivals you!⁵

She was a proud young goddess who was proud of her body, which felt like a high-lying field, hillock land, well watered in readiness for ploughing. A goddess who took to her beloved Dumuzi, or Tammuz, and delighted in him at first glance. But that was centuries later. By then she had already become less potent, and it was no longer considered to be Inanna who held full power of judgment and decision and the control of heaven and earth, whose eye was Ama Usum Gal Ana, Mother Serpent Great of Heaven, a lioness in battle with heifer horns adorning her holy head. Great had been her powers, and great was the yearly festival of sacred mating, when Inanna's high priestess had chosen a new lad to be shepherd for the year, a new Dumuzi, a new true son, consort of the Goddess.

How could this Goddess have become a maiden pining for a favour from her glorified beloved? She, who was goddess of infinite variety - who had once been able to set her mind from the great above to the great below.

The answer is: patriarchy decided so. Inanna's dethronement matters, for it casts an interesting light on the de-powering of women, if not actual, then at least mythological dis-empowerment. A dis-empowerment which needs to be noted in relation to a woman's experience of bereavement. We must not forget that due to women's greater longevity and the fact that there still is a tendency for women to marry slighter older men, the majority of bereaved people, especially later on in life, are women. The preparation for this likely event, whether social, economical or emotional, is virtually nil. As has been said before, many women, when their husband (who is often the main income-earner) dies, experience a painful drop in social status and an increase in financial worries, as well as substantial loneliness. Furthermore, a woman who has lost her spouse is exposed to many expectations with regard to her behaviour, which do not apply in equal measure to men who have lost their wife. Now, as in the past, in Britain as abroad, bereaved women carry the greatest burden of mourning, the display of acts which are expressive of grief. Many such acts are inspired and prescribed by the cultural/religious group we belong to. Less then a hundred years ago the eyes of the world rested very heavily upon the rich and poor widow alike. Whereas a century ago the rich woman had to wear deep mourning for a year or more, with none of the materials used for her clothing allowed to reflect even a shimmer of light, her poor counterpart probably had to turn to inadequate Poor Law and to Charities for help, charitable bodies made up of men who felt that they could divide bereaved women into two groups, namely:

1. Where the mother is weak in mind and body, and consequently will always need help in some form until the children can earn money.

2. Where the mother is a person of energy and resource, whom temporary help will enable to support the family.[6]

Only the latter group qualified for meagre assistance, the others were left to their own devices; after all one should remember 'the carelessness of the poor to provide against sickness and death'.[7]

It is not necessarily true that much has changed in these last hundred years, and we need to be aware that we ourselves may be in danger of making similarly crude value judgments. To this day a stigma is associated with death which informs our ideas and guides our perceptions. In his study of grief in adult life Colin Murray Parkes says that 'It is as if the widow has become tainted with death in much the same way as the funeral director ... In the circumstance it is not surprising that many societies have found it most convenient to send the widow into the next world with her husband ... We do not burn our widows, we pity and avoid them.'[8]

This experience is painfully described in the words of Amber Lloyd, whose husband died suddenly at the age of 58. She says:

> Death of a spouse brings a loss of identity to the survivor. Without realising it, you constantly measure yourself against your partner; you see yourself as part of a whole. Afterwards you have no framework to set yourself in. In addition there is the loss of role. From playing full-time, glamorous, starring parts of wife, lover, companion and friend, you can suddenly find yourself demoted to a part-time, drab, supporting role of granny. It takes some time to rebuild your self-image and see yourself in a new and worthwhile role.[9]

When the glamour and the confidence, the strength and the sense of self-worth are primarily derived from the role of 'wife to this man', bereavement is a terrifying experience. Then we experience more than the gap caused by the absence of intimate interaction, which was once rooted in our 'instinctual need for pair-mating and brood-rearing',[10] for then the supplies of information, money, societal security and therefore a degree of protection, are also closed down when the spouse dies. This adds to our fear and bewilderment.

Even if none of the above was actually true about the relationship between us and our partner, the prevailing cultural illusion of male providers and care-takers may still have placed a further burden upon our shoulders, demanding that we not only mourn our unusual marriage, unusual by choice or most reluctantly, or because we now tie ourselves into emotional knots, feeling that we ought to pay our dead spouse a kind of posthumous honour by pretending that we have actually lost the traditional man around the house.

There is no escaping from the reality that images of woman-hood are closely connected with images of widow-hood. Let us therefore return to our journey with Inanna, the goddess whose powers were taken away from her. A goddess who was made to lose weight, both literally and metaphorically. Whereas in the early days of ancient Sumeria the emphasis had rested with Inanna's sexual and reproductive powers, as time progressed the myths tell us primarily about Inanna's erotic power. Consequently the goddess' attention is made to shift from child and son, to lover. Once she is endowed with erotic energy, she is attributed with 'the beautiful woman's ability to lure the powerful man to his own destruction'.[11] One wonders, why would she want to do such a thing. Unless of course, she has been wounded.

When I was fifteen years old we read in our English class Wordsworth's famous poem *My heart leaps up*, which includes the line 'The child is father of the man'. During the ensuing discussion of the poem's merits I raised my hand and asked 'Sir, is the child also the mother of woman?' The teacher did not waste a moment. He replied: 'No, women are either children or mothers.' Laughter ran through the class. I did not think it was that funny. What he said seemed to have an importance beyond the complexity of the moment. For if women were either mothers or children, then what was a woman's life? After all, a hero is demi-god and a heroine merely a most worthy lady.

As the years passed by I lived and encountered many more images and experiences of childhood, motherhood, womanhood. Yet I continued to be struck by the difficulty which surrounds any attempt to describe what womanhood might entail. The pull of both child and mother seemed to draw so many of us into a symbiotic world, which consisted of an all nourishing mater omnis with a devouring child, or a devouring mother with an eternal child. To be a woman, who found an identity which was not exclusively formed by the embrace of masculine requirements regarding the female, was obviously difficult. How to struggle beyond the image of a woman, who was required to be a lady in the street, a maid in the kitchen and a whore in bed?

It so often seemed that women and men were still listening to Richard Brathwait's advice, given in the seventeenth century that a woman could best occupy her thoughts with:

— what habilliments doe best attire her,

— what ornaments doe best adorne her,

— what complements doe best accomplish her.[12]

Was this a description of the editorial policy of some of the women's magazines of childhood days? Did not even the poet Yeats wish his daughter to think that 'opinions are accursed', with the ultimate desire expressed in a father's most sincere wish, namely: 'that a bridegroom bring her to a house.'[13] And did not many people quietly agree with Ben Johnson who wrote: 'Say, are not women truly then, styled but the shadows of us men?'[14] So many women who seemed to be but shadows of what was possible, discerners of a distant light who appeared to lack the strength to journey and who like the author Ann Oakley, so often ended up making mere lists of the things they most wanted in the world. Desiring, not acting. Wishing, not doing. Ann Oakley created such a list shortly after the birth of her second daughter. It included amongst others:

— A wig for the baby

— Some gin

— A new bath hat

— A push chair

— A cleaning lady

— A portable television

— Some huge meals in posh places.[15]

It took her a while to realise that she was deeply depressed. She too was a woman, who might say with Celie, in *The Colour Purple*:

I can't even remember the last time I felt mad...After a while every time I got mad, or start to feel mad I got sick. Felt like throwing up. Then I start to feel nothing at all.[16]

When we start to feel nothing at all, we have arrived in the land of No Return of which the Sumerian poet says:

(Yonder) he shares in food that is no food,
shares in water that is no water,

> (yonder) are built cattle pens
> that are no cattle pens.[16]

It is a realm of shades, a world devoid of real substance, of things and experiences. In this world we meet the Celie's who have started to feel nothing no more. The men and primarily the women whose solution to the riot of confusion which dances in their head, is NOT to utter the scream which hasn't stopped for so long now. In this world we encounter a rigid adherence to lists. Lists of things to do, people to contact, items to buy. Here we face compulsion, bitterness and guilt. It is truly the dark night of the soul. No wonder Patrick Kavanagh warns the child not to go into the dark places of soul, for there the grey wolves whine, the lean grey wolves. Of course we can listen to his warning and wait and hide. Avoidance is a real option. But we also have the choice to face the events and circumstances of our life. To choose a path of intentions which can be realised, with power which is accountable. Maybe once upon a distant time such longing inspired Inanna's decision to embark on her journey.

Inanna's powers were taken away from her when a new order of civilization ruled in Ancient Sumeria. Dethroned, she visits her father (a father who was once her son) to ask:

> The Annunaki, the great gods - their fate
> Enlil placed firmly in your (hand),
> Me, the woman, (wh)y do you treat differently?
> I, the holy Inanna - where are my prerogatives?[17]

Her complaint and request are simply put aside, as so many a woman's complaint has since been put aside. Enki responds:

> Lo, the inundation has come,
> the land is restored.
> The inundation has come,
> The land is restored.[18]

The Sumerian word for water also means semen. His inundation has come. She however has been deprived of her prerogatives. It was not too much to ask an explanation, and yet to have to ask is in itself a pain.

Inanna, ancient female goddess, needed to reclaim the strength which is hers, the responsibility which is hers. Standing on the corner chanting 'I ain't scared' simply would not do. Like Little Red Riding Hood, we might then betray ourselves by disbelieving our reliable perceptions. Swallowed by the wolf, we either end up dead, or, in the rectified versions of the tale, rescued by Daddy or the Green Hunter, only to be told never to go into the forest again.

Of our ancient Sumerian goddess it is said that:

> From the Great Above, she opened her ear to the Great Below.
> From the Great Above the goddess opened her ear to the Great Below.
> From the Great Above Inanna opened her ear to the Great Below.

> My lady abandoned heaven and earth to descend to the underworld.
> Inanna abandoned heaven and earth to descend to the underworld.
> She abandoned her office of holy priestess to descend
> to the underworld.[19]

Many are the ways in which the tale of Inanna's descent to the Underworld has been explained, amongst others as a metaphor for the replenishment of food supplies, or as a complex astrological myth, containing precise scientific and technical information.[20] Such interpretations offer us numerous insights and alternative understanding which add to our appreciation of the astounding intricacy of apparently simple stories. The resonance which we are seeking here is the way in which the myth may speak to us about death and loss and the return to life.

When Inanna descends to the netherworld she is ceremonially robed with all her power, the seven divine laws: the Sugurra (a kind of crown), a measuring rod and line of lapis lazuli, sparkling stones, a gold ring, a breastplate and a pala-garment, the garment of her lady-ship. Later we shall discuss what these various ordinances may represent, at this stage it is important to note the sense of balance and clarity of purpose which are hers. This is no hasty packing of a few bits and pieces for a journey undertaken on the basis of a whim, as has been some suggested by Thorbald Jacobson[21]. Inanna knows what she needs to take with her. Not her second best shoes, or her old dress, for after all 'things are likely to get dirty in the underworld'. She takes the best in her.

Just so it is the best in us which is at stake when we grieve deeply. This much we know too.

Once Inanna goes towards the netherworld, we witness by her side her messenger and trusted handmaiden, Ninshubur, who is also known as Ninshubur Amamu: Ninshubur, who is also my mother (Following the further dis-empowerment of the goddess Inanna and of women, Ninshubur too is reported to be a man. In the earlier versions of the tale, though, she is definitely the handmaiden). To her Inanna says:

> Ninshubur, my constant support,
> My sukkal who gives me wise advice,
> My warrior who fights by my side,
> I am descending to the kur, to the underworld.'[22]

'Constant, favourable and true', these are the words Inanna uses elsewhere to describe Ninshubur. This is a relationship of trust and respect. It is based upon experience and knowing. Once more Inanna shows herself to be aware of who she is, what her values and perceptions are. She is a woman, capable of recognising someone who is bond-worthy (in Bowlby's terms), able to initiate a bond and to maintain it. As Stith Thompson says, 'Of the qualities which bring about universal admiration for a character in fiction, none is more compelling than faithfulness.'[23] Faithfulness from a wife who seeks her husband (in later versions of the Inanna tale she becomes precisely such a woman), faithfulness from a sister towards a brother (Dumuzi's sister Greshtinanna fulfills this role is some other important variations of our story), and last but not least the servant, who demonstrates fidelity and commitment. It is a dangerous task, for just when all seems well, the treasure has been acquired or the dragon is killed, then the moment of true peril for the servants comes. They may be turned into stone, get killed or in other ways disposed of, until the master or mistress, recognising the error, makes a sacrifice and restores the servant to his or her proper status.

Ninshubur too faces this danger. Thus to be entrusted with the role of the faithful handmaiden is a mixed blessing indeed, for the journey which lies ahead parallels her mistress's route as regards danger and distress. The only protection available is born from an unswerving commitment to grace, constancy and truth, qualities which, at a later time in the history of humankind, were ascribed to the go-between god or the Christian Holy Ghost.

This power, this force within Ninshubur, is the power Inanna has to trust. But it is not a trust without direction or application. She is fully aware of the dangers ahead of her. She therefore instructs Ninshubur, saying:

> If I do not return, Set up a lament for me in the ruins.
> Beat the drum for me in the assembly places.
> Circle the houses of the gods.
> Tear at your eyes, your mouth, at your thighs.

Dress yourself in a single garment like a beggar.
Go to Nippur, to the Temple of Enlil.
When you enter his holy shrine, cry out:
'O Father Enlil, do not let your daughter
be put to death in the underworld...

If Enlil will not help you,
Go to Ur, to the temple of Nanna. Weep before Father Nanna.
If Nanna will not help you, Go to Eridu, to the temple of Enki.
Weep before Father Enki.
Father Enki, God of Wisdom, knows the food of life,
He knows the water of life;
He knows the secrets.
Surely he will not let me die.'

Inanna continued her way, then she spoke and said:

Go, Ninshubur,
The word which I have commanded thee, do not neglect.[24]

This moment of parting between Inanna and Ninshubur is awe-inspiring. For the first time it has become obvious that Inanna is aware of the journey which lies ahead. She will meet death and hopes for resurrection. The hope is founded on the belief that ultimately one of her fathers will protect her and come to her assistance. She has not much ground for such trust. It is a leap in the dark. In addition to the unknown factor of her fathers' willingness and ability to come to her aid, Inanna has to rely on her servant and that within her which knows constancy, grace and truth. She can but hope that Ninshubur will not be overwrought with despair when she fails to return on the third day, but shall maintain the capacity to act under dire circumstances. In addition, Ninshubur will have to be able to remember the instruction. Their parting therefore constitutes a 'barbaro momento'. It is the time of contemplation, which the oracle-book, the I Ching describes as the moment 'when the ablution has been made, but not yet the offering. Full of trust they look up to him.'[25] In ancient China this moment of time between ablution, libation and the offering of the sacrifice, was the most sacred of all, because it was reflective of the deepest inner concentration. For if the demonstrated piety is sincere and expressive of real faith, the contemplation of this moment will have a transforming and awe-inspiring effect on those who witness it.

Inanna says to Ninshubur, 'Go Ninshubur, the word which I have commanded thee do not neglect.' Once more we hear the resonance of the garden of olives, and witness the eternal leap into faith.

Before we accompany Inanna on her journey into the netherworld, we need to dwell for a while longer in the upperworld, to bring to the fore some of the images of fatherhood which are veiled in the gods Enlil, Nanna and Enki.

Following the death of the person we love, we too shall re-encounter the internalised images of our parents as well as the actual nature of our relationship with them. For the death of a partner evokes memories of all earlier intimate relationships, experiences which involved living together and then letting go. All being well, the processes of separation were lived through with our mother and father some time before we encountered the person to whom we made a long-term commitment and who has now died. If not, then the confusion caused by our relationship with both parents, or with our mother or father specifically, is likely to be brought back to life by the pain we experience in our bereavement.

In the Inanna myth, we are introduced to three mythical images of fathering, images of parenting which stand out in their early harsh, nearly crude complexity, but which to this day persist in stories the world over. They are the three primary masks of mythological fathers.

Enlil is the god whose name means Lord Wind

In ancient Sumeria nature appeared to be barren in springtime, the storehouses were empty and the people tired from lack of food. Under those circumstances the winds which heralded spring were very welcome. A hymn to Enlil sings:

> O mighty one, you hold the rains of heaven
> and the waters of earth,
> Enlil, you hold the halter of the gods
> (of nature)
> Father Enlil, you are the one
> who makes the vine grow up,
> Enlil, your (warm) glow brings in the deep
> the fish to maturity,

> you let the birds in heaven, the fish in the deep,
> eat their fill.[26]

Without this god's warrant, the warrant of the great mountain, Enlil, no city could be built, no population settled therein, no cattle-pen built, its sheepfold not set up. He is the god of providence. His decisions are his own. Nobody can help him, for nobody could begin to understand the complexities which he alone can grasp. He is, however, more than a calculating provider. Enlil is also the dreaded power in the storm. Indeed, the spring winds may be balmy and fructifying, but the people also knew a different kind of wind, one which devastated their lands and their dwellings, which was relentlessly and recklessly destructive, a wind which blew and howled and tore apart until it settled down of its own accord, in its own good time.

As lord of the wind, Enlil is the father who listens not for pleas for mercy. Instead he closes his heart like an earthen box. He seals his ears with his fingers, lays his head upon his knees and covers his head with a cloth. Thus he hears not, sees not and feels not, whilst he pummels his people till they perish. People who pray to their god:

> O father Enlil, whose eyes are glaring (wildly),
> how long till they will be at peace again?[27]

We are undoubtedly familiar with this pater familias. The constant provider, who determines what may or may not happen in 'his' house, who rules wife and children with an iron rod, and who through violent outbursts, lasting as long as he chooses them to last, controls all those who ever dare to question his omnipotent wisdom. He is the father of Anton Chekhov who writes of his earliest memories: 'My father began my education or, to put it more simply, began to beat me, before I reached the age of five. Every morning as I awoke, my first thought was, "Will I be beaten today?"' He is also the father, the man, about whom a girl like Sofie says: 'All my life I had to fight. I had to fight my daddy. I had to fight my brothers. I had to fight my cousins and my uncles. A girl-child ain't safe in a family of men.'[29]

The ancient god Enlil displays his deadly blind force with the stunning ruthlessness of a divinely cruel and truly heartless man. He is the first father whom Ninshubur is told to visit.

Nanna is the god whose name mean Princeliness

If Enlil does not offer help, Ninshubur needs to appeal for help to Nanna, who is Enlil's firstborn son, the Moon-god. His essential function, apart from the measuring of time and the provision of fertility, is to create light in the darkness. On the day of the month when the moon is invisible, the day of lying down, Nanna travels to the netherworld to decide law-cases. Being a just god, the people trust him because he enables the heart to know the proper things. In addition to being the power of the moon, Nanna is also the god of cowherders and spring-floods. But his powers are circumscribed: 'he controls the rise of the waters, the growth of the reeds, increase of the herds, abundance of milk, cream and cheese.'[30] However, all these powers are granted to him by his father Enlil. They have an intimate, unchallenged relationship. Nanna is the perfect son, whose obedience is exemplary. He brings his father presents; in return Enlil gives him presents, though these, of course, reflect the son's subordinate position.

In every respect Nanna is a father's child. Without doubt he is kindly and well-intended, but he will never challenge the father's wrong-doings, tame the untamed spirit. Because he never evokes the rage, he may not even notice it. This god cannot be relied upon to defend your case, or anyone's case. He is a friend in time of peace, a potential enemy in times of danger, for his unquestioned loyalty to his father renders him suspect, and therefore merely trustworthy in times of plenitude.

He is the second father to whom Ninshubur must turn in order to ask for help. If Enlil cannot be roused to compassion and Nanna cannot either, then Ninshubur's last hope is the god Enki.

Enki is the god whose name means Cunning

Enki is Enlil's younger brother, and also Inanna's grandfather. Their relationship has been complex, for at an earlier mythological time, Enki was also once Inanna's son.

He is the cleverest of the gods, the manipulator, one who does not like too much power, because it does not suit him. He achieves his ends through trickery, persuasion and evasion. Enki is not only the god of sweet water, of rivers, marches and rain, he is also the true seed emitted by the great bull. The elegist proclaims about him:

> The Tigris surrendered to him, as to a rampant bull.
> He lifted the penis, brought the bridal gift,
> brought joy to the Tigris, like a big wild bull,
> rejoiced in its giving birth.[31]

He is the god of male sexuality, rampant and at times even dangerously uncontrolled in an over-whelming fertilizing desire. His energy is, however, not violent in a confrontational way, for he is willing to appear moderate in order to get around corners. He is the water in the abyss, moving through, never clinging, bringing both form and pliability to all he encounters. As such Enki is also the god of cleansing and purification, a masculine mythical image who stays in close relationship with his feminine counterparts.

This is a god who is potent in the world, who enters into relationships, makes mistakes and recovers from them. Though there is frequently unease between himself and all who surround him, ultimately Enki will try to do his best, for his love of life determines all his decisions. He will be Ninshubur's last hope.

Let us now return to Inanna, who is progressing on her way to the nether-world. The old story tells us that Inanna upon arriving at the gates of the underworld, acts evilly. She is on the 'clay tablet' record as having spoken evilly, imperiously demanding right of entry. She says:

> Open the house, gatekeeper, open the house,
> Open the house, Neti, open the house, all alone I would enter.[32]

This is no timid knocking at the door. She is determined to enter all alone. The word 'evilly' in the text has puzzled many authors. Some suggest that she is an imperious young queen used to exercising her power, others say that she knocks out of despair. It may however be that Inanna was simply menstruating and therefore thought to be evil, for in later Babylon the evil day was the day of Ishtar's menstruation, which day coincided with the full moon. On this day everyone had to take a complete rest, no journeys were to be undertaken, no cooked food eaten. 'Sabbatu', which is how the day was called, meant 'heart-rest'. As time passed each of the four quarters of the moon was designated a rest day.

Therefore the evil deed which Inanna may have committed was to journey on the prescribed day of rest, the day of bleeding and therefore the day of the full moon, thereby breaking the rules imposed on women.

The story continues with Neti, the chief gatekeeper of the underworld, asking 'who are you?' Our great Queen, goddess of Heaven and Earth, replies:

> I am Inanna, Queen of Heaven, On my way to the East.

Neti responds and says:

> If you are truly Inanna, Queen of Heaven,
> On your way to the East,
> Why has your heart led you on the road
> From which no traveler returns?'

Inanna answers:

> 'Because. . .of my older sister, Ereshkigal,
> Her husband, Gugalanna, the Bull of Heaven, has died.
> I have come to witness the funeral rites.'[33]

In this myth a great deal is apparently at stake. Inanna has gathered the seven ordinances and dressed in holy preparation. She has instructed Ninshubur what to do in case something goes amiss, and has taken leave of her with those most serious of words: 'Go, Ninshubur, the word which I have commanded thee do not neglect.' She knocks at the gate, demanding to be given entry. Her purpose is questioned. This is the first examination of her motivation. So far we have encountered a description of her journey. Neti however, offers Inanna the opportunity to change her mind. There is time to return yet. She need not enter this dark place, all alone. Without hesitation she states her reason for her travel. She has come to attend the funeral rites for Ereshkigal's husband, the lord Gugulanna. It is hard to know whether to believe her or not. By stating that she has come for a visit, she indicates her intention to leave again, yet she knows this is the land of No Return. By indicating that she wants to honour the funeral-rites, it is hard to refuse her the permission to attend.

Lord Gugulanna is the great bull of heaven. The name used is, however, also an epithet for Inanna's own husband, An, in the days when she was still queen of heaven. Have they both been demoted to lesser glory? Is she travelling in order to reclaim earlier powers or to become reconciled to her loss? Ereshkigal, Inanna's elder sister rules this nether world which was imagined as a city ringed securely by seven walls, and which therefore had to be entered through seven successive gates. The gates kept the living

separated from the dead. As the fear of ghosts was substantial in Ancient
Sumeria, the gates were very important. They helped Ereshkigal prevent the
dead from flooding those who were still alive. At first Ereshkigal ruled this
dark domain by herself, but when she married Gugulanna, they shared the
power. She is the woman who once said to her father:

> When I, your daughter, was little, and since
> I never knew girl's play,
> I never knew the frolicking of little ones.[34]

Ereshkigal makes a connection between herself as a child who due to
circumstances was never allowed to be a child, who had to grow up too soon
and who consequently remained childless. Ten thousand years later this link
is being tentatively explored in current research into the causes and treatment
of infertility. As such the myth also offers us food for thought as well as
insight.

Ereshkigal bemoans her pain of being without child. She rules a dark,
dead world. Inanna tells us that this lonesome woman has now also lost her
husband (a husband who may have been shared between the two sisters as
other versions of the myth suggest.)

Neti speaks with Ereshkigal. Apparently he has been instructed to allow
Inanna to enter for she is invited to pass from one world to another. The
journey into darkness begins in truth. The option of premature return is now
foreclosed. What is done cannot be undone. An irrevocable choice is made.
This is made abundantly clear to her when at the FIRST gate the crown of
the plain of her head, the Sugurra, is removed. She expresses her surprise,
saying: 'What, pray is this?' and is told:

> Be silent Inanna,
> the ordinances of the nether world are perfect.
> O Inanna, do not question the rites of the nether world. . .'[35]

Until this moment in the story Inanna has been in full control. She herself
gathered the ordinances, she instructed Ninshubur, knocked on the door and
decided to enter. Now her power is taken away from her in a three-fold way:

— The Sugurra is removed
— She is told not to question the rites
— She is told to be silent.

These three injunctions are the first contractions related to the expression of
self. The diminution begins as she is required to be silent.

The crown which was removed from Inanna's head, is the first divine law. The awareness of being at one with 'One', with a godhead. The number one often signifies primordial unity and universal awareness. The crown of the plain of her head is also likely to refer to our first chakra (energy centre), the crown chakra. This is the energy-centre which is linked with the pituitary gland, the upper brain and the right eye. When the Sugurra is removed, this is the first sacrifice Inanna makes.

When she comes to the SECOND gate, the measuring rod and line of Lapis Lazuli are taken from her. Amongst the ancient Sumerians' proudest discoveries and creations were the measuring rod, geometry and mathematics. Without such knowledge it would not have been possible to build the structures they built, to develop their advanced agricultural society. These tools of civilisation are removed. The second divine law of which she is stripped is, however, also her awareness of duality, of opposites. Duality enables us to conceive of the transitory, of that which passes. When we lose our awareness of time as a passing phenomenon we enter a certain kind of grace and a certain kind of hell. The second chakra (or energy-centre) is thought to influence the left eye, ears, nose and nervous system. This second removal thus disables her even further. Then she comes to the third gate.

At the THIRD gate the lapis lazuli stones from around her neck are taken away. In an early hymn to Inanna, there is a reference which suggests that this necklace is connected with her role as a sacred prostitute, a woman whose sexuality is not (yet) connected with pro-creation. The number three however was associated with Venus herself: the morning as well as the evening star. Often the number also refers to the three dark days of the moon, during which it cannot be seen. At this time many initiation rites used to take place, partly because during this extended period of relative darkness, 'All' could be experienced. It is interesting to note that three is the first number to which the concept of 'ALL' can be applied; as such it is heaven, earth and water.

To remind ourselves: at the first gate Inanna's awareness of the godhead, of an omnipotent self was removed; at the second gate she had to relinquish her awareness of 'I and other', and at the third gate she is asked to let go of her awareness of Self. The third chakra is connected with the throat, which influences digestion, the bronchia and vocal chords. Lapis Lazuli is the gem/colour associated with the throat chakra. This energy-centre enhances the expression of our unique sense of self. It is therefore considered to be the container and seat of personal creativity. This too Inanna has to abandon.

At the FOURTH gate she has to remove the twin stones at her breast. The number four is often seen as a solid figure, static. It is frequently regarded as the ordering principle of the manifest world; obvious references are then made to the four elements and the four cardinal points. In Buddhism the number suggests the four boundless wishes of compassion, affection, love and impartiality.

The fourth chakra is the heart-chakra, the energy-centre which is concerned with blood and circulation. In terms of relationships, this centre is linked to our involvement with the group, our awareness of being part of a social environment. Having let go of the godhead, of the other (who can be thought of as the parental couple), and of her sense of self, Inanna is now being stripped of her group-awareness.

We, who accompany her on this journey, can see how we are also witnessing a journey which shows distinct parallels with the steady progress of profound depression, during which, one by one, all interest and investment in outer and inner events is relinquished and during which the bonds which connect us with life are severed. But let us stay with Inanna for a while longer.

At the FIFTH gate she is ordered to remove the gold ring at her hand. The ring is a succinct symbol for completeness, representing the whole. The number five came to be associated with the Sun God Apollo, the god of golden light. It is a number which is often thought to refer to the 'hieros gamos', the marriage of heaven and earth; as such it stands for quintessence. The years of Venus too are counted in groups of five, and in ancient Qabbalism, with its root in Sumerian esoteric knowledge, the number five represents fear.

Many people, when they experience fear, feel the panic in their stomach, which becomes knotted up with fright and panic. The fifth-chakra rules the stomach, liver and gall as well as the entire nervous system. It is intimately linked with the heart-chakra, and responds strongly to the frustration of will and desires.

At the SIXTH gate Inanna's breastplate is taken away. The plate which says 'Come, man, Come'. In our language the word to come has acquired many meanings, one of which is: to have an orgasm, the little death. The sixth chakra, which is thought to be located in the holy bone area, is closely related to our sexual energy and to the womb, the gonads and the genitals.

It is possible that the removal of the breastplate at the sixth gate suggests the end of sexual longings, the end of the wish also to conceive and give birth to a child; the desire to continue life beyond herself is taken away.

Then - at the SEVENTH gate - the pala-garment, the garment of her ladyship, has to be dropped. Seven is the number which above all signifies completeness. It often represents the macrocosm: three as heaven and soul, four as earth and body.

The seventh chakra is located at the base of the spine. Here dwells the physical life-force, the urge to existence, as such it is linked upward to the crown of life. This too is removed.

Thus Inanna has relinquished:

— the awareness of the universe,
— the awareness of duality.
— the awareness of a creative, expressive self
— the awareness of being a member of a group
— the desire linked with fulfilment of self, individually and within the group
— sexual and pro-creative energy
— the will to life

The depression is complete. But the indomitable Inanna speaks beyond the imposed silence and says:

> Pray what is this?

Once more she is told:

> Inanna, be silent,
> the ordinances of the nether world are perfect.
> Do not question the rites of the nether world.[36]

Then Inanna bows low and the pure Ereshkigal, seated upon her throne, accompanied by the Annunaki, the assembly of the gods and the seven judges of the nether world, pronounce their judgement. Fastening their eyes upon her, the eyes of death, they speak their word, the word which tortures the spirit and, as the story tells us, 'The sick woman is turned into a corpse.' A corpse which is hung from a stake.

All the forces which determine life have decided that Inanna must die. At every single gate which Inanna passed a judgment was pronounced and executed. Our goddess from the great above, who decided to descend to the great below, has been stripped to the core of her being to be hung from a stake, a rod which crucifies her spine from her anus to her throat. In this condition she stays for three days and three nights. If the myth is indeed also a representation of a sacred rite of initiation into higher states of consciousness, then the three days and nights are significant, for they represent the amount of time which an initiate can dwell in a state of 'bardo'. This is the condition where our astral and ethereal body is separated from our physical body, enabling us thereby to gain insight into other aspects of 'Being'.

When Inanna does not return at the agreed time, Ninshubur becomes alarmed.

First she goes to speak to Enlil, the father who exercises ultimate control over the household of the world, who rules with an iron fist, whose will is law and whose tempers are violent, yielding not to cries for mercy. Before Enlil, Ninshubur weeps:

> Oh father Enlil, let not thy daughter be put to death in the netherworld.

Enlil replies:

> My daughter, she has asked for the 'great above', she has asked
> for the 'great below', the ordinances of the nether world,
> the ordinances, the ordinances, she has reached their place.'[37]

Father Enlil stood not by her in this matter. What else could we possibly have expected? He was unlikely to relent. His daughter had chosen her destiny, had committed the outrageous deed of travelling on the 'evil' day to go to the nether world, of all places. Why should Enlil offer support? To this day we can hear the resonance of his thought.

Then Ninshubur turns to Nanna, and of course Nanna refuses, availing himself of the same arguments his father Enlil had produced. He too says:

> My daughter, she has asked for the 'great above', she has asked
> for the 'great below', the ordinances of the nether world,
> the ordinances, the ordinances, she has reached their place.

He will not defend Inanna and take her side. Until the end, he shall be the obedient son.

Then Ninshubur goes to Father Enki. In Erdu, the house of Enki, she weeps:

> O father Enki, let not thy daughter be put to death in the
> nether world. let not thy maiden, Inanna, be put to death in the
> nether world.

Enki responds and says:

> What has happened to my daughter? I am troubled.[38]

Every child and every adult needs to know that another human being is
prepared to be troubled on their behalf. Each of us also needs to know that
we ourselves shall be concerned about ourselves. As one of my clients once
said: 'I have learned to care for me, myself and I.'

Enki's capacity to be troubled about Inanna safeguards her. His concern
when combined with her knowledge, and Ninshubur's unswerving commitment, facilitates Inanna's return to life. Had he not been a god of compromise
as well as of cunning, the story would have ended here. But Enki's willingness to deviate from the predictable, his ability to be committed to a
relationship, when linked with Inanna's courage, ingenuity and trust, enable
this extra-ordinary story to continue.

For having been troubled, Enki brings forth from beneath his fingernail
some dirt and some red paint from the top his nail. Out of these two he creates
the mysterious food of life and the water of life. Then he instructs the food
of life and the water of life as to their tasks and how to behave themselves
in order to accomplish their mission.

The Kurgurra (the food of life) and the Kalaturra (the water of life) are
instructed to go to Inanna and to sprinkle themselves onto her body sixty
times.Bearing in mind the precision of ancient Sumerian calculations and
their cultural preoccupation with numerical accuracy, this figure too is likely
to have numerous esoteric associations, most of which have been lost behind
the veil of time.

Once the Kurgurra and the Kalaturra have sprinkled themselves onto
Inanna's body, she returns to life. She arises. This is the truly mysterious
moment; a moment for which we have no words. How to explain the return
of strength after long illness, the return of hope after periods of utter
darkness? A process of healing was at work, and it worked. There had been
a singular devotion to purpose in Inanna's acceptance of the rules of the
underworld. This unswerving commitment to intention, when combined
with Ninshubur's ability to act and with Enki's willingness to be troubled
resulted in the creation of the food of life and the water of life, food and water

which travelled towards her, acted upon her, so that the woman who had abandoned so much regained life. It is important to remember that Inanna been deprived of:

— her will to life
— her sexual and procreative energy
— desires linked with the fulfilment of self
— awareness of being a member of a group
— awareness of her creative expressive self
— awareness of duality
— awareness of the universe

When all these had been removed and the inner decay seemed total, the turning point came. Then the powerful light that had been banished returned. The change was not brought about by force, but by the steadfast commitment to the journey's intention, namely, to descend into the great darkness, so that the old might be discarded and a transformation achieved.

In some later versions of the myth we are told that following Inanna's return to life, the Annunaki flee. They cannot tolerate the presence of the reemerging life-force. But the little ones, the underling gods, will not allow Inanna to return peacefully. 'Verily', the story says, 'the dead hasten ahead of her'.

When Inanna re-awakens, the journey home is begun. At every gate one of the divine laws, one of the life-forces, is returned to her. One by one she re-covers the forces which inspire her life. We can recognise this progression, when thinking about the processes which mark our own renewed consent to the events and circumstances of life following bereavement. The return of our consent may not have happened in the same sequence, but the chances are that sooner or later we too re-experienced the mysterious emergence of a new will to life. This emergence is frequently experienced as a movement, a stirring within. About this process the I Ching says: 'Movement is just at its beginning; therefore it must be strengthened by rest, so that it will not be dissipated by being used prematurely. This principle, ie of allowing energy that is renewing itself to be reinforced by rest, applies to all similar situations. The return of health after illness, the return of understanding after an estrangement: everything must be treated tenderly and with care at the beginning, so that the return may lead to a flowering.'[39]

When Inanna arrives in the upperworld, she meets her trusted hand-maiden, Ninshubur, who sat in dust and was dressed in sackcloth as if she had not left the place. The demons say to pure Inanna:

> O Inanna, let us carry her off.

But Inanna answers the demons and says:

> My messenger of favorable words, my carrier of true words, who
> failed not my direction, neglected not my commanded word, who
> filled the heaven with complaints for me, cried out for me in the
> assembly shrine, rushed about for me in the house of the gods,
> she brought me back to life. . .'[40]

The faithful servant is honoured as well as protected. Ninshubur had acted in accordance with Inanna's instructions. The trusted handmaiden is the one who became responsible for bringing Inanna back to life. History must not be repeated, for the cycle of life and death and life is now complete.

Here the Sumerian myth ends (In later Akkadian and Babylonian versions the demons are not satisfied with Inanna's refusal to let them abduct Ninshubur to the underworld and they continue their journey to find a replacement for her.[41]).

The myth of Inanna's Descent in its Sumerian form embodies the ancient vision that humanity can only be awakened through an entry into profound darkness. It conveys to us, beyond the confines of time and space, that humankind cannot develop unless we have the courage to die to a vital part of ourselves, become willing to risk and to experience such dying, protected only by our trust and hope that we shall be safeguarded by that within us which is humble and faithful, which has the capacity to weep and which, at a later stage, is able to stir into compassionate action those aspects of ourself and our surrounding world which are prepared both to be troubled and to act in order to enable the mysterious rebirth of our will to life, a rebirth to life which is both natural and mysterious, straightforward as well as complex.

At this stage in our journey we need to return to our Tewa myth of Creation. We left the early people as they struggled to make their way towards a new world, which Mole had dimly sensed during one of his travels. At this point the way back has been closed off. No longer can the early people return to the world which they once inhabited; the only way is onward towards the unknown. After a long time has passed, Mole stops his tunneling and the people come to the surface of this earth. They are covered in light.

It is everywhere. There is such abundance of light that they become very frightened. They throw their hands in front of their eyes and hide their faces in the palms of their hands, fearing that they will be lost to blindness. They say to each other that nothing has changed. The darkness was hard and the light is hard too; maybe they should give up and try to go back to where they have come from. After all they are used to that world. They stand there, the early people of the long-ago time. They argue and speak fiercely with each other. Then they hear a little voice. It is the voice of a woman. It speaks to them and says:

> Be patient, my children and I will help you.' The oldest man of the people asked her, 'Who are you my mother?' Then she answered him, 'Take your hands away from your eyes, but do it slowly, slowly. Now wait a minute. Move them a little bit farther away. Now do it again. And again.' Four times in all the people moved their hands. At last their eyes were freed and opened, and the people could see who had been talking to them. She was the bent little old Spider Woman, the Grandmother of the Earth and of all living things.'[41]

We meet in Ninshubur, 'who is also my mother' in Ancient Sumeria, and in Spider woman, 'who is also the earth's grandmother' in North America, the everlasting images of quiet nurturance and wise mothering. We desperately need such images when our trust in life is wounded due to our encounter with sudden, violent or early death. When our depression is fierce and our will to live low, it is to be hoped that we too shall generate 'alarmed' concern, a concern which helps us with our very own journey through the darkness and beyond the pain. The responsibility for the journey remains ours, but we can be given the support to stand still long enough so that we too may hear a small still voice, which encourages us to act wisely, until we have once more become accommodated to the strength of the light of day.

References

1. Marriott, A. & Rachlin, C. K., (1968) *American Indian Mythology*, Mentor Books, p. 88-95.
2. Thompson, S., (1977) *The Folktale*, University of California Press, (repr. of 1946, ed.)
3. Radin, P., (1943) *The Road of Life and Death*, Pantheon, p. 23.
4. Henderson, J. L., (1963) *The Wisdom of the Serpent, Collier Books, p. 18.*

5. Jacobson, T., (1976) *The Treasure of Darkness*, Yale University Press, p. 140.

6. Loch, C. S., (1883) *How to Help in Cases of Distress*, Longmans, Green & Co., p. 62.

7. Loch, C. S., *op. cit.*, p. 43.

8. Parkes, C. M., (1976) *Bereavement*, Penguin, p. 23.

9. Lloyd, A., (1982) Easing grief for oneself and for other people, *Relaxation for Living*, p. 3.

10. Parkes, *op. cit.* p. 24.

11. Thompson, W. I., (1981) *The Time Falling Bodies take to Light*, St. Martin's Press, 1981, p. 165.

12. Braithwaite, R., (1631) *The English Gentlewoman*, Alsop and Fawcet.

13. Yeats, W. B., (1977) *Collected Poems*, Macmillan, p.212.

14. Schelling, F. E., ed., (1903) *A book of Elizabethan Lyrics*, Ginn & Company, p. 156.

15. Oakley, A., (1984) *Taking it Like a Woman*, Flamingo Press, p. 67.

16. Jacobson, T., *op. cit.*, p0. 52.

17. Thompson, W. I., p. 164.

18. Thompson, W. I., p. 165.

19. Wolkstein, D. and Kramer, S. N., (1983) *Inanna, Queen of Heaven and Earth*, Harper & Row, p. 52.

20. See: Von Dechend, H. and de Santillana, G., (1969) *Hamlet's Mill, An essay on myth and the frame of time.* Boston: Gambit.

21. Hacobson, T. W., *op. cit.*, chapter 4.

22. Wolkstein, D. and Kramer, S. N., *op. cit.* p. 53/54.

23. Thompson, S., *op. cit.*, chapter II.

24. Wolkstein, D. and Kramer S. N., *op. cit.* p. 53/54

25. I Ching.

26. Jacobson, T., *op. cit.*, p. 99.

27. Jacobson, *op. cit.*, p. 102.

28. Troyat, H., (1984) *Chekhov*, Hamilton, 1984, p. 1.

29. Walker, A., (1983) *The Colour Purple*, The Women's Press, p. 38.

30. Jacobson, *op. cit.*, p. 122

31. Thompson, W. I., *op. cit.*, p.162..

32. Kramer, S. N., In: Henderson, J. L. and Oakes, M., (1971) The Wisdom of the Serpent, Collier Books, p. 111.36.

33. Wolkstein, D. and Kramer, S. N., *op. cit.* p. 55.

34. Thompson, W. I., *op. cit.* p. 163.

35-38. Kramer, S. N., in: Henderson, J. L. and Oakes, M., *op. cit.* p. 113-116.

39. C. F. Baynes, (1965) *I Ching*, or *Book of Changes*. The Richard Wilhelm translation. Routledge and Kegan Paul, p. 98.

40. Kramer, S. N., in Henderson, J. L. and Oakes, M. *op. cit.* p. 113-116.

41. Marriott, A & Rachlin, C. K., *op. cit.*

O my God, hear my cry;
Or let me die.

Henry Vaughan

CHAPTER FOURTEEN
Death's dangerous pull

Our child has died. Our parent died, or the person with whom we shared the intimate intricacies of our days and nights has died and sooner or later we are likely to ask ourselves why we would we wish to continue living. Should we not go where they have gone? Join them in the place of death? Unusual is the person who does not fleetingly consider the possibility of travelling voluntarily to death's abode. We do not wish to be separated by death. Especially not when death came unannounced, abruptly thwarting our plans for life. In a Welsh traditional verse a woman laments:

> I shall not go to my bed tonight, my love is not in it;
> I shall lie on the gravestone - break, if you must, my poor heart.
> There is nothing between him and me tonight but earth and
> coffin and shroud; I have been further many a time, but never
> with a heavier heart.'[1]

In a thousand tongues and calling to gods with a hundred different names people the world over have pleaded for a speedy release of their body from earthly bonds following the death of their beloved. Especially during the first weeks or months of bereavement our pain may be such that we cannot imagine how life will ever again be worth living now that our child, our partner or parent has died. Deprived of a vision of a possible future and with all other options seemingly foreclosed, we may then not only feel death's pull but, welcoming it, take the decision to end our life.

We can but hope that our welsh lady did not quite get round to resting on the gravestone at night and that if she actually went to the cemetery the cold of night helped her to decide to return home. Or that maybe people went out to look for her and called her name. Encouraging her to stay with them in the land of the living for a while longer yet, for their sake as well as for her own sake.

But what if no one came, and what if no one cared. Might then the urge to die not triumph over the urge to life? Might not exhaustion as a result of earlier pain and other troubles lead to the conclusion that there is nothing to expect and no way of recovering from the blows received?

Any of us might indeed decide this. If we are able then to reach out to someone who will meet us where we are, namely on the threshold between life and death, then we stand a chance of returning to life. Alternatively, we may be helped by the internalised voice of the dead person who may tell us in no uncertain terms that we need to continue life, not brokenheartedly but wholeheartedly, not merely with our eyes on the past but with devotion to the present and to the future. When this happens, when we hear this inner voice, we stand a better chance of counterpoising the other inner pull towards controlling self-destruction. Then it may be possible to engage with our despair, due to the fact that the angry-concerned voice inside us encourages us to live. The Kwakiutl people of British Columbia tell us what happened to one of the women of the Koskimo tribe in this process:

> The ghosts dwell in four lodges, each one below the other. A woman from the Koskimo people cried and cried because her father had died. He had been buried and she lay on his grave, crying and crying for four days and nights. The people tried calling her back home, but she did not want to leave his grave. When the fourth day came, she heard another kind of voice which called and said: 'Weeping woman, come down. I am calling you.' She got up quickly and the ghost spoke again, saying: 'Come with me.' He went into the earth and she followed him. They arrived at the lodge called Hemlock-Leaves-on-Back. They went inside the lodge where an old woman sat near a fire. The old woman said: ' Ah, Ah, Ah, Ah. Come and sit by the fire.' Dry salmon was cooked over the fire. It was put on a small mat, broken into small pieces and then they offered it to Weeping Woman. She was about to eat it, when someone came and asked her to go to the next lodge, which is called Maggots-on-Bark-on-Ground. The old woman from the first lodge, cried again: 'Ah, ah, ah, ah.' Then she said: 'Go with this woman. They are of higher rank.' Weeping Woman went with this person who had asked her to come along to the second lodge. She went inside and again she saw an old woman sitting by a fire. She looked similar to the one she had met in the first lodge. She too cooked her food in a kindred

way, and offered her some food. Again, just when she was about to lift it into her mouth, a new woman came to her, inviting her to the third lodge, which is called Place-of-Mouth-Showing-on-Ground. Again the woman in the second lodge advised her to leave and go to the third lodge. When she came to this place, she saw the same old woman and the same fire. Once more food was cooked and when she had opened her mouth to eat, another woman came in, inviting her to the fourth lodge, the Place-of-Never-Return. Once more she was told to go and accept the invitation.

When Weeping Woman came to this lodge, she saw her father who sat in the back of the lodge. As soon as he saw her he was angry. He spoke and said: 'What made you come here? Do you not know that from this place nobody returns. When you enter the first three lodges you may still go back. But whosoever comes here, must stay. Do not eat what is offered to you and go away. Hasten back home.'

He summoned the ghosts to accompany her on her homeward journey. She lay beneath the grave-tree and seemed dead. The ghosts had sang the following song as they came upwards: 'hama yahahaha.' Her father had told her that they would sing a song so that the Koskimo people would hear about her homecoming. The Koskimo people did hear the ghost's song, but they could not see them. The woman lay on a board. Her people took this board to the Winter dance house. A long time ago the song belonged to the Koskimo people, but since then it has travelled to the Newettee and to the Nakwado peoples as well.[2]

In our story the woman's father tells her in no uncertain terms: Go back and return to the land of the living. Through him, the story advises us all to cry and weep but not to allow ourselves to be carried away by grief into the realm of overwhelming sorrow where the only remaining wish is the desire to embrace death. Equally, the tale reminds us that when we enter such a state of utter abandonment, we sever the bonds with the people who care for us. Whereas the Koskimo people at first called the woman, their voices fell silent when she accepted the invitation to travel downwards. The ghosts had to announce her return to the land of the living by singing a song so that the Koskimo people would be alerted to her arrival. When she was found she was as good as dead, in a state of severe shock. Not only had her father's death caused her substantial pain, her own response to his death had traumatised her even further. Consequently, her recovery would take a substantial amount of time. In the house of Winter such renewal might happen. There she would be given another chance, slowly and gradually to come to terms with her grief, which as C. S. Lewis says:

> still feels like fear. Perhaps, more strictly, like suspense. Or like waiting; just hanging about waiting for something to happen. It gives life a permanently provisional feeling. It doesn't seem worth starting anything. I can't settle down. I yawn, I fidget, I smoke too much. Up till this I always had too little time. Now there is nothing but time. Almost pure time, empty successiveness.[3]

Thus we wait if we can, if we have the courage to hang on and don't get swallowed by the restlessness or dumbed by the squalid aloneness. We who once felt we knew it all. We were probably aware of death before it entered into our intimate circle, having witnessed its occurrence in other lives. Maybe we had even believed ourselves to be inoculated against the fierce harshness of this pain when and if it were to happen in our life. Thinking, possibly not that long ago, that we would cope much better than Mr S or Miss M, not feeling any great compassion when judging the pain which marked their faces. For we secretly thought that 'really, they should have got over it by now.' How come then that we hurt this much, now that we ourselves are wounded? We, who maybe have to admit that once we too secretly called ourselves:

> One flesh. Or, if you prefer, one ship. The starboard engine has gone. I, the port engine, must chug along somehow till we make harbour. Or rather, till the journey ends. How can I assume a harbour? A lee shore, more likely, a black night, a deafening gale, breakers ahead - and any lights shown from the land probably being waved by wreckers.[4]

We might have been so much less panic-struck if someone explained to us that our response is the normal response to a traumatic occurrence. Whenever we live through a traumatic time, such as the time of bereavement, initially we dread the days and dread the nights. This dread is, amongst others, caused by the very exposure to an overwhelming event which resulted in a felt sense of great helplessness. In the case of bereavement this event may well be the witnessing of the way in which our partner, child, or parent faced the danger of death. The intolerable anxiety we then felt was probably paralysing. We may have tried not to become emotionally absent, but in spite of ourselves we may have fled to a hidden corner deep within, so that we did not need to know the full measure of our fear, need not acknowledge the full depth of our fury. We did not want them to die and it happened nonetheless. No wonder part of us remained back there at the time when our suffering happened. Part of us may still be attached to the memory of the drama during which we could not act in the way we wanted. We may still need to utter what we could not speak even though there was so much that we desperately wished to say.

When there is a great deal of unfinished business, we cannot leave the dead beloved. We stay with them until somehow we have found a way of doing what had to be done, of saying what needed to be said. It may seem strange but we are not free to leave the actual or symbolic graveside until we have completed the incomplete scene and given voice to the unspeakable. Then, and only then, are we free to continue life for life's sake. Otherwise we shall continue to feel existential despair, assuming responsibility where none was ours to carry, and apportioning blame where none existed. This life-limiting effect of bereavement is precisely sketched in a Chinese tale from the fifth century:

> One night an attendant of the governor of Wuhsin, a man called Tsou Lan, followed the troops with a boat full of firewood. It was a rainy evening, and as Tsou's boat offered no place to shelter, he was glad to see a lighted window across the bay. When he arrived Tsou found a thatched hut. Inside were a man, who was about fifty years old, and a boy of ten, who was crying bitterly. Tsou asked if he could spend the night in the hut; the man willingly agreed. All night long the boy cried. The man attempted to comfort him, but to no avail. At length Tsou asked why the boy was so distressed. The old man explained that the boy was his son and he cried because his mother, whom he missed, wanted to marry again.

> Just before dawn broke, Tsou departed. When looking back he did not see a hut, but two graves which were overgrown with brambles and bushes. Nearby he met a woman. She was surprised to see him, and asked where he had come from. Tsou told her what had happened the previous night.

> The woman then said that she had been on her way to see the graves in order to say goodbye to her husband and son, as she was planning to marry again. With tears in her eyes she then went to the graves. She burst out weeping. She gave up her second marriage.[5]

The past held her within its tight embrace. Although there is no timetable for the human heart, she had believed herself ready and willing to make a new commitment in life and thereby a new commitment to life. Then her grief returned, voiced by a man who needed shelter from torrential rain. Maybe she had been wrong in believing that she could say a final good-bye to this earlier part of her life, for as soon as she heard that her son was crying for her, she abandoned her plans to remarry. Maybe, therefore, she had made her decision too soon, ignoring the need to look back a little longer, to acknowledge the searing memories. There was probably much that still needed to be shared in some way or another with her dead husband and son. An 'internal' son who, in the story, was terrified to let her go, probably anticipating that he would be abandoned now that his mother had found new joy and was about to start another family. If only we could accept our loss as part and parcel of whatever happens next, and therefore, if only the woman had not come to say good-bye to the graves, but had come to visit in order to let her 'internal' husband and son know that she loved them none the less, especially so because she had found further happiness.

All of us need to accept that the death of people we love is a serious event. We will miss them greatly, and because we miss them so we may well experience a deterioration in our physical and mental health which contributes to our sense of vulnerability. Of course there are many factors which influence our response to bereavement, such our age, socio-economic status and gender, as well as our religious convictions, the kind of person we are, and our life's events before we became bereaved. In addition, we shall have to bear in mind how the person we love, died. There is no doubt that sudden, unexpected and untimely death wounds us more fiercely than those which we have been able to anticipate for a longer period of time. It speaks for itself that violent death forces us not only to come to grips with our loss, but frequently also with the reality that the death was caused through the action or negligence of other people. This contributes to our pain.

Amongst all these losses, death through suicide is the harshest death to come to grips with. Nearly all deaths due to suicide are sudden and untimely, but frequently they are not unexpected. This is partly because the act of taking one's own life is often preceded by periods of depression and a range of stressful life-events. When someone we love has killed him- or herself, we are not only faced with our feelings about the death and the choice to die, but we also face an inquest and reports in the press, which are sometimes obnoxiously intrusive into the events of our private life, and with having to deal with such matters as correspondence with life-insurance companies who argue that the suicide has put the entitlement into jeopardy. Invariably, those who are involved from a distance believe that the 'survivor' is in some unspecified way to blame for the death, thinking without saying that the death might have been prevented, and that anyhow it is a shameful occurrence.

The cumulative effect of these experiences adds to the burden of the grief which has come our way.

Whereas it is difficult to cope with death through suicide, it is especially hard for a child, at any age, to experience the death of both parents within a period of days or weeks. This may happen when our mother or father commits suicide just before or just after the death of their life-partner, or our parent dies like the woman about whom Sir Henry Wotton said:

> He first deceased; she for a little tried
> To live without him, liked it not and died.[6]

Alternatively, our mother or father, wounded by the loss of their partner, much against their will has to surrender to their own serious illness and dies, pained to the core by the knowledge that their child (or children) now have to continue life as 'an orphan'. When we experience our parents' double-death, whatever their cause, our response can initially be little other than a profound sense of anger, guilt and bewilderment, sometimes tinged with relief because it is all over. When the first impact of shock has faded away, the fact that we have become orphaned may well contribute to a sense of feeling destitute, as the Greek origins of the word, imply - forsaken and comfortless, someone without a place. But, therefore, also someone who can truly search for a place which can become our own in new and unexpected ways. As such, being an orphan may, at a later stage, also be experienced as a substantial gift, the gift of life in a true sense. Much depends on the bond which we had with our parent. Much too depends on the resources which are ours to use, for better or, sadly, for worse.

For worse, when we collect a last bit of energy and try to kill ourselves, or to move in our thoughts from considering whether or not to kill ourselves to the stage of actively planning our death. Also for worse when we implement our decision to die at a stage in life when much was still within our reach and when our pain could have been substantially relieved.

Following a serious bereavement many of us may well be sorely tempted to create our own death. It is therefore important to reflect a little on the forces which may be at work when we consider the death option, and on various ways in which we may be helped to refrain from enacting our despair with life.

In an old Cheyenne story, *The Ghost-owl*, we are told that:

> A little girl sat crying in her mother's lodge. She was angry because her mother wouldn't let her do what she wanted to do. It was night time and her mother told her she couldn't go out of the lodge. Finally, the mother got so exasperated that she picked the little girl up and put her outside. 'Go on', the mother ordered, 'The owls can have you if they want you.'[6]

In the tale we then encounter a young girl's journey into the dreaded night, which includes a stay with the ghost-owls. These are believed to be the ghosts of the dead returning to earth for many different reasons, including revenge, to complete incomplete tasks and to fulfil physical needs which were not satisfied in life. The ghost-owls are the sins of the fathers which are visited on the children. They also represent the numerous forms of disturbed behaviour in both adults and children which compensate for the experienced family dynamics.

The child in the story cries and is angry because she cannot do what she wants to do, namely to encounter the great darkness. Her mother does not want her to meet the spirit of death. The girl has to remain within the firm embrace of the home, a home which may be good or bad, but where, so the parent believes, the ghost-owl does not dwell. It lives outside the lodge, sitting in a tree where it waits for a mouse or a rabbit to come along unless its most favoured prey, a human being, were to dare to go out into the night. Then the great owl swoops down and the nightmarish encounter with the ghosts from the past may begin.

My client (let us call her Mary) was hardly thirteen years old when she had a bitter row with her mother, a woman in her mid thirties, who had felt drained for some time. Her own mother had died several months ago, and somehow she just wasn't feeling quite herself since then. She had not been particularly fond of the old woman - to the contrary. 'Granny' had once looked after her wee daughter by herself, having been deserted by the child's father. Never having recovered from the pain of the desertion she became profoundly embittered, trying to hold her daughter in tight reins. The daughter escaped as soon as she could into an unhappy marriage. The marriage broke down when her children, too, were fairly young. In this family Mary grew up. She had not been close to Granny, and her death seemed to leave the grandchild stone cold.

This rainy night in November, Mary was 'simply' outraged that she was not allowed to go to the school-disco. Word followed word, scream followed scream and hands hit her hard. Without a coat or money she was finally thrown onto the streets with the words 'Don't you dare come back. You can go to your father's house. I don't want to see that snidy little face of yours ever again.' It was a wet and windy evening some time in late November. She wandered around the estate. Didn't dare knock on anyone's door, not least her father's who had beaten her before now. She no longer wanted to go to the disco either. She had no money for the bus and looked awful. Late the following morning her young brother found her in the attic. She had sneaked back into the house when everyone appeared to be asleep. Then she had gone to the bathroom and had swallowed a range of tablets from the medicine cupboard. The attic seemed to be a good place to go to sleep for ever more. When her brother woke her up, she felt very ill. Pretending she had caught a cold, she stayed drowsily in bed for many days, not telling anyone that she had tried to take her own life that night. It became yet another of her secrets. After a while life resumed as if nothing much had happened. More fights and more demands and yet more fights, until she grew silent most of the time, altogether silent. She did not die and yet she did not remain alive.

When at last she came to talk about the row with her mother that rainy night in November she said: 'Don't get me wrong. I didn't try to kill myself because of that. It wasn't that bad a row. It had happened before. Don't forget that. I did it because I had thought of killing myself for a long time. Do you understand? For years. That row was the last straw. I couldn't cope no more. It broke my back that row. It was just that I had only been thinking about doing it. I hadn't yet planned it. There weren't enough tablets around. Now I know what it takes to kill yourself properly. I don't really want to do it, but when it's bad, I do. Next time I'll do it well. I know I will.'

Her voice sounded businesslike, devoid of all emotion. She said in no uncertain terms that past and present were combining into an unbearable burden. The anticipation of a miserable future only added to the load. As the *I Ching* says: 'The ridgepole sags to breaking point. It furthers one to have somewhere to go.' Somewhere to go indeed, but where? Her only way forward was to meet the darkness.

Mary's family background was typical of those dynamic factors which are frequently found in the families of children (and adults) with suicidal tendencies.[7] These have been identified as:

— crisis-proneness in the family
— the presence of a suicidal parent in the family
— the demand by the parents that the child assume responsibilities, which the child perceives as beyond his or her capability
— a lack of satisfying relationships with adults.

In addition, Mary had, as so many of us do, a deeply paradoxical perception of death. On the one hand believing that being dead equates with a state in which all needs are satisfied, which makes it highly attractive, and on the other hand being very frightened of both death and dying. Next to the urge to death she wanted to stay alive, in spite of the feelings of desperation and depression. But she had trouble finding a form for the dim, blind wish to live.

This tension between the fear of life and fear of death, and the love of life and love of death, is a frequent characteristic of many people who consider ending their life. It speaks for itself that the presence or absence of this pull is likely to constitute an important difference between those children or adults whose suicide attempt is successful and those whose attempt fails. We must, however, never forget that such paradoxical feelings are exhausting. Luther once said that the difference between hell, purgatory and heaven was the difference between despair, near-despair and security. If we apply this analogy to the suicidal child or adult, then most of their life is experienced as either hell or purgatory and they long to reach heaven, if only for a little while.

When we consider killing ourselves, we often do so because of our despair of ever being able to reach some kind of stability and security, because we can no longer cope with being in a state of hopelessness. This utter barrenness of the inner landscape, and the absence of any worthwhile images to encourage the pursuit of our journey, combine into the feeding-ground from which emerge the wish and ultimately the decision to commit suicide.

Experience suggests that all of us need a good enough, internal image of a possible future. Like Dante we need our Beatrice and like Odysseus we need a vision of a home reach. When we are suicidal we have to arrive at such a vision all the more urgently. We must not forget that the suicidal child or adult has lived for a long time in the hope that someone will come along who will recognise their despair and outrage, someone who is willing to hear how bad things really are. The hope is kept alive against the most painful odds and ferociously clung to until, one day, it is abandoned.

The act of giving up hope often parallels the decision to commit suicide. There is no doubt that the suicidal child and adult have enacted their pained disturbance: difficulties with attendance at work or school, staying in bed till early afternoon and being unable to go to sleep at night, fighting the darkness by staying awake. Alcohol and drugs are used partly to explore alternatives but mostly to keep despair at bay. Meanwhile, their language has borne witness to the distress, the outrage with the world. When this too isn't heard, the ultimate weapon - the curse of boredom - is used. During the French student-revolt of 1968 some graffiti read: 'The prospect of being pleased tomorrow will never console me from the boredom of today.' The child or adult who considers suicide nourishes no prospect of being pleased tomorrow, holding firm to the belief that tomorrow will be as bad as today. Today is unbearable, and therefore exhausting. Consequently, tomorrow will be even more unbearable. Life can be ended, and because it is too much to bear, it must be ended.

This decision is also inspired by the cruel pain of the prevailing cultural myth of the happy childhood. This is an illusion which persists, even though it is a well known fact that the childhood years of many people are very painful indeed. Nonetheless children frequently hear adults say: 'You think you've got it bad now? Wait until you've grown up and have kids', or 'Cheer up, it'll only get worse', or 'You're wasting the best years of your life'. Such comments do not take into account the fact that these children's lives are already saturated with tortuous impotence. Too young to have the power to act in their own right and interest, many children live through interpersonal hells in which they are ignored, maltreated and abused, while they are surrounded by images which suggest that these are the 'glad years of innocent youth'. Sadly, many children also find ample evidence for the apparent truth of the statements that things will only get worse, for they rarely witness contentment and happiness in the lives of the adults they meet. This prospect of a life without satisfaction, devoid of joy and the security of rewarding relationships, slowly undermines the last images of a possible future to which the suicidal child and adult have knowingly or unknowingly clung.

The steady depletion of hope is closely connected with the increasingly narrow perception of alternative solutions to the experienced troubles. This narrowing of the perception occurs primarily because all known solutions have been tried and found inadequate. A redefinition of the problem might result in the finding of a solution which is efficacious. However, as long as the problem is defined in established terms, and as long as the suicidal person knows that all previous attempts at solving the defined problem have failed, so long will the girl or the boy, the man or the woman, continue to plan and attempt suicide - especially because suicide is perceived as the only remaining solution.

As Orbach's research has shown, cognitive functioning in suicidal people indicates that there is a significant correlation between the attraction to death and the inability to give an alternative solution to a dilemma about life and death that is different from one's own.[8] Their world is closing in. Having experienced through bereavement that death is indeed inevitable, irreversible and causal, the preoccupation with fantasies about death, killing and violence start to dominate the imaginative-emotional life. The judgment that suicidal people then reach is, however, based on the application of the concepts of 'inevitability and irreversibility' to life and not to death. My experience suggests that suicidal children and adults believe that suffering is universal and unavoidable. It is concluded, after many hours of morose reflection, that the damage done is irreparable. The only perceived solution is the solution of killing oneself. Under these circumstances the motivation behind the act is not to vent anger and to seek to alter behaviour in others, but to circumvent the perceived and felt reality of existence; namely to be doomed to suffering which is insufficiently alleviated.

When someone has become convinced that all known solutions are useless, when everything that could be undertaken is perceived to lead to the failure and suffering, when the distress is shown in acting-out behaviour and the repeated declaration that nothing is any good and everything truly boring, then there is time yet to discuss the likely preoccupation with death and dying. But time is running out. For one day an apparently minor event, such as missing the bus or losing some money, may combine with the desire to leave a final mark upon the world by making the one decision which can be and will be truly one's own, namely to choose to take our own life. The power of this desire needs to be acknowledged and its legitimacy brought into the open. For we know that, if this desire and sorrow are not given voice, then 'the grief that does not speak, Whispers the o'erfraught heart and bids it break'.[9] The suicidal person's grief is born out of profoundly disturbed family dynamics, troubled parent-child relationships, and out of a prevailing sense of inadequacy and deadlock. But it is the unacknowledged and unexpressed nature of the grief over this situation which leads the suicidal person to follow Cleopatra's path, when she says: 'My desolation does begin to make a better life. It is great. To do that thing that ends all other deeds, which shackles accidents and bolts up change.'[10]

For it is the certain conviction that one knows what it means to be dead which inspires many a suicide attempt. Such children and adults do not agree with Heidegger when he says: 'Death is a strange alien thing, that banishes us once and for all from everything in which we are at home.'[11] To the contrary, they have a firm conviction that they know what death and after-life are about. This certainty facilitates the performance of the suicidal act. It is therefore important to note that this apparent certainty is frequently both unexamined and unexplored. Their death concept, though inclusive of the awareness of the universal presence of death, the irreversibility and finality, the causality and the link with ageing, is used to refer to phenomenon which occur in life. This is important to note, for it leads to the mistaken conclusion that the pain caused by the death of someone we love is inevitable, irreversible and irredeemable. And consequently unbearable. Frequently the death-concept of people who feel suicidal does not (yet) incorporate thoughts about the nature of death itself, or ideas as to what happens after death. For the experience of bereavement, and therefore the encounter with death, has not necessarily led to an awareness of feelings about our own mortality, a feeling-response which may well be determined by a yearning for immortality, an unacknowledged longing for a deeper and more enduring life, the desire to embrace a finite existence by conquering death in life and thereby to transcend it.

Our mortality and our sexuality are forces which motivate us in unknown ways beyond all personal goals. Whenever we feel suicidal, or work with suicidal people, a careful exploration of the awareness of our own mortality is called for. In addition, we need to be helped to internalise a good-enough 'other', to develop more attainable ego-ideals and to diminish our attachment to an ideal self and a harsh super-ego, so that healthier identifications can be facilitated and aggressive responses to frustrations and disappointments altered. It speaks for itself that those areas of family-conflict which contribute to our distress need to be brought out into the open and, where possible, worked through. Siblings and parents, partners and children need to be encouraged to develop their relationship with the suicidal person and to exercise their competence. Of course, any practical issues which demand attention need to be taken care of and appropriate action taken. All these can only serve to strengthen the suicidal person's awareness that his or her distress is taken seriously and that thoughtful action actually makes a difference for the better.

Meanwhile, however, the longing for death which leads to the formulation of a suicidal intention or attempt has to be explored and the fascination with death as a solution overcome. When we have encountered death we somehow experience ourselves as being granted a special vision. In order to win back life, we need to surrender this charm of otherworldliness. For the alternative is to live in a state of dreamy indolence, an indolence which will once more lead to a profound impoverishment of actual existence. The spell therefore needs to be broken, the pull undone.

For many people who actually attempt suicide and live through the experience this occurs of its own accord. My experience of meeting and then working with people who had tried to kill themselves more than once suggests that their fascination with death 'as a subject and not necessarily as an experience' was neither recognised, acknowledged nor overcome. Yet, in order to regain a commitment to life, it is important to address the fascination with the numinosum of death and dying so that the embrace of a finite existence is no longer equated with an identification with a tamed and domesticated kind of person, and the embrace of death with an identification with the image of the tragic hero or heroine, a doomed and fated person.

It may be stating the obvious to draw attention to the fact that the awareness of mortality *per se*, does not necessarily incorporate an awareness of the longing for immortality or the desire for something which will endure. Many are the research-programmes which attempt to find identifiable clusters of predisposing factors which suggest increased suicide risk, clusters which will enhance the possibility of creating efficacious modes of intervention (Henderson, 1977, Touriel, 1988, Withers & Kaplan, 1987 and Chabrol & Moron, 1988). The search for pre-disposing factors, as well as the description of the circumstances of a person's life in the year preceding the suicide attempt, have resulted in an apparently 'clear' picture of the kind of conditions which are likely to foster the intention or even the determination to kill oneself. Most of these factors have been mentioned earlier.

However, one predisposing factor which is frequently overlooked, either because the wrong questions are asked, or because the therapist decided not to wish to know, is the suicidal person's identification with the doomed person, who embraces death as the heroic outcome of a predestined journey. On this journey the hero or heroine will have the courage to travel to the nether-world to slay the dragon, which is 'life' itself. Because the dragon represents life as it was experienced and as it is anticipated, there can be no return from this journey. For life itself must be and then was 'killed'. Such a hero or heroine believes that life deserves to be killed because it has become synonymous with pain, isolation, violence and suffering. Were there to be a glimpse of a life which is gentler, surprising and rewarding, then the attack might still need to happen, but defense too would be required.

In my work with people who contemplate or have attempted suicide, I have tried to create many stories of a fated hero or heroine and to develop the image of the life which needs to be killed, to explore what the hero or heroine needs in order to undertake such journeys and battles and who or what might intervene in order to assist both life and its assailant. We discuss which obstacles must be overcome, and why the hero or heroine is compelled to embark upon this heroic quest in the first place. Villains who put unexpected obstacles in the way are encountered, as well as helpmates who provide new insights and solutions. It speaks for itself that, in the pursuit of such a quest, the character of the One who is to be Slain changes. No longer is Life experienced as a threat, but the threat is represented by another 'internal' external Beast.

The hero or heroine in all such stories follows the path of all other mythical heroines and heroes. The journey is begun as a result of someone's abstention, or due to the violation of an interdiction. The hero/heroine is either a seeker who has set out upon a quest, or a victim, upon whom a tragic fate has befallen. Having abandoned home and hearth a further misfortune befalls our story-character, whose reaction to the misfortune will influence the continuation of the tale.

It is then that the temptations begin: the 'tell me where's', the careless acts, the offers of magical potency, the deception and coercion. Our hero/heroine may or may not become an accomplice to some villainy, either by performing an evil deed, or by abandoning consciousness through falling asleep. The opponent, often the Beast in disguise, then has a wide range of harm at his or her disposal. These aspects of the story tend to arouse great interest and excitement, as they provide a vicarious satisfaction for felt rage and fear. Thus the imagined harm often includes plundering, bodily injury, the casting of spells, the removal of power, attempted murder and torments at night. At each stage of these stories the decision whether or not to continue with the tale needs to be made, especially at this point the temptation to give up looms large, for now the hero/heroine has to decide whether or not to make the villainous matter known and to request mediation.

It is then, and only then, when the predicament has been exposed, that the counter-action can begin. The temptation to end the tales at this stage is substantial but, on the other hand, the purpose of the suicidal person's quest is to confront death as well as life and our story-hero/heroine is not quite so easily defeated by a bit of opposition. The decision to carry on with the story is volitional and a reflection of the exercise of choice and will. It is therefore likely to be made.

The next stage of the stories then includes an encounter with someone who will test our hero/heroine, and who bestows strength and determination. This character is called the donor.[12] The testing takes many forms, from interrogation, to the demand that service to the deceased is performed, to a request for mercy, or engagement in combat. Once more the hero/heroine's reaction matters. Is he or she capable of showing mercy, of making decisions? Able to engage in combat and to withstand the testing?

If the hero/heroine succeeds, then some powers are bestowed and the hero/heroine is made aware of the whereabouts of the Beast (whatever this Beast may be). Thus fortified, our story-character continues the journey, until the hero/heroine and the main villain meet in order to engage in direct combat. The struggle is always intense. And after some very troubled moments, and maybe after repeated engagements in battle, the hero/heroine succeeds. The Beast is defeated. The hero/heroine is branded or marked in unpredictable ways. Though the original misfortune and lack have been liquidated, the marking has occurred. Then the return journey begins.

Here again, the person who is creating the story is likely to give up; after all, the battle has been won. Great strength was demonstrated, but what next, whereto and wherefore? Luckily the story-hero/heroine's desire to confront the homefront with the outcome of the journey often outweighs the client's longing to give up. For the vanquished villain has bestowed upon the one who is victorious the wish to make the deeds known, to bear witness to the event. Thus the return journey is undertaken, sooner rather than later.

Then the pursuit and chase by evil characters carry our story-character along. Once more wit has to be exercised, whilst strength continues to be tested. For the little devils make many attempts to prevent the hero's or heroine's return, and many, therefore, are the solutions which have to be found.

When the place of return is reached a further disappointment lies in wait. The hero or heroine is not recognised. Frequently a usurper has taken his or her place, claiming all honour for deeds they did not do and courage they did not demonstrate. This is the most difficult task of all. How to cope with the false hero/heroine? In order to discern false from true, new tasks are set. Once again he or she has to undergo an ordeal. Was it not enough? The encounter with the original suffering was bad. The villain wounded our hero/heroine. Then the helpmate demanded testing. This was followed by the direct struggle with the villainous Beast and the marking. We were chased during the return home, endured the disappointment of not even being recognised, and then, when we are really exhausted, a further demonstration of our cleverness and endurance is demanded. Only, and often only when the hero/heroine has undertaken these final tasks, is true recognition offered. The false hero/heroine is exposed and either pardoned or punished. Then our hero/heroine is rewarded, with, amongst others, the knowledge that their strength is truly theirs and that therefore they shall live comparatively happily ever after.

In our therapeutic work with people who are suicidal, we may work with tales which are thus patterned, in various ways:

1. Clients may be told a traditional folktale which has as its theme a heroic journey in which great danger, and therefore death, is faced.

2. A traditional tale may be shared, and the client is engaged in expression related to the tale. This expression takes the form of structured exercises, such as painting, writing, enactment.

3. The client/group is guided through a series of creative tasks, which parallel the journey undertaken in an ancient tale, thereby permitting the super-imposition of the client's imagery and life-experience onto the original story-base.

The identification with a character who is at once 'I and not-I' enables each of us to let go of the singularity of our interpretation of experienced difficulties. We can then also hide behind the obvious possibility that it was only and merely a story, one which bears no relation whatsoever to our daily reality. This identification at one remove offers us a safeguard, and therefore the freedom to project onto our story-character important personal material, which we need not introject if it does not suit us right now.

Many people relish the chance to listen to a tale. As such, each story is a gift for us, especially because it need not be about us - at least not in a way which we have to acknowledge although the bashful identification with a hero or heroine who has the courage to persist and the strength to prevail can vicariously nourish our at times brittle sense of self.

People who wish to use stories in their work need to have not only a love of stories but also an awareness of the structural properties of a tale and knowledge of the conditions under which the tale was told, as well as knowledge of the purpose associated with the telling in days gone by. Those who wish to create story-making structures must be at ease with a range of creative-expressive activities and familiar with the power of the material which can be evoked. It is true that such evocation will be contained by the functional and structural properties of the traditional tale, but an inexperienced therapist, social worker or teacher may well be tempted to change the story around a bit, so that it seemingly better reflects the presented predicament. Such tinkering with the basic structure of an old tale only works when the storyteller has a deep love and knowledge of tales, and therefore makes a well informed judgment.

We may assume that an old story was passed from generation to generation, in the form in which it was recorded, precisely because this form fulfilled an important emotional and psychological function. The distillation process with regard to this underlying form therefore resulted in a well established problem-solving format. If we wish to apply this format to present-day predicaments which relate to our human suffering, we may at first want to give the existing sequences and interrelationships a chance. If they fail us, we can always create entirely new stories which may more accurately reflect our current situation.

Before drawing this chapter to a close, we need to lift to the fore some parallels between the heroic journey described in many myths and tales and the story of a person who has experienced a troubled childhood or serious difficulties in the process of recovery from bereavement.

Such a person (and this may even mean most of us), is likely to have experienced a substantial degree of absence and abandonment by caretakers. These separations were often accompanied by periods during which strict injunctions were imposed as to what may or may not be done. Such injunctions were probably contradictory and confusing. Almost certainly several violations of the authority's prohibitions and commandments were committed, violations which resulted in threats and or punishments, and imagined or actual further abandonment. The search for reparation of some kind or other will have been embarked on, but further misfortunes occurred. The child or adult is now likely to have experienced him- or herself as having been delivered to a villainous world. In spite of repeated efforts to accommodate the self to a confusing and disturbing environment, ease could not be found. Instead there was a growing awareness of trickery and unkindness.

At this stage the child or adult may have decided to become an accomplice - to agree to ferrying drugs, to participate in early sexual activities, to submit to physical and emotional abuse or to perpetrate such abuse on younger siblings and friends. Actual harm is being caused. The full horror of the situation is felt and, if a reasonably trustworthy adult were to be available, help may well be sought. When help is offered, our person may or may not be able to make use of it. Being insufficiently aware of what it means to be helped and the accompanying increase in difficulties on the home-front (the second appearance of the villain) may result in the forsaking of help, engaging instead with a blind lonesome struggle with darkness which may well be lost, given that the child or adult is already exhausted and ill-supported. It is at the height of this struggle that suicide is attempted. If the attempt is successful, then the heroic journey finds its tragic end.

If the attempt has failed, then the question 'what now' has to be faced, unless, like Orpheus, he or she simply wants to stay by the side of the river Styx, forever mourning, forever unable to accept the invitation to celebrate the Festival of Dionysus. It is likely that the struggle with darkness needs to be returned to again and again. After all, it needs resolving. If this is not understood, then we shall have to witness the painful reality of renewed attempts to meet death within, to murder life-as-it-has-been-known within. Once the great, beastly darkness within has been successfully encountered, the return-journey begins. The events of his or her life are then likely to show marked parallels with the pursuit of the little devils, about which the stories tell us. Equally, they may well encounter the lack of recognition and the sense of acute alienation, the temptation to collude with the home-stayers' desire to pretend that everything that happened, happened to somebody else. A false hero or heroine is presented to the world. The newly discovered strength and authenticity still need testing and trying out. These tests feel distinctly unfair and they demand a great deal of wisdom and patience from everyone involved; slowly and gradually, however, a more authentic self will prevail and the false hero can be sent a'wandering. Then we will indeed have moved a long way and further journeys may begin.

It is self-evident that those people who are familiar with such processes of change, their dynamics and resistances, are more likely to be able to endure the trials and tribulations of a complex bereavement journey than those who, in addition to the difficulties of the bereavement process, have to deal with a real lack of 'sensed' knowledge regarding the processes of sorrow and change.

It is equally true that since time immemorial metaphor and the story's sequential imagery have been used to activate people's emotional and cognitive ways of coping, story-imagery which, due to the purposeful sequentiality, could be easily remembered in times of pleasure and times of stress.

Therefore, it may be suggested that the telling of traditional tales, which involve the struggle with various dilemmas has a rightful place in death education and in the support and treatment of people who live through a troubled bereavement response. If nothing else, the telling of the tale creates a temporary bridge across which two people meet, whilst each can thank the other for engaging in the sacred act of keeping a story 'alive'.

References

1. Hurlstone Jackson, K., (1979) *A Celtic Miscellany*, Penguin Books, p. 134.
2. Retold by the author. Contemporary source: Bierhorst, J., ed., (1976) *The Red Swan*, McGrahill.
3. Lewis, C. S., (1961) *A Grief Observed*, Faber, p. 29.
4. Lewis, C. S., *op. cit.*, p. 29.
5. Retold by the author. Contemporary source: Yang Hsien-Yi, Yang, G., (1958) *The Man who Sold a Ghost*, Peking: Foreign Languages Press.

6. Marriott, A. & Rachlin, K., (1975) *Plains Indian Mythology*, Mentor Books, p. 43.

7. Orbach, I, Rosenheim, E., Hary, E., (1987) Some aspects of cognitive functioning in suicidal children, *Journal of the American Academy of Child & Adolescent Psychiatry*, 26(2) 181-185

8. Orbach, I., et al., (1987) Sequential Patterns of five sub-concepts of human and animal death in children, *Journal of the American Academy of Child & Adolescent Psychiatry*, 26(4) 578-582.

9. Shakespeare, W., *Macbeth*, Act 4, scene 3.

10. Shakespeare, W., *Antony and Cleopatra*, Act 5, scene 2.

11. Heidegger, M., (1961) *An Introduction to Metaphysics*, tr. Ralph Manheim, Doubleday Anchor, p.133.

12. see: Propp, V., (1984) *Morphology of the Folktale*, University of Texas Press.

Part V

On Stories and Storymaking

If there were dreams to sell
Merry and sad to tell,
And the crier rang the bell
What would you buy?

Th. Lovell Beddoes

CHAPTER FIFTEEN

On ancient stories and storytelling

Many years ago I worked in Harlem, New York with angry teenagers who lived in a drug-addiction treatment centre. Their life-stories read like catalogues of crimes, deaths, desertions, loneliness and betrayals. They had few reasons to trust anyone, let alone themselves. The world had given them a raw deal and they had helplessly paid it back with suffering for suffering, violence for violence. Now they tried to stop the habits of their young lives and to begin to trust someone, somehow. But where to start, when so much had been hurting for so very long?

One afternoon I sat in the blazing hot sun at the edge of the basketball court when one of our members, a black girl called Deirdre, came and sat by me. Deirdre never talked about the past nor about the future. If she spoke at all, it was about the heat of the sun or how long the game would continue. I pondered her name, and given my own love of stories, it was not surprising that the ancient Irish tale of 'Deirdre and the sons of Usnach' came to mind.

When I first heard this story I had been fourteen years old, a lonesome teenager in a new town. Perhaps, therefore, in the sharing of the tale, despite the other more obvious differences, there might be the sharing of the experience of loneliness.

I heard myself say 'Do you know the story of Deirdre and the sons of Usnach?' Not surprisingly, she did not know the story and she wouldn't mind if I told her. That afternoon whilst the other children played their gracious game of basketball, I told the ancient Irish tale. Slowly but steadily Deirdre who hated being touched, snuggled up beside me; she cried without saying why. The following day she told her own painful tale. How her mother and father had fought and drunk a great deal. How she had been only nine years old when her mother had suddenly died. Life had rapidly gone from bad to tragically terrible. Between her sobs she cried: 'I wonna make it better. That other Deirdre. I wonna make it better. I wonna live.' The old Irish story mattered to a young girl born in Harlem, New York, partly because it offered her a fairly accurate representation of her own life experience and therefore of her inner world.

Deirdre's response to the Irish tale resembles what happens to many of us when we listen to a tale in a time of sorrowed trouble. We hearken to these tidings not only because we wish to be distracted but also because we long to be comforted and to find a way through our difficulties, hoping to discern the kernel of a possible answer in the ancient tale. Let us therefore look at the nature of such stories and consider why they are important to all of us.

From generation to generation: guarding the story-child

Tales of the ordinary and tales of the mysterious have spellbound people the world over irrespective of their age, learning or social status. To this day descriptions of marvellous adventures can be heard at many a dinner table. Most children (and adults) love to be told a story at bedtime, sermons and lectures are now as ever richly illustrated with new and old anecdotes. In most pubs and clubs time is whiled away with tales of wonder and the extraordinary antics of fate. Stories are thriving.

In this book only a very narrow band of all possible stories is represented, namely those tales which have been passed from one generation to another, primarily orally and sometimes in recorded form. The term folktale is used to describe the tales which were handed down through the centuries often from one storyteller to another. Whenever such an old tale is retold the storyteller's faithfulness to the received material matters, for the tale bears witness to the distilled wisdom of generations of people. The storyteller's decision to change a tale consequently needs to be inspired by similar wisdom, experience and knowledge.

The Ekoi-people of Nigeria say that a long time ago stories were like story-children. These story-children were woven from whatever was seen in the house of the world. The storyteller, or guardian of such a story-child was entrusted with four special responsibilities.[1]

— The first task was to ensure that the story-child had a beautiful gown of her own, which was distinct from and yet connected with all other story-children.

— The second task was to allow the story-child to be inspired by all which is hidden. To know about the rich and the poor, day as well as night.

— The third task concerned the ongoing nourishment of the story-child's authenticity and veracity. She had to be helped to speak her own truth. No more, but also no less.

— Finally, each and every story-child had to be allowed to run free. This could be done in one way only. Namely by giving voice to the story. Thereby the story-child was given life and could remain, perhaps forever, on earth.

The fourth task was acknowledged to be the most difficult one. It was known that sooner or later the storyteller pays a price for each and every story told. Like deeds which cannot be undone, the wisdom contained within the tale cannot be unknown. Yet, how to live one's life in relation to these truths? However, there was also comfort to be drawn from the realization that the price paid for electing not to repeat a tale would always be greater. Silence about important issues invariably creates serious difficulties.

The ancient people addressed this predicament, which might be described as 'to tell or not to tell', by creating numerous stories about the birth and acquisition of tales. Such tales describe how the story-children came into the world accidentally or following many trials and tribulations or because someone used a trick. Of course these stories are also reflective of the hierarchical organisation within a given society, the distribution of status and power between men and women, the wealthy and the poor, as well as the skilled and the unskilled. As such they offer us insight into the functioning of a community and its attempts to describe the status quo in story-form.

The Ashanti people tell us how in those long ago days, before the birth of stories, Kwaku Ananse, the now famous Ananse, went to see the Skygod, Nyan-Konpon. This is what happened.

At that time Ananse was still only an ordinary spider, who had the audacity to tell the Skygod that he had come to buy his stories. Upon which Nyan-Konpon exclaimed:' What makes you think you can buy them?' And the spider answered: 'I know I shall be able!'. Nyan-

Konpon said: 'Great and powerful towns like Kokufu, Bekwai, Asumengya have come, but they were unable to purchase them, and yet you who are but a mere masterless man, you say you will be able?' The spider asked: 'What is the price of the stories?' and then the Skygod replied: 'They cannot be bought for anything except Onini the python; Osebo the leopard; Minoatia the fairy and Mmoboro the hornet.' The spider said: 'I will bring some of all of these things and what is more, I will add my old mother Nsia, the sixth child, to the lot.' The Skygod said: 'Go and bring them then.'

Ananse returned home. He told his mother about his promise to give her to the Skygod. Then he asked his wife for help. She did this by giving him a riddle-like instruction, so that he could capture python, hornet and leopard. Ananse himself thought up a way to capture the fairy. When he had done so, his mother gladly agreed to be given to the Skygod. Then, accompanied by all he needed to buy the stories, Ananse returned to Nyan-Konpon. When Nyan-Konpon saw that the spider had brought everything he had asked for, he called his elders and he put the spider's case before them, saying: 'Very great kings have come, and were not able to buy the Skygod's stories, but Kwaku Ananse, the spider has been able to pay the price which the Skygod asked. He also gave and added his mother to the lot.' Then Nyan-Konpon said: 'Sing his praise'. The elders all shouted 'Eee!' The Skygod said: 'Kwaku Ananse from today and going on forever, I take my Skygod's stories and I present them to you. Kose! Kose! Kose! My blessing, blessing, blessing!' No more shall we call them the stories of the Skygod, but we shall call them Spider stories.[2]

Here the story ends, but the ancient storyteller adds the following words: 'This, my story, which I have related, if it be sweet, or if it be not sweet, take some elsewhere, and let some come back to me.'

This final plea can be heard the world over in numerous variations. The storyteller knows that the listener passes a judgment upon the tale, maybe it was liked, maybe not, but whatever that judgment is the audience has to be urged to continue the telling. For retelling guarantees a story's life. Not to be retold means the end of the story. Storytellers thus have a dual task: to protect the act or even the art of storytelling and to safeguard themselves as the precious container of tales.

For whenever a story is set free by having been handed over to the listener(s) a certain emptiness dwells inside the teller, an emptiness which must be acknowledged. Not only because within this receptive space new tales emerge, but also because initially the emptiness feels raw and somewhat frightening. The declaration of the need for 'becoming a listener too' may then encourage others to share their tale. Thus the nourishment which is sought can be provided.

As the ancient stories pass from mouth to mouth some are like errant children, who transform and yet persist, finding ways to adapt to different environments and, where necessary, becoming faithful servants to alternative meanings and purposes. The original form of any folktale therefore remains a matter of conjecture. Studies have shown that the same feats can be ascribed to a Trickster-character in one area, a God somewhere else, or to a Fairy in yet another place. The deeds have remained the same, even though the hero or heroine has changed. The rules and regulations which surround the retelling of a given story vary greatly from region to region; what is held sacred by one society may serve as entertainment with another tribe.

The oral story's propensity to alteration, addition and embellishment has inspired the storyteller's art since time immemorial. However, this tendency also threatens the long term survival of a tale. Consequently, each story is potentially re-told beyond recognition or reference to the original tales unless the storyteller has placed certain injunctions upon the re-teller. Such injunctions usually refer to the actual permission to re-tell a tale. For example, there are stories which can only be told by parents to their own children or by the elders of a society to young men and women about to be initiated. Or the injunctions refer to the circumstances under which a tale may be retold. Some stories may thus only be retold after the sun has set at certain times of the year during specific ritual events.

This latter category of tale is often referred to as myth or sacred story.

A folktale or a myth?

Ancient stories are frequently divided into two categories: myths or folktales. Even though it is often surprisingly difficult to determine whether an ancient tale belongs to the realm of the sacred, or to that of instruction/entertainment tales. The lines of category-specificity blur and the delineation is far from clear. Times also change and what was once considered sacred has long since moved into the domain of the ordinary. Additional confusion is generated by the temptation to presume that, if a story deals with a so-called serious subject, it therefore must be sacred. Or vice versa, that its humorous style places it squarely in the entertainment category. This may not be the case at all. Anthropologists, who aim to understand a story in its cultural context, tell us that we need to comprehend each story's relationship to ritual, as well as the myriad ways in which its content informs behaviour and values, before we should dare to pronounce such a judgment. They debate with folklorists and historians of religion as to whether exact delineations between myths or folktales can ever be made, since strict classification-systems have so far proven to be unworkable.

However, it is also clear that every society and possibly even each person differentiates between that which is held sacred and that which is considered profane. This act of differentiation, which arises from the need to delineate, matters.

All of us have difficulty in finding words to express that which is most precious to us. Mystery is beyond language. Intuitively, we sense that it may also be dangerous to frame the impenetrably mysterious within the narrow confines of verbal utterances, unless such words are open to multiple interpretations and associations. The story, and especially the sacred story mediates between our experience of the known and our intimations about the unknown. It has, therefore, to make use of multivalent language. Language which evokes, and through evocation inspires. Such inspiration enhances our vision. This we need, oftentimes desperately, in days of pain and turmoil.

In spite of this inability to create firm demarcations for the kinds of subjects which are dealt with in folktales and those which are addressed in myth, we can say with a degree of certainty that most mythological stories speak about the world before it became the way we know it nowadays. The primary purpose of these myths is to convey the preparation which occurred long ago for the present and future order of affairs. As such, all myths form a 'constitution' of a certain kind by introducing us to a Creator-God or to the Original Principle which inspired creation. Often the myths also explain the origins of the wind, waters, animals, people and the universe, the emergence into being of all creatures and phenomena, their eventual functioning and demise. Important events as we experience them today can then be explained by reference to these imagined or revealed earlier happenings, and important information is thereby given about the puzzling human condition.

Certain human experiences and situations are universal, as are our preoccupations with issues surrounding life and death, suffering and healing, luck and bad fortune. The particular form through which these basic concerns are addressed varies, of course, from person to person, tribe to tribe and time to time. But the central themes stay remarkably similar: how can we relate to that which imbues creation, beginnings as well as endings, in such a way that our life is enhanced? The answers to this central preoccupation are given in a society's myths, which offer a framework both for the experience of reality and for the interpretation of this experience.

Both tribal and non-tribal people, western city-dwellers and inhabitants of the remotest rain forest tend to believe that their particular 'sacred narratives' are true, that the ancient story relates to actual, and not necessarily to symbolic events which occurred in the distant past. Most people in ancient and in modern times feel deeply uncomfortable with the possible thought that their sacred story might not relate to actual history but aim to approximate sensed potentiality; 'It may have been', rather than 'It was'. Speculation, instead of the recording of facts; hypothesis, instead of revelation.

Many of us wish that the essential condition preceded the actual condition. We long for the security of the thought that once-upon-a-time the present existed in a state of pre-scribed or given potentiality, in *statu nascendi*. For if this were to be the case, this selfsame unfolding force, guided by the power and direction of the original creative intention, would continue to direct and thereby to affect our own life to this very day.

This idea or belief is important, for there is a great deal at stake. If such an overall, once-given plan were to exist, then we too could presume to be part of an original scenario and we could thereby find our place both within history and in the universe. This is felt to be reassuring and we need to remember that such reassurance is offered by most sacred narratives, precisely because they contain descriptions of an all encompassing 'once upon a distant time' design and recognize a designer. These sacred narratives therefore protect us against the consideration that in the beginning neither intention nor meaning existed; there was no pre-planned higher purpose to life in general or to our life in particular. Whatever sense of meaning we generate, it is no more and no less than the outcome of intention and interaction. Many of us shudder at the immense responsibility and aloneness of this idea, and therefore many people refrain from contemplating its consequences, preferring to hold firm to our sacred myth like ivy to a wall.

Whichever path we choose, and however much we may oscillate between certainty and uncertainty, we also need to remember that we all grow in wisdom and generosity through the nurturance of beliefs which are worth risking.

Some further considerations

When we read a myth or sacred narrative we are not only confronted with the reality that its content may be diametrically opposed to our own cherished belief, but we also need to be aware that the text is an incomplete representation of the myth. This is due to the fact that whenever a myth is recited it consists of spoken or chanted words and sounds which are accompanied by equally important prescribed facial expressions, gestures, music and the ritual use of ornaments and space. Thus we have the 'mythos', which is the myth *per se*, as well as the 'dromenon', which refers to the set of parallel and integrated acts or actions, which are an essential part of the myth. Together, and only together, these constitute the mythical, ritual event.

Each myth derives its potency from both correct preparation for participation in the ritual and the correct performance, or more accurately, the precise execution of the prescribed ritual deeds. Therefore, it will come as no surprise that the recorded myth, to which we have access in an article or book, frequently appears to be fragmentary. To put it simply, it is incomplete due to the absence of the 'dromenon' or the action. Therefore we need to remember that, although a myth has been carefully recorded and faithfully transcribed/translated, it is only part of a greater story. The recorded text inadequately, and thereby inaccurately, conveys the myth's potency.

It also speaks for itself that our own cultural biases and presumptions profoundly influence the way in which we relate to the material. We tend to bring a whole range of barely conscious presumptions to many myths and tales, which consequently appear to be strange and incoherent. If we take time to consider our pre-judgments, we may well find that there is much to discover in stories which initially seemed alien and inaccessible.

While several stories in this book can be described as myths 'proper', most are in the category of the folktale. Broadly speaking, we can say that such stories were told for entertainment, instruction or inspiration. As suggested before few constraints are placed upon the retelling of the folktale. A lawyer might use it in court to support her plea, an elder to admonish a child, a friend to clarify his situation. Whenever a folktale is recounted the listeners or audience, tend to feel free to question the storyteller. The main character in a folktale can so to speak, be called upon to justify his or her deeds and omissions. The listeners and particularly children feel free to stop the telling of a tale in order to make a comment or to demand an explanation. After all, the folktale is both true and not true, 'for real' and yet not 'for real'. These frequently witty interruptions and interpolations lead the storyteller to expand upon the tale and thus the process of alteration in character, incidents and plot begins.

As the Nigerian Ekoi-people said, the story's life depends upon being told. However beautifully a story is retold in a book, the written story is not changed by the act of reading, even though the reader may well be changed. The reader's relationship with the printed word is private and solitary, whereas the oral tale thrives on company and context. Even if no word is added or changed, the atmosphere of the telling-place, the quality of the listening, as well as the desire to pass on this story to these people here and now generate a new vitality to the tale. They give it life again as well as anew.

This rebirth into freshness constitutes both the myth's and the folktale's potency. The recitation is their life-breath. When the story is such a gift between teller and listener, everyone emerges replenished.

References

1. Talbot, P. A., (1912) *In the Shadow of the Bush*, London: Heinemann.
2. Retold by the author. Principal source: Radin, J. and Sweeney, J., (1952) *African Folktales and Sculpture*, New York: Bollingen Foundation.

They are not long, the days of wine and
    roses;
Out of a misty dream
Our path emerges for a while, then closes
Within a dream.

Ernest Dowson

CHAPTER SIXTEEN

Bereavement counselling through storymaking

It is lovely to tell stories when life is good. Then we entertain ourselves and others with tales of years gone by, knowing that a captivating yarn gives a special kind of glow to the hours spent in the company of friends as well as strangers. Temporarily, the story will provide a link between us, a sense of unity as well as a common frame of reference. Each story calls forth other tales, memories of expeditions and adventures, or recollections of old folktales cherished and loved beyond the 'once upon a time'. Thus the cup of human companionship is passed amongst all who dwell in this certain place at this specific time. These are the gentle gatherings. However, we also know other times when the coming together is clouded with pain. Then we meet not in order to be entertained, but because we badly need people who will understand, who may offer consolation. During such hours many painful emotions struggle within us for acknowledgment and expression while we search for the words to say it. The burden of silence must be overcome if we want to find a way through. Our very survival depends upon the establishment of contact.

When we have been hurt, and we were hurt badly when someone we love dies, we often long for greater relief than can be offered by our meeting with other people. We want to move our understanding of what has happened beyond the personal towards the transpersonal and to place our pain into a larger framework. We do this amongst others by referring to similar events in other people's life or by remembering an old story which relates to our

situation. Intuitively, we know that reassurance is to be found in the awareness that people in other places and times encountered kindred sorrow, and
were able to live through their pain, eventually to be healed. We also realize
that if we were to be able to get involved in such a story it might take our
mind off things. Thereby we would have the chance to stop, to take a little
break. This could be restful. In addition, such a story may offer us some ideas
about how to approach our own situation, for nearly every tale deals with
difficulties and with ways of surmounting them. When listening to an ancient
tale we do not have to declare that we experience similar problems; we may,
but we do not have to. This freedom liberates our willingness to consider
possible alternative solutions to our experienced trouble. The anonymity of
a folktale or myth grants us the permission to identify with the story-char-
acters and their life-events to our heart's content. The identification frequently inspires us with new energy, especially if the story is the 'right' one for
this moment. Thus we gain vicariously in strength and courage.

Meanwhile, the storyteller simply offers us the gift of a story, told to us
and for us, here and now. A thread of wonder is woven; a bridge of
companionship is built. We need this contact, often greatly, when we suffer
the aloneness of grief. Alternatively, we may be as disinterested in the story
as we like. When we are recently bereaved our memory and concentration
do not function at their best and although our inability to focus may unsettle
the storyteller a little, it is definitely not the end of the world. At least our
mind-wandering does not upset someone who also needed to have their
life-story heard; nor do we feel guilty when we listen to the tale, as if it were
merely a transcription of our personal troubles. We can absorb its tidings
with complete self-centredness; we are even encouraged to do so. If the story
grips our attention it softens our preoccupation with our own situation.

Thus there are numerous reasons why stories are told in times of trouble
and consequently we may expect to find many stories which deal with intense
emotional states and the resultant self-absorption, and indeed we do. All over
the world we find story-cycles, series of stories, in which a troupe of
storytellers helps a weeping man or boy, woman or girl to stop crying, to
smile and finally to laugh again. Such storytellers told one story after another,
until they succeeded in lifting their listener's burdensome sorrow and
renewed interest in the world was demonstrated. It speaks for itself that at
the end of such telling the troupe reaped ample rewards. After all, it is no
mean achievement

— to help the silent to speak,

— to motivate those of us who are swallowed up by apathy,

— to make the withdrawn curious,

Such, though, are the powers of stories and such is the domain of storytelling.

Humankind has long since known that it is dangerous for us to build walls of silence around ourselves and to resist the effort which is made to draw us into communication. For if were we to succeed in our resistance, we risk severing the bonds with the world which is ours to inhabit and explore. Ancient stories speak to us about this tricky human propensity and help us cope with our disturbing behavioural tendencies.

Disturbed tendencies which become part and parcel of 'normal' behaviour, whenever we experience the stress of bereavement. When we lose someone we are very close to, we are only too aware that their death deprives us of all the pleasures and comforts, rhythms and complexities, which our relationship with them provided. This hurts, to put it mildly. We become tense and anxious, and we may even wonder whether we are going crazy, asking ourselves if such pain will ever go away. The stress is caused by a number of unavoidable factors:

— Though we may have anticipated the death for a long time, it is surprising how much suddenly has to be decided and done. These are often unfamiliar decisions and acts. This is in itself stressful.

— Our previous rhythm is thrown completely off balance. Old habits need to be changed. The table now has to be laid for three people instead of four. We need to take the car to the garage ourselves. The subscription to specialist magazines, membership of clubs and organisations has to be cancelled. The list of adaptations and alterations is endless.

— Consequently, predictability and reliable expectations seem to be words from a distant past. This adds to our sense of disruption and confusion.

— Endless bits of information come our way. Some of these are contradictory. Equally we are surrounded with a great deal of advice. It is often difficult to discern what is useful and what is superfluous; this is a further burden.

— Decisions are being made for us, either because we dilly-dally, or because well-intentioned but nonetheless interfering busybody's make decisions on our behalf. Bureaucracies and large organisations, such as hospitals, banks and town halls, move at their own pace, a pace which may well be too fast or too slow for us, thus adding to our sense of loosing control.

— We are forced to use previously untapped resources. Though some of these may make us feel surprisingly good, it is also bewildering to feel good whilst we feel bad. Such ambivalence can add to our sense of being stressed.

To encapsulate:

The early stages of bereavement represent a crisis situation, with all the concurrent physical and emotional responses. These lead to three pre-dominant modes of reaction to stress, which are known as Fight, Flight and Freeze. (Ayalon, 1989)

fight: A vicious circle of frustration - anger - aggression - attack - destruction - frustration.

flight: A regressive mode instigated by fear and insecurity, which may be followed by denial - flight into fantasies - retreat into illness - dependency - passivity.

freezing: A mental and physical paralysis and shock, followed by depression - helplessness - self-blame - fatigue - apathy.[1]

The first task we face in a crisis-situation such as bereavement is to survive it as best we can. The second, if at all possible, is to gain from the way we manage to live through these frightening times. When we are in the eye of the storm both of these may seem like tall orders.

When we have been diminished by the death of someone we love, our hope, courage and resourcefulness are at a low ebb. Of course they are. Maybe we discern vaguely that they could be replenished by the expression of grief but how and in which way is a mystery to us, even though we know that the only way forward is to experience our bereavement for what it is and to feel the full measure of our loss.

Though the road is difficult, with more than a little help from our friends most of us find our way through our bereavement. There are weeks and months, sometimes years during which we take flight, fight often and bitterly and freeze, but in time we repair our hurt and regain a sense of vitality.

But some of us find the going very troublesome indeed. This may be because the pain of earlier losses adds to the burden of our present bereavement or because the circumstances surrounding the death were particularly awful. Events may also have compelled us to deny our sorrow, even though we know that we pay a heavy price for success in the game of 'let's pretend that I'm not broken-hearted'. After all, we have not only lost this person but also our special way of being with them. 'No longer will I be the one I am and was with this one, let alone whom I might have been and who we might have been if only there had been time yet'.

Numerous reasons may have led us to keep our grief under tight control and therefore to wait incessantly or we may have been forced to run away from our mourning and thereby never rest again. Either way, it will be as if the very act of breathing constitutes a deed of betrayal.

When we are thus knotted up inside ourselves, preoccupied with words spoken and deeds done or words unspoken and deeds undone, we may at last seek help, or help may be offered.

Then the hour has come when we are wholeheartedly encouraged to tell the story of our grief to people who are able to hear, stories which embody our experience of life and stories which transcend this experience. And the AIM of this telling?

— to express our feelings and emotions
— to experience 'being heard'
— to have our grief acknowledged and shared
— to receive support
— to let go of our unnecessary long-term accommodation to high levels of stress
— to allow the ordinary to return

Ultimately, we achieve reconciliation with our irrevocable loss, and therefore with a life which is complete only in its incompleteness.

The bereavement-journey involves tears and protest, silence and readjustment. It also demands the retrieval of a past which can be remembered with a degree of pleasure, while it is inclusive of our grief, so that we may discover a new 'imagined' future, one which encompasses hope and inspiration, as well as a belief that benign changes are equally possible.

Along this journey we invariably encounter a great deal of fear, such as the fear that we shall be devoured by the intensity of our feelings; for it hurts to acknowledge how much we have lost and it also hurts to dare to hope again. When we tell the stories of our often hellish interpersonal experiences our earlier withheld emotions tear at us. But we also know that, to overcome the 'rending pain of reenactment of all that we have done and been', we need to mourn the life lived and the life that was not lived. Only then can our future become more than the mere realization of a blueprint created in the past. To achieve such true 'transcendent unknowing', we must consent to the essentially unpredictable process of change. This consent emerges from the crucible of experience.

For us, the important question is how we may facilitate this process of healing through story-telling and storymaking in groups.

This question is answered in three ways:

— by describing the conditions which foster a healing atmosphere in a counselling group

— by indicating why creative-expressive activities matter

— by discussing some specific characteristics of storymaking.

A climate of sharing

Let us first focus on those conditions which foster a climate of sharing in a self-help or counselling group aimed at helping the group members to work through grief. With such a group we may presume that every group-member has experienced a bereavement, either recently or at some time in the past. Though the specific motivation to join the group will vary a common reason is simply that it is hard to cope by oneself. When we suffer it is often reassuring to be with people who have gone through comparable experiences. Because each of us brings to the group a unique pattern of experiences and responses we soon find that there are common ways of coping as well as alternative ways of going about things. Different interpretations of some-one's behaviour or hurtful comments are possible. New insights can be gained which help us to predict possible setbacks and confusions. We receive encouragement on both bad days and good days, and we soon discover that though we are alone in our grief, we need not be alone with our grief. There are people to whom we can talk, who will actually understand, partly because we are living through a shared fate. Thus we offer each other a hand when needed and especially when it is not needed but still very nice to receive.

In these various ways such groups help us to find norms for our experiences. Frequently, we are very confused by what happens during our bereavement. The group then provides us not only with an actual structure due to its weekly, bi-weekly or monthly pattern, but other people's descriptions of their toil and turmoil give us a frame of reference by which to assess the severity of our particular situation.

Thus we learn to trust again, to tolerate our self-doubts, to express our feelings and to cope with our anxiety. Above all else we learn to make a bond again, a link with people who matter because of who they are and what they are going through, people like ourselves - a bond, therefore, also with ourselves. We begin, albeit hesitantly, to repair our relationship with life, the life which hurt us so because someone we love died.

Bereavement counselling groups, whether self-help or facilitator-led, are organised in various ways. Most, however, adhere to similar patterns and understood ways of functioning. These are some of them:

— the group meets on a regular basis in an agreed place

— new members are welcomed, either at each session or at certain intervals. Likewise members leave either at each session, or at specific intervals

— consequently, membership of the group is time-limited. It is presumed that at some point after the grief has been worked through regular membership of the group will end, though informal contact may well be maintained

— the group has explicit or implicit rules about 'confidentiality'. Members can trust that details of their life-experience will not be discussed with people who are not group members

— though membership of the organisation is unlimited, the group itself is likely to be limited to between six and fifteen people, in order to enhance sharing and support.

Beyond these basic patterns many things are possible. Some groups may plan outings together, encourage friendships, offer practical advice and guidance, while others stay with more formal patterns of interaction, have no breaks for coffee or tea and concentrate primarily on the actual experience of the pain of bereavement.

It is always important to remember that we joined the group in order to work through our grief and to reclaim some sense of 'consent to life'. From time to time we therefore have to ask ourselves whether the group is still meeting our needs and if not, how we can address this in the group. If all else fails, we need to discuss with the group what we are looking for and how to find alternative sources of help or support. If we decide to end our membership before we have come through the major stages of the bereavement-journey it is important to arrange adequate alternatives. It also matters to say good-bye to the other group-members for their sake and for our own sake.

Why creative-expressive activities matter

While many bereavement-counselling groups work on the justified assumption that 'talking and listening' are good enough means of help in some counselling-groups additional ways of seeking relief are explored. These alternative means can often be summarized under the heading 'creative-expressive exercises'. There are various reasons why creative-expressive activities are particularly beneficial for people who experience emotional difficulties.

These are some of them:

— symbolic expression, through painting, sound-making, movement, drama or story-telling helps us to address our predicament in an indirect way, thereby gently easing our attempts to control the healing process.

— because we temporarily concentrate on making something new, we are freed from our preoccupation with ourselves and become more able to explore alternative solutions to our everyday situation. The act of making something also furthers our sense of mastery, and paradoxically helps us to consent to 'newness'.

— the permission to express ourselves symbolically enhances our sense that we are allowed to express ourselves directly. This matters when we have been holding onto a lot of feelings.

— by giving a symbolic form to the 'unthinkable', our ability to tolerate the 'actual' is increased. it helps us to resolve affective conflicts.

— the process of symbol-making, and the products which have been made raise our awareness of ourselves and others. We learn to see and hear differently.

— it is indispensable to our affective and intellectual equilibrium to have access to an area of activity where we are not expected to adapt to reality but where we are helped to assimilate reality to ourselves.

— activity implies a structured approach to time; this helps us to experience a degree of control.

— when we are engaged in symbolic-expressive activities we do not have to accommodate ourselves to external demands or models; there are neither coercions nor sanctions and this enables the assimilation and therefore the transformation of experienced reality. When this reality is grievous it is of even greater importance that this process occurs.

This much we know. Even though theoreticians and practitioners from a wide variety of backgrounds continue to speculate on the why's and wherefore's of the efficacy of symbolic-expressive activity. The assumptions they make reflect their theoretical orientations. However, they all agree that the creation of symbols at will fulfills an essential human need and thereby contributes to our well-being. The making of a symbol which is generated by oneself and which expresses felt trouble is deeply satisfying. Such satisfaction is especially important when life is painful. We can therefore safely say that the restoration of the capacity to create 'symbolic' utterances results in the easement of tension and contributes to the healing of pain.

Many bereavement counselling groups therefore engage in 'symbolic-expressive' activity to do some painting, to make music or write poetry whilst in some groups improvised drama is enjoyed. When such modes of work are introduced the group facilitators are likely to adhere to the following guidelines:

— The free-flow of ideas and associations is encouraged. Early judgment of any of these ideas as either better or worse, acceptable or unacceptable is actively discouraged. Every contribution matters and is valued for what it is.

— A climate is fostered in which difference is enjoyed. The similarities and differences between various ways of coping are recognized as a source of wonder and stimulation. When commonality occurs it is noted but not necessarily praised.

— prescriptive answers and solutions to the experienced problems are avoided. It is taken as given that each of us has to find our own specific way through, a way which is right for us.

— genuine, warm interest in one another's work is encouraged. Praise or criticism of the formal quality of someone's contribution is limited. What truly matters is the expressive activity/product, the act of engaging with something; the 'how' and to a lesser extent the 'what'.

— the courage to express is acknowledged and stimulated.

— especially during the early stages of the group work, every member receives an equal share of time and attention. Silence is also considered to be a contribution worthy of interest.

The environment within which such a group meets needs to be conducive to the kind of work the group is engaged in - a spacious, quiet room with comfortable chairs, tables for writing and painting and a large enough empty area for movement/drama work. In addition, the group needs to have access to some simple musical instruments, a few props like scarves and skipping ropes, plus ample writing paper, paints, pens and modelling clay. None of these are prohibitively expensive and, if needs must be, all kinds of alternative low-cost solutions to the use of more expensive materials can be found. All that is required is a basic willingness to engage in symbolic expressive activity; the rest follows.

Specific characteristics of storymaking

In which ways, then, do storymaking sessions differ from other group-meetings, during which people become involved in creative-expressive activities? The most obvious difference is the high degree of prescribed structure.

Let us presume that you are by now familiar with the stories and the storymaking structures in this book. You will have noticed that every structure has opening exercises, a 'central' task, and ending exercises. You will also have become aware that each structure has a specific focus which is closely related to the story. The telling of the story is part of the session-structure as are a wide range of activities and so-called response-tasks. Though there are individual differences between the storymaking-structures you probably discovered that most structures follow a similar pattern. This is:

— welcome
— initial focussing exercises
— individual/pair/group tasks based on the theme
— sharing of experiences

— the story
— group/pair/individual tasks based on the story
— sharing of experiences with specific response-tasks for the other group-members
— reflection and connecting of metaphoric material to individual and group ways of being.
— ending

The movement within most structures is from the individual to the group, back to the individual from the external story to the internal story; from old material to present material. Links are established between individual and collective fantasy, memory and knowledge, between the past, the present and the anticipated future. During the session the group will explore images, memories and longings/fantasies which are evoked by the theme. In some structures a parallel story is created, in others certain aspects of the ancient tale are developed in metaphor. Attention is then devoted to the creation of links between these self-created metaphors and the group members' actual life-experiences.

The stories and the storymaking structures have been chosen because they address some basic experiences which each of us is likely to live through when someone we love has died. Though many of these experiences are the same for most people, we face them in our own way and at our own time. However, in the storymaking work the focus of a session is pre-selected. It is crucial to bear this in mind. The group-facilitator and/or the group members need to take responsibility for the decision to work around a given theme. This decision consequently has to be made with full consideration of the group's developmental needs, its strengths and weaknesses. The therapeutic competencies of the group and the facilitator also need to be noted. Each structure is likely to generate strong feelings. Though various ways and means of containing such feelings have been built into the storymaking structure this does not reduce the demands placed upon the therapeutic sensitivity and skill of the group members towards one another and of the facilitator to the group.

This very same sensitivity and skill will be drawn upon when judging whether or not a given story/theme is appropriate for the group at this moment. Whenever the facilitator(s) take the responsibility for selecting a given story or structure, it is important to read and to re-read and actually to do/perform as best one can, every exercise in all THREE structures which are connected with the story. Only such careful homework will inform you of the potency of each story and each specific storymaking structure, and therefore of their potential value to the group with whom you work.

In so far as the group has access to the stories in this book, the decision to work with a certain story/theme can be shared. A group may choose to explore the material in this book in an alternating pattern:

- one week, a 'talking' group, at the end of which next week's story-theme is selected.
- the other week a 'storymaking' group.
- then a 'talking' group, etc.

Once a specific story and structure has been chosen the group members need to agree to participate in this particular storymaking-journey. Such agreement is important for the purpose of each task within the structure is not necessarily clear to the participants, and the group members are therefore asked to invest a substantial amount of trust in the structure's healing potential. This trust is given in good faith.

The faith is probably based on presumed competence in the design of the structures, and on the fact that the work has been tried and tested with other people. Even though the first is hopefully true and the second is a reality, the trust which the group members invest needs to be acknowledged.

Group members must also be reminded that, whenever they feel that they do *not* want to engage in a certain exercise, they have every right to sit out. Their first responsibility is towards themselves. They need to take care to protect their own boundaries, even though the group-facilitator also has the task to try and encourage each group member to ease these boundaries.

In the storymaking workshop the group members are introduced to an ancient tale which they are likely to be able to recall and retell many years later. This is paradoxically easier if the story is unfamiliar. This was therefore one of the criteria by which the stories in this book were selected.

Another guiding principle was the decision to look for some tales created by people whose way of life is severely threatened or which has already been destroyed. Previous group members have often expressed their genuine surprise at the astounding beauty of an Inuit, Bushman or old Japanese tale. Because each tale bears witness to the knowledge and the wisdom of the people who voiced it, the re-telling of such a story then also contributes to the raising of our awareness with regard to our prejudices. So much the better, then, when the story becomes a bridge across which people from different places, in different times and with other predicaments meet to address their shared longing for a good enough life.

During each session the group member will have painted, moved, written, talked. But the story itself will stand out in its own unforgettable imagery. Imagery which resonates long after the actual telling of the tale.

The stories in the book have been retold in an unembellished, straight-forward way. Where possible, several versions of each story were collected. These were compared with one another and with original source-material. Then the obvious 'individual' variations in the versions of the story were removed. The story was retold using only those events and factors which were the same in every version. As such, the stories are presented in a 'bare-bone' manner.

Each facilitator is strongly encouraged to get to know this basic version inside out, then to re-tell the tale. This should present no other difficulty than possible initial shyness. The chosen stories have a certain 'memorable' quality due to their pattern and structure. This inherent logic aids the retelling. In many respects you will find that the tale re-tells itself.

When retelling a folktale I have often found it helpful to remind myself that I am truly no more than a servant to the story and not a performer who needs to impress my audience with verbal skills and oratory excellence. None of this matters; I am simply given the time to share a story which has touched me. If it is a story worth knowing it needs be told without my getting in its way. I noticed that the story's poignancy and beauty benefit most from sincerity. Once I realised this, the story became a gift which I was allowed to pass on - no more, no less. I became as much a listener to my own retelling as the others. All of us captivated by the tale, all of us glad to be in this telling-place, to receive this story which had already survived centuries of living and which with our help will survive a great deal longer.

So much about the telling of the stories, let us now return to the storymaking structures.

The storymaking work is based on the premise that almost everyone who is more than two years old has the capacity to create a 'new' story and to communicate it. It is also presumed that at first there will be difficulties in doing this, which can be eased. The working-method therefore has to take account of these early hesitations and be geared towards the facilitation of the group member's ability to express him- or herself.

All exercises have been specifically designed with this principle in mind, but they also had to contribute to another process. The stories which are to be created during a session have to be relevant to the predicaments which the group member experiences. Not only must there be some way of voicing the felt dilemma, the newly made story also has to include attempts at conflict-resolution and to free the potential for healing.

When faced with the question 'tell me a story' many of us feel tongue-tied. When this question is rephrased as 'tell the group a story, which will bring relief to your current situation and which will show you a possible direction to resolve your felt problem', most of us would not know where to begin. It seems an impossible task. However it is not, provided we have a method to approach it.

It is important to note that this methodic approach is embedded in the *entire* storymaking structure. From the very first exercise to the final activity, the storymaking structure is geared to the facilitation of the group member's ability to give form and voice to experience. Simply to express is, however, not enough. It is a beginning which needs to be followed by attempts to come to grips with the experience, to introduce new ways of relating and to open up further avenues for exploration. Courage and hope must be increased, consolation and reconciliation offered.

In the storymaking workshops the group members are guided through a series of purposefully sequential tasks. The specificity as well as the sequence of these tasks matters. They have been designed because the performance of the exercise or task enables the group member to undertake part of the journey which is embodied in the story-pattern. The 'story' of the entire session always portrays one of the strands in the group member's life. The goal of the session is to bring knowledge and awareness of this felt reality to the group members whilst simultaneously bringing relief through the creation of access to possible ways forward.

When engaged in the various exercises, the group member becomes the one who speaks of his or her own woundedness, the one who finds the remedy and the one who heals. These shifts occur at times surreptiously, at times explicitly. In the design of the structures these processes have been taken into careful consideration.

As will be remembered from the reading of the storymaking structures, the response-tasks fulfil a crucial function. Whenever a tale is told or writing shared the other group members are given a specific task which has to be done immediately after each 'home-made' story is told. Seeing the group at work for oneself and in relation to the contribution one has just made, confirms to the group and to the individual that he or she has been listened to. This matters a great deal especially when you have every reason to feel that your troubles were not heard at a time when you really needed it. To risked telling a story and then to have noticed that your listeners are absent-minded or preoccupied with their own tales would have been a further most unhelpful experience.

The response-tasks are therefore constructed in such a way that the listener is drawn into 'enjoyable and healing' listening. Through this each group member simultaneously acquires and practices the ability to interact with a story (including, of course, their own) through metaphor. The group member's skill in responding in a meaningful way to both the stories and to one another is also substantially enhanced. Through the response-tasks the group members learn to give each other attention as well as care at a time when everyone feels vulnerable and exposed and the 'giving' is followed by the experience of receiving nurturance and considered attention. Many people find this a deeply moving experience. Within an atmosphere of renewed trust and confidence it then becomes possible to share the actual life-events which inspired the stories. Then the words can be found to describe what previously could not be described and the chaos of once-upon-a-time overwhelming experiences can be encountered within the safety and boundaries of an established group. New pathways towards healing are discovered and gradually internalized.

One final note of caution: the integrity of each storymaking structure matters. The tasks are carefully chosen. Their sequentiality is for specific reasons. I therefore urge you not to alter the exercises, or their sequence. If you are tempted to introduce your own exercises (and why not) then please design an entirely new structure. You may find the process of designing a structure interesting. But the structures in this book have their own inherent logic. They have been tried and tested, and as such can be vouchsafed to work. Tampering with their inherent logic will lead to confusion which none of us needs when the going is already tough.

That said, we can trust the rekindling powers of ancient stories and new tales. The potential for positive, projective identification between a story-character and oneself does inspire new ways of being, whilst the emergence of individual and group creativity enables us all 'to make our dream of life come true'. Therefore we too may add our voice to the Zuni Indian invitation:

Come, ascend the ladder: all come in: all sit down.

> We were poor, poor, poor, poor, poor,
> When we came to this world through the poor place,
> Where the body of water dried for our passing.
> All, all come, all ascend, all come in, all sit down.[2]

References

1. Ayalon, O., (1988) *Rescue*, Nord Publications, p. 13.
2. Rothenberg, J., (1969) *Technicians of the Sacred*, Anchorbooks, p.3.

Part VI

The Stories and Storymaking Structures

The Stories

Note: Please do not attempt to use these structures without reading the previous chapter.

Enkidu's dream

As Enkidu slept alone in his sickness, in bitterness of spirit he poured out his heart to his friend. 'It was I who cut down the cedar, I who levelled the forest, I who slew Humbaba and now see what has become of me.

Listen, my friend, this is the dream I dreamed last night. The heavens roared, and earth rumbled back an answer; between them stood I before an awful being, the sombre-faced man-bird; he had directed on me his purpose. His was a vampire face, his foot was a lion's foot, his hand was an eagle's talon. He fell on me and his claws were in my hair, he held me fast and smothered; then he transformed me so that my arms became wings covered with feathers. He turned his stare towards me, and he led me away to the Palace of Irkalla, the Queen of Darkness, to the house from which none who enters ever returns, down the road from which there is no coming back.

'There is the house whose people sit in darkness; dust is their food and clay their meat. They are clothed like birds with wings for covering, they see no light, they sit in darkness. I entered the house of dust and I saw the kings of the earth, their crowns put away for ever; rulers and princes, all those who once wore kingly crowns and ruled the world in the days of old. They who had stood in the place of the gods like Anu and Enlil, stood now like servants to fetch baked meats in the house of dust, to carry cooked meat and cold water from the water skin. In the house of dust which I entered were high priests and acolytes, priests of the incantation and of ecstasy; there were servers of the temple, and there was Etana, that king of Kish whom the eagle carried to heaven in the days of old. I saw also Samuqan, god of cattle, and there was Ereshkigal the Queen of the Underworld; and Belit-Sheri squatted in front of her, she who is recorder of the gods and keeps the book of death. She held a tablet from which she read. She raised her head, she saw and spoke: 'Who has brought this one here?'

Then I awoke like a man drained of blood who wanders alone in a waste of rushes; like one whom the bailiff has seized and his heart pounds with terror.'

Gilgamesh had peeled off his clothes, he listened to his words and wept quick tears, Gilgamesh listened and his tears flowed. He opened his mouth and spoke to Enkidu: 'Who is there in strong-walled Uruk who has wisdom like this? Strange things have been spoken, why does your heart speak strangely? The dream was marvellous but the terror was great; we must treasure the dream whatever the terror; for the dream has shown that misery comes at last to the healthy man, the end of life is sorrow.' And Gilgamesh lamented, 'Now I will pray to the great gods, for my friend had an ominous dream.'

In: *The Epic of Gilgamesh*, English Version by N. K. Sandars, Penguin Classics, 1972, p. 91-93.

Text:	ENKIDU'S DREAM
Focus:	Friendship, in good and difficult times
Time:	90 minutes

Recall: Something you noticed this morning, which you have not yet shared with anyone.

Talk: Describe this to the group. Use a few sentences only.

Pairs/Talk: Having listened to everyone's contribution, share with your partner an experience/event which you now remember.

Paint: Using fingerpaints, create a picture around the theme of 'friendship'. Remind yourself of important friends. You may decide to use 'symbols' to represent these friends. Make sure you find a space/form for those people, who are or have been important to you.

Reflect: Imagine that you can see your friendship with each person in bird's eye view. Scan the ups and downs of your relationship with each other. Allow the bad, good and neutral times to flow past your mind's eye.

Return to the circle

Share: Your painting with the group, include some of your reflections on friends and friendship in your life.

Read: The story of ENKIDU'S DREAM. Introduce the story by telling the group that this text is a fragment from one of the world's oldest stories, *The Epic of Gilgamesh*. It is at least

5000 years old, written in very early writing (cuneiform) on clay tablets (Some of these are in the British Museum). The story describes the friendship between two strong young men. When our part of the story begins, they still live in that glorious sense of indefatigable youth, believing that the world is theirs and that life is limitless. Then Enkidu has a dream.

Remind: Yourself of occasions when you and your friends shared a similar sense of an imminent dark future. You may find yourself torn between conflicting feelings, such as regret, gratitude, relief, sorrow. Let this be.

Write: Now imagine that shortly after having heard the dream, Gilgamesh decides to write his friend a long letter, amongst others to offer him encouragement. Please write this letter.

Read: This letter to the group.

Response-task: Each group member has as many small, colourful cards, as there are group members. When a letter has been read, write/paint something on a card, which is a response to the letter's expression of friendship. When all group members have read their letters, distribute the cards.

Look: At the cards you received.

Connect: Recall this session's work: the painting of your friendships, your reflections, the story, the letters and the cards.

Select: One statement/idea which you wish to share with the group.

Reflect: Upon the entire session.

Text: ENKIDU'S DREAM
Focus: Preparations
Time: 120 minutes

Mime: Create, through mime, a small, imaginary suitcase. Pass this round the circle. When you receive this small suitcase, open it, look at its imaginary contents and add something else needed for a journey of two weeks. Then close the suitcase, pass it to your neighbour, who opens it, etc. When every-thing is packed, the imaginary suitcase is put in a corner of the room.

Walk: Group members walk round the room. Approach each other with the kind of questions we may ask our part-ner/children/friend, before setting out on a journey, eg:
                     - did you check the taps are off?
                     - did you leave the phone number with the neighbours?
                     - have you got our tickets?

                Return to the circle

Share: Briefly share your reflections on these exercises.

                In pairs

Talk: About the things you do/don't do before going to sleep at night. Try to be detailed.

                Return to the circle

List: On a roll of paper list those preparations which are similar to going on a journey and to going to bed to sleep (eg saying goodbye and saying good night).

Paint: On a small piece of paper fingerpaint or draw the image evoked by a bad dream or nightmare.

Reflect: On how someone might have been able to help you, when you woke up from this bad dream.

Response-task:	As each group member talks, record what he/she says about HOW someone might have been able to help. Make sure that you write this list!
Read:	The story of ENKIDU'S DREAM.
Write:	Using your list of 'How someone might help', write a note of advice to Gilgamesh.
Share:	Your writings with the group.
Select:	As you listen to these writings, select one idea which feels pertinent to your current life-situation.
Share:	This idea with the group.
Connect:	Reflect on all activities in today's session: the packing of the suitcase, the journey questions, the preparations for sleep, the bad dream painting and the kinds of help that could be offered, the story as well as your advice for Gilgamesh.
Select:	One thought/feeling which you want to share with the group.
Imagine:	That you repack the imaginary suitcase, this time not with concrete objects, but with 'qualities needed for a journey'. What would you then pack? Retrieve the imaginary suitcase from the corner of the room where it was left. Open it up and pass it round. Each group member packs their chosen quality. When it is fully packed, suggest that each group member will take away just such a small 'imaginary' suitcase.
Reflect:	Upon the entire session.

Text:	ENKIDU'S DREAM
Focus:	Becoming aware of mortality
Time:	90 minutes

Notice:
: Look carefully at one another. Notice clothes, hair-style etc. One group member is chosen to change something in their appearance. All others close their eyes. Then the change is made. The group looks to see what has been altered. The change is described. Then the next person is asked to change something in the way they look, etc.

Contact:
: Hold hands. Be still for a moment. Make eye-contact. Let go of hand contact.

Read:
: The story of ENKIDU'S DREAM.

Recall:
: Think back to the time when you first realized that people you loved would one day die, and/or that you yourself will die. Do not discuss this experience. Allow yourself to re-member.

Give:
: Each group member as many sheets of newspaper (cut to A4 size) as there are group members, and an equal number of sheets of A4 writing paper.

Talk:
: Each group member has exactly TWO minutes to talk or to be silent, in which to share their experience.

   nb: It is important that the group member is helped to stay within this time-boundary. Remind the group member when time is nearly up.

Response-task:
: When a group member has finished speaking tear a small or large hole in your sheet of newspaper. Place this sheet on top of the A4 writing paper. Within the irregular, empty space which now emerges, write a brief poem, which reflects your response to his/her contribution.

   nb: This may seem a difficult exercise. It is not, provided group members are helped to work within the rhythm of the time boundary.

Write such a poem, irrespective of whether a group member chose to speak or to remain silent during his/her two minutes.

Give: The poem to each group member concerned.

Read: The poems you received.

Connect: Reflect on this session's work: the 'something has changed' exercise, the story, the memories and your sharing, the poems you wrote and those you received.

Share: Some of your thoughts/feelings with the group.

Reflect: Upon the entire session.

The woman from the stars

In the early days there lived a man who had captured a beautiful herd of cattle. He loved them very much. Every day he took them out to graze and in the evening he found them a place to shelter near his home. One morning, as he came to milk the cows, he noticed that the udders were dry and wrinkled. Thinking nothing much of it, he took them to a better place for grazing, and that evening he left his beloved cattle in their shelter as usual. The following morning the udders were dry again. Then he knew beyond doubt that his cows had been milked. When evening fell, he decided to wait and see, whether anyone would come to milk them that night.

About midnight, he saw a strong rope coming down from the stars. Down the cord climbed the young women of the people of the stars. They carried baskets and calabashes, whispering with excitement as they very lightly made their way to his herd of cattle. He followed them, and indeed, the star-women began to milk his cows. But as soon as they saw him, they sped back to the rope, and were gone.

However, one star-woman had not rushed to the rope as fast as the others. He was glad she had been slow to run away, for she was the loveliest of all. She said that she would live with him, on one condition. He was never to look inside the basket with the beautiful lid which she had with her, the star-basket. At least, never to look inside it without her permission. The promise was readily given, and thus they began their life of herding the cattle and gathering food in the fields.

The basket stood in a corner of their dwelling. They both nearly forgot about it. But one day, as the man came home early, and the star-woman had not yet returned, the man's eyes got hold of the basket. He felt pulled towards it. Then he lifted the star-basket's beautiful top. He laughed.

In the evening when the woman returned, she knew what had happened. She just knew, and said: 'You've looked in the basket.' Again he started to laugh, and said: 'Yes, I have. You silly woman, there is nothing in it.' She asked: 'You saw nothing in the basket?' 'No, nothing,' he said. Looking very sad, she turned her back upon him. It was the time of the evening sunset when she vanished.

Retold - Principal source: Van der Post, L., (1962) *Patterns of Renewal*, Pendle Hill Pamphlet Number 121.

Text:	THE WOMAN FROM THE STARS
Focus:	A promise broken
Time:	90 minutes.

Circle: Sit in a circle, and hold hands. Then let go.

Again: Reach out to hold your neighbours' hands. Make sure you look around and establish eye-contact with every group-member. Then let go.

Write: List all the words which come into your mind related to the word 'promise'.

Place: As many TWIGS as their are group members in the middle of the circle.

     nb: When selecting the twigs, make sure each one has a lovely shape.

Choose: Ask each group member to select a twig.

Draw: Create a free drawing/painting of the tree or bush, which has lost this twig. Place the twig near your drawing.

Walk: Walk around, and have a look at everyone's painting/twig.

Response-task: On a small piece of paper write a promise you imagine this tree/bush could have given to the twig.
eg   - I'll always be here
       - I shall remember you
       - You're always welcome.

     Ask group members to leave this 'promise' near the paintings.

Return: To your own place in the circle. Do not yet read the 'promises' which have been left near your painting.

Tell: The story of THE WOMAN FROM THE STARS.

Write: Your immediate response to this story. Focus on your
                intuitive sense of what went amiss (if you feel that anything
                did go amiss).

Read: The 'promises' which were left near your tree/bush
                drawing.

Select: One or two which feel pertinent to your life-situation.

Place: A chair or cushion at one end of the room you are working
                in. Group members move their seating, so that they sit in a
                horse-shoe shape near this chair/cushion.

Speak: One by one, the group members will take place in the
                chair or cushion, taking their twig with them. The twig func-
                tions like a 'talking-stick'. They hold it quietly. Then they
                will speak a few sentences about 'promises and the break-
                ing of promises'. The other group members listen silently.
                When all group members have spoken, the chair or cushion
                is removed. Group members return to circle.

Paint/write: Re-read your writings and look once more at your
                painting. You can add whatever you want, and have a few
                minutes to do so.

Share: Any thoughts/ideas/feelings which need to be shared
                at this stage.

Reflect: Upon the entire session.

Text: THE WOMAN FROM THE STARS
Focus: Years later
Time: 90 minutes

Talk: Think of your handbag, purse or any pockets you may
              have in your clothing. Mention one quality which you ap-
              preciate about your bag, purse or pocket.

              *nb In the unlikely case that a group member has none of these,
              ask them to speak about one they have, or have had, at home.*

Write:	On a piece of paper, three numbers between one and ten.
Create:	A painting of a beautiful basket, which has a snugly fitting lid.
Tell:	The story of THE WOMAN FROM THE STARS
Look:	At the three numbers, which you wrote down earlier.
Write:	Imagine that the man continues to live on his farm, and that the numbers represent the number of years which have gone by since the day he looked into the Star-woman's basket. Imagine too that he keeps a diary. Write a diary-entry, which he made ....years, ...years and ....years after the Star-woman vanished.
Read:	The diary-entry writings to the whole group.
Response-task:	Create as many pieces of paper as there are group members. Having listened to a diary-entry, draw/paint/write a gift on this piece of paper, which you believe the farmer in their story might like/need to receive. Write the name of the group member who told this story, on the other side of drawing/ writing.
Give:	When all group members have shared their writings, distribute the gifts.
	nb: If a group member elects not to share their writings, please ask the others to create a gift for the farmer's untold story.
Open:	All the gifts.
Look:	At the earlier basket-painting, and re-read your writings.
Connect:	Make some connections between these and your actual life-experience.
Share:	Some of your reflections with the group.
Reflect:	Upon the entire session.

Text:	THE WOMAN FROM THE STARS
Focus:	In her own words
Time:	90 minutes.

Clap: Start a rhythm, which all group members will also clap, until someone changes it. Then the group follows this rhythm until a group member changes it, and so on, until someone says 'stop'.

Clap: This time everyone will clap their OWN rhythm. We do this by one person after the other joining in. Each clapping their own rhythm. When everyone is clapping, the person, who first started, stops, then the next one, and so on. In order to get the hang of this exercise, the group may wish to do it, a couple of times.

Tell: The story of THE WOMAN FROM THE STARS.

Write: Re-write the story from the woman's point of view. Use first person singular, or more simply 'I, The Woman from the Stars'.

Tell: These stories.

Response-:
task   Create as many small pieces of paper as there are group members. Having heard a story, write on a piece of paper a character-trait/quality you appreciate in this Star-woman, as well as a character-trait/quality you believe she needs to develop/nurture. Make clear which is which,
eg - I appreciate your honesty.
      - Develop your gentleness.

Give: These writings to the respective group members.

Select: One or two of the responses which feel pertinent to your actual life-experience.

Share: This with the group.

Reflect: Upon the entire session.

The fate of the unhappy Sura

A long time ago there lived a clever Sultan, who could foretell what kind of future lay ahead for people. One day, the Sultan saw amongst his soldiers a thin, sad man. At once the he knew that the man had been born under unfavourable stars. His life was difficult and it promised to remain so.

But the Sultan took pity on him. He decided that he would try to help him a little. Maybe things could get better for this sorrowful man.

The Sultan called for the soldier to ask him about his life. It was, as the Sultan had expected, full of trouble and loneliness, for Sura did not have enough money to pay the bride-price. It was a woe-filled tale indeed. Upon hearing the soldier's story, the Sultan's wish to help him was even stronger. Therefore he asked Sura to deliver a letter on his behalf to the Chief of a nearby village. It was a great honour to be trusted with the Sultan's sealed letter, and Sura promised he would take care of the letter as best he could. The Sultan then gave him two silver coins for food and drink on the journey.

But the day was hot, and the road seemed long, and soon Sura felt thirsty. He began to get tired. When he came to a little village, he could not help himself, he had to rest a while. Then it so happened that his fellow-soldier, Reksa, saw him. Sura was glad to tell him the whole story of being called to see the Sultan, and of the request to deliver the letter. But now it was so hot, and it was such a long way. Reksa was surprised. Wasn't it a great honour to be asked to deliver the Sultan's letter? He himself would not have minded doing so. Hardly had Reksa said that he would have been only too pleased if the Sultan had asked him to take the letter to the Chief, than Sura had handed him a silver coin, as well as the Sultan's letter. As far as he was concerned, it was too hot and too far.

On Reksa went, until he came to the Chief's house, where he insisted upon delivering the letter in person. When the Chief read the Sultan's message, he looked at Reksa in surprise. His friend had written to suggest that this young man might be a suitable husband for the Chief's youngest daughter. As the full bride-price was included, and Reksa seemed strong and lively, the Chief ordered that the best food be made ready to receive his future son-in-law. When Reksa at last discovered his good fortune, he was well pleased. As was the Chief's youngest daughter, who took delight in the young man. It was a joyous wedding-feast.

Forty days later the young couple came to offer their respect to the Sultan, who then saw who had married the Chief's youngest daughter - something he had been keen to find out, having already discovered that Sura, the sad-looking soldier, had returned to work as normal. And Sura? When he heard how Reksa had been able to marry the Chief's youngest daughter, he could have been knocked over with a feather. And who would blame him?

Therefore when the Sultan asked to see Sura some time later, he went to the court with great trepidation. The Sultan, however, received him kindly, and gave him a large watermelon, saying: 'Here Sura, take this home and eat it. It is very sweet.'

Sura was filled with gratitude. He had not expected such gentle treatment. But again, the day was hot and on his way home Sura passed a tobacco shop. He so much wanted a smoke and a drink, and he had no money. Nearby sat an old widow, a fruitseller. If only he could sell her the watermelon, then he would have enough money for some tobacco and a drink of coffee. He bargained hard with the old woman. Finally they came to an agreement, and he sold her the Sultan's watermelon for forty cents, even though she told him that he was a fool for selling her the Sultan's melon. He ought to treasure it.

A little time passed. Then the woman wondered what kind of watermelons the Sultan might grow. Maybe it would be very nice. She cut it open, so that she might have a taste herself. What? The greater part of the melon's flesh had been scooped out, and there sparkled the most beautiful jewels and gold coins.

The news that the old widow had suddenly become rich after having bought Sura's melon, spread like fire through the village. Sura nearly lost his mind. Whilst he was still tearing his hair out over his unlucky fate, a messenger came from the Sultan. He was ordered to come to the court immediately.

This time Sura hastened along, determined to do exactly what the Sultan asked. Another letter had to be delivered. This one had to be given to the Village Chief.

Sura wondered, what would it be: promotion, coins, a possible marriage? He hurried along. Anticipating all the goodness that might come his way. The village-chief read the letter aloud:

> 'Sir, The man who hands you this letter has twice disobeyed my orders. He must be put in prison for two months. His imprisonment begins immediately.'

Poor, poor Sura had but one thought: 'Why am I so unlucky?'

Retold - Principal source: Siek, M., (1972) *Favourite Stories from Indonesia*, Heinemann Educational Books (Asia) Ltd.

Text:	THE FATE OF THE UNHAPPY SURA
Focus:	Destiny and choice
Length:	90 minutes

Write: Word associations around the theme 'destiny'.

Pass: Your word-associations to another group member.

Read/paint: Read these word-associations. Take some paper and finger-paints or crayons. Re-read the words you were given. Then, in a few minutes, paint the image evoked in you by this collection of words.

Return/give: The word-associations to the person whose words you received. Please give them your painting as well.

Look: At the painting you too have received.

Share: Talk about the feelings which the painting evokes in you.

Response-task: Take some paper and crayons. Feel free to draw or doodle, whilst the story is told.

Tell: The story of THE FATE OF THE UNHAPPY SURA.

Imagine: That you are either: The Sultan, The Chief whose youngest daughter married Reksa, The Woman who sold water-melons, or The Village-Chief, who imprisons Sura for sixty days. Choose one of these.

Write: Take some paper and a pen. Write on the paper which one of these four you are. Think how you would be dressed. What kind of things you like. Where you might be sitting, when you are going to write a letter to Sura, who is about to be released from prison. You wish to let him know your thoughts and feelings. There may also be advice you wish to give him. Write your letter, please.

Fold: Upon having written your letter, fold it up and place it in the middle of the group.

Return to the circle

Take: Each group member takes one of these letters. Read it quietly. If you can't read the handwriting, make sense of it your way, like you might do with any other letter.

Response-task: On a piece of paper, create as many spaces as there are members in the group. After a group member has read a letter draw or write in one of these spaces, something which you wish to remember from the letter, they have just read.

Read: The letter to the group, which you received to the group. You may keep this letter.

Retrace: When you have made your last drawing/writing, retrace all you have done during this session. The word-associations, the paintings, what you said/heard about the feelings these evoked/the story you heard and maybe the doodle-painting/the letter you wrote and the letter you received/the various drawings/writing you have just done in response to listening to the letters.

Connect: Ponder on some of the links all these have with your actual life-experience.

Share: Try to share with the other group-members some of your reflections.

Select: One thought/idea/feeling which you especially wish to remember from this session.

Share: This thought/idea/feeling with the other group members.

Reflect: Note any other statements which need to be made right now.

Complete the session

Text:	THE FATE OF THE UNHAPPY SURA
Focus:	I can't be bothered
Time:	90 minutes

Share: Think of all the other words and phrases which are similar to 'I can't be bothered', such as:
- too much hassle
- forget it
- I don't care any more
- I've given up.

Paint: Take a roll of wall-paper, and as if you were spray-painting graffiti, using large letters and working closely together, write several of these words/statements onto the wall-paper.

nb: You may find that several group members want to add tough language, to push away those who are perceived to be pushing them into action; apart from the obvious four-letter words these might be:
- *leave me alone*
- *get off*
- *up yours.*

Paint: Having written the words/statements, decorate the banner, so that it looks good. Do this together.

Return: To the circle, having washed hands if necessary.

Write: Take paper and a pen, and think back to a time when you felt really tired. It might have been today or this week, or much, much longer ago. Write about this time of tiredness.

Share: Your writings.

Response-task: As you listen to these writings, imagine that it was you who was this tired. Think of what you might really need, to help you to become less tired. Allow yourself to think of unusual ways of restoring vitality. When you have thought of a way to remedy the tiredness about which you heard the group member speak, write your idea on a piece of paper. Fold it double and write the group member's name on the outside. Keep your 'remedies for tiredness' gifts with you at this stage. They'll be distributed later.

Tell: The story of THE FATE OF THE UNHAPPY SURA.

Doodle: Encourage group members to draw or doodle as they listen to the story.

Share: The 'remedies for tiredness'.

Read: Your gifts.

Select: One gift, which might have been very helpful to Sura. Choose one gift which is important to you at this stage in your life.

Paint: Take a new roll of wallpaper. Using the graffiti-style, using large letters, write your chosen gifts unto this paper.

Decorate: Having written the statements, decorate the banner, so that it looks good. Work together.

Look: Place both banners side by side, and look at them.

Reflect: On the differences and similarities between them. Make connections with your tiredness writings, and the gifts/remedies you received. Ponder on those remedies, which you might not have thought of.

Connect: Make connections with other life-experiences. Reflect upon the entire session.

Text: THE FATE OF THE UNHAPPY SURA
Focus: Nothing will ever change
Time: 90 minutes

Whisper: In turn, the whole group GENTLY whispers every group member's first name. The group member listens quietly. They may wish to close their eyes, as this heightens the experience.

Talk: A little about this exercise.

Whisper: As in Chinese whispers, into one group-member's ear 'nothing will ever change. . .'. The group member in turn whispers this statement to their neighbour.
Work with great concentration, and go round several times.

Speak: Then ask the group, to repeat with strength the words: 'nothing will ever change.' Do this several times. Then divide the group into two. Position both groups opposite each other. In choral exchange, ask each group to experiment with different ways of saying: 'Nothing will ever change.'

Give: Each group member some pottery-clay, ready for moulding.

Tell: The story of THE FATE OF THE UNHAPPY SURA.

Invite: Group members to create something out of their piece of clay whilst they are listening to the story, or just after the story is finished.

Share: Clay-modellings with the group. Remind yourself of the feelings evoked by the 'nothing will ever change' exercise.

NB: Some group members may choose to do nothing with their piece of clay. They are invited to reflect on their decision NOT to change the clay.
Alternatively, some group-members may feel very uncomfortable with clay. Invite such a group member to write a brief poem about the story.

> *Try to be firm about this. You may be surprised at the result. If the group member insists and insists that they will not write, then invite their drawing, or comment on the importance for the group of the presence of a group member who listens quietly without doing anything.*

Select: One thought/idea/feeling, which you wish to reflect on further.

Share: This thought/idea/feeling with the group.

Reflect: Upon the entire session.

Sisiutl

Someone stands by the sea, overlooking the wide water. A person stands and looks at the sea.

There are rocks on the coast and trees. Trees which are twisted and stripped of bark. Rocks which are twisted, as if in pain. Turning, turning away from the sea. The trees and the rocks are screwed into agonised shapes, because they tried to flee from where they could not move. They saw Sisiutl, the gruesome monster from the sea. Sisiutl who has two heads, one at each end of his body. Heads which fill us with the greatest fear we shall ever know.

Whosoever sees Sisiutl, knows but one blind urge. To run. To run as fast as feet will carry, as far as the land will reach. For the Monster who dwells deep in the sea is terrifying to behold, and fills our heart with frozen, haunting terror.

This is how it is.

You stand on the beach and see Sisiutl. You want to run. And yet, you know that if you run, you shall be like the trees and the rocks. Turning, twisting, spinning, lost. Forever wandering. Forever terrified.

Meanwhile the waves will carry Sisiutl towards you. The mouths cast cutting panic into your soul. All thoughts cease. You want to tear yourself away. The heads come closer, and you know that if you run, you shall run forever. The wind too holds its breath. The air you gasp is filled with Sisiutl's foul stench. No rescue anywhere. Nowhere to go. No way of going. And the devouring mouths come closer. Whatever you do, stay firm. Do not run away. If you know words of protection, say them, and above all else, stay firm.

The next wave, and Sisiutl's heads close in upon you. This you know. They reach towards you. Closer and closer. Both mouths open. One more move, and they shall fasten upon you. Fasten upon you forever. And in spite of this, stand firm.

The last wave. Both heads turn towards you. Then this happens. Just before the twin mouths touch you, each head suddenly sees the other, because you are there. Because they both want to be near you, Sisiutl sees his other face, and whosoever sees the other half of Self, sees Truth.

Sisiutl, the gruesome monster of the sea, spends eternity in search of Truth, seeking those who dare stand firm. Who will let him look into his own eyes, into his own other face.

Then Sisiutl will bless you with his truth. Truth which will be yours forever. And the vision people will visit you often, reminding you of the place where truth may be found. You are no longer alone.

Retold. Principal source: Cameron, Anne, (1984) *Daughters of Copperwoman*, The Woman's Press Ltd

---

Text:	SISIUTL
Focus:	Blessings for a time of fear
Time:	90 minutes
Breathe:	Sit in a circle, and guide group members into stillness. Focus the attention on breathing. Where possible, help the group members to achieve belly-breathing.
Recall:	Any songs you know and like.

Share:	Some of the melodies/words of these songs with one another. Sing them. Hum them. If you know any rounds, try singing some, such as:
	    - Ah, poor bird, raise thy flight.
	    - My dame had a lame tame crane.
	    - Hey Ho, nobody at home.
	    - London's burning
	    - Row, row, row your boat.

Write:	On four separate small pieces of paper, a blessing for someone, who is about to embark on a difficult journey.
Collect:	The various pieces of paper. Shuffle and redistribute, four for each group member.
Write:	Read these four blessings, and sequence them for inclusion in a short blessing poem. Write this poem.
Share:	Ask each group-member to share their blessing-poem in the following way:

Walk: Decide upon a certain area in the room you work in, which will be the blessing-place. Ask the group-members quietly to walk around the room. Upon hearing the drum-beat, they stand still, and turn to their face to the blessing-place. Once the blessing-giver has spoken he/she re-joins the walkers. Then another person enters the blessing-place, until every group member has given their blessing.

nb: Use a drum-beat to indicate that the next speaker will enter the blessing-place, and share their blessing-poem.

Return: To circle.

Tell: The story of SISIUTL.

Silence: Introduce another brief period of silence.

Circle: Join hands, and keep holding hands for a little while. Establish eye-contact with other group members. Let go of hands.

Reflect: On the experience you went through whilst listening to the blessings and to the story.

Connect: Take time to make connections with your actual life-experiences. You may also find yourself thinking about the blessings you were NOT given, and those you yourself did not give. Try to share such experiences with the group.

Stand: Ask the group to stand in a circle, about a foot away from one another. Remind group members of their journey during this session: the songs, the rounds, the blessing-creation, as well as the giving and receiving of blessings, the listening to the story and the life-experiences which were shared. Then focus on the journey home or back to the rooms, which the group members are about to start. Maybe they wish to give each other a blessing for this journey as well. Create an opportunity to share/sing/give such blessings.

Thanking group members for their contributions, the session then ends.

Text:	SISIUTL
Focus:	And you shall not be alone again
Time:	90 minutes

Circle: Guide Group members through a simple hand-massage, during which they will use their left hand to massage their right hand, and vice versa. Massage with circular movements on the palm and top of each hand. Move along every finger, as if you were stripping off a tight pair of gloves.

Choose: A partner.

Draw: Place both your hands on a sheet of paper. Ask your partner to draw the outline of your hands onto this paper. Do the same for your partner.

Write: Write inside the outline of your hands everything you value about them, as well as things you do with your hands.

Share: Your writings with your partner.

Circle: Return to the circle, and fold your hands together by intertwining your fingers as if for prayer. You now have a small cupped opening between your hands, in which you could nearly hold or hide something. Each group member in turn will say what they might hold thus safely in the hollow of their hands.

Pairs/Focus/   Choose a new partner. Sit opposite them, maybe hold hands.
Talk: Decide who is A and who B. B will begin by describing A's face. Do not use any 'evaluative' words such as beautiful, or troubled, or sad. Simply describe - colour, lines, shapes, marks. Do so gently, with great attention to detail.
After a couple of minutes, indicate that A will now describe B's face. Emphasize again that this needs to be done attentively and caringly.

When you have completed the exercise, spend a couple of minutes talking with one another about the experience.

Return to the circle

Reflect: On your experiences so far.

Tell: The story of SISIUTL.

Circle: Give each group member a small piece of paper (approx. 3" x 4"). The theme of this painting is an image evoked by the words: 'And you shall not be alone again'. Some group members may wish to write these words onto their painting.

Give: Then ask each group member to give their painting to another person in the group. Do this one after the other. Each person can only receive one painting.
Encourage the 'giver' to address the receiver by their first name, and to allow time and attention for the process of giving and receiving.

Connect: Look at your hand-writings, remind yourself of the 'cupped hands' exercise, the description of your face, as well as of the way in which you described your partner's face. Remember the story, the feelings it evoked. Then remember the 'you shall not be alone again' painting, and the process of giving this away.

Reflect: On all this and allow yourself to remember any actual life-experiences which are demanding attention.

Share: Some of these life-experiences.

Circle: Hold hands once more. Make eye-contact around the circle.

Thanking the group members, acknowledge that this is the end of the session.

Text: SISIUTL
Focus: Places of fear and serenity
Time: 90 minutes

Recall: A place outdoors, which give you a sense of peace.
               Maybe yours is the seaside, maybe the high mountains, a
               meadow, moorlands, or a river.

Describe: Your place to the group, using just a few sentences.

Response-   As group members describe their beloved environment, paint
task: or draw either that environment, or the feelings/image it
               evokes for you.

Tell: The story of SISIUTL.

Paint: On a large roll of wallpaper, ask group members to paint
               the images and feelings evoked by this story. They are en-
               couraged to work cooperatively. Use finger-paints and
               crayons. Try to complete the painting within fifteen minutes.

Share: When the painting is finished, invite group members to
               sit around it in a circle and to reflect on the process they
               have gone through.

Invite: Group members to make connections between this
               experience, and their bereavement.
               Allow ample time for the sharing of feelings/events, fears
               and hopes.

Reflect: Upon the entire session.

In the dreamtime

In the dreamtime darkness covered the earth. In this darkness, the great spirits Baiame and Punjel made mountains and rivers, animals, birds and the people of the early time. They all lived by the light of the stars and the moon.

Then Emu and Eagle-hawk, two of the animal-people, quarrelled. It was a real quarrel, with much squawking, and feather-pulling, snapping and screeching. At last Emu rushed away with some of the food over which they had been fighting and Eagle-hawk wandered back home. She stumbled upon a nest, Emu's nest. In the faintly glimmering light she saw that there were eggs in the nest. Eagle-hawk seized one of Emu's huge eggs, and hurled it up to the sky. There it smashed into the great wood-pile of the sky, which Punjel had been building, and the entire wood pile burst into flame. Then the brilliant white and gold flames of Emu's egg lit the world.

Baiame and Punjel, the great spirits, looked on in wonder. Their creation was this beautiful? They decided that every day they would make such a fire of light.

When they were ready, they asked Morningstar to tell the creatures of the earth that day was near. But only the animals who were already wide awake, saw her. So Baiame and Punjel knew that they had to find another way of awakening the animals and, above all, the people of the early time. They pondered and wondered. Then they knew that they needed a sound to announce the new day, to call the sleepers to awaken.

They thought and thought. Then, one evening, they heard the sound of cackling laughter. Goo-goor-gaga, the kookaburra, was floating through the air. He made the sound they needed.

Baiame and Punjel asked Goo-goor-gaga, if from now on he could watch for a star in the eastern sky. A little later he would see that the great sky-fire was being lit. And please, would he then awaken the world with his laughter?

This happened. This is happening. Baiame and Punjel were well pleased.

From this time onwards the animals and the people hear a voice when they are called to awaken, and the voice is filled with laughter.

Retold. Principal source: Reed, A. W., (1984) *Aboriginal Myths, Tales of the Dreamtime*, Reed Books.

Text:	IN THE DREAMTIME
Focus:	Between dusk and dawn
Time:	90 minutes

Write: Word-associations connected with darkness and word-associations connected with light.

Small groups/pairs

Share: Your experiences and ideas related to 'Dusk' and 'Dawn'.

Move: In your pair/small group move as far as possible away from the others. Stand near each other. Establish eye-contact. Stand very still. Imagine that you will now begin to move. This is the dance of dusk and the dance of dawn. This is initially most easily done by mirroring your partner's movements, and then introducing your own movements.
Practice your dance.

Show: The other group members your group's dusk-dawn dance.

Return to the circle

Reflect: On your experiences.

Tell: The story IN THE DREAMTIME.

Write: Take a large sheet of paper. Write at the top: 'In the darkness. . .' Write at the bottom: '. . .There is light.'

Then write all the sentences which belong in between these words. Use big letters if you wish. Fill the entire page.

In pairs

Read: Your writings to your partner. Then switch.

Response-task: Then ask your partner to read your text to you.

Select: One sentence from your writing, which is especially important to you. Share this sentence with your partner.

Return: To the circle.

Share: These sentences with one another.

Write: Sequence the group's sentences so that they form a whole.
               Discuss the sequencing. (Some connecting words may need
               to be used.) Then write the group's 'Darkness...Light' text
               on a large sheet of paper.

Recite: Practice reciting this text together, chorus-style.

Connect: Re-read the darkness-light word associations, recall the dusk-
               dawn memories and the dances. Remind yourself of the
               story and your writings, plus the experience of mak-
               ing/speaking the group text.

Reflect: On the links between your work during this session and
               other life-experiences.

Share: Some of these.

Closure: Hold hands. Try to visualize a beautiful star-strewn night.
               Stars which fade away, due to the first light of dawn. Let go
               of hand contact. Establish eye-contact. End the session.

Text: IN THE DREAMTIME
Focus: Alarm or awakening
Time: 90 minutes

Contact: Hold hands. Slowly count from one to sixty in the
               following way: One person says 'one', the next person says
               'two', etc.

Move: Remain in a circle - stand or sit.
               Make circular movements with your:
                   - hands/arms/shoulders
                   - toes/feet/ankles/legs/hips
                   - eyes/head/neck

- the top of your body.
Do this in clockwise and anti-clockwise directions.

Draw: On a large sheet of paper, draw circles. Practise
           drawing in clockwise and anti-clockwise directions. Also
           draw circles simultaneously with both hands.

           nb: Circles will overlap. That is fine.

Draw: Turn your sheet over. Look at its emptiness. Take a crayon
           or pen in your hand. Decide whereabouts on the paper you
           will put it down. Think before you do this. Remember that
           the paper will be irrevocably changed once you have made
           your mark. Then make your mark and keep your crayon
           still. Once the story begins, allow your pen to meander
           slowly along the paper. Do not lift the crayon of the paper
           until the story is finished.

Tell: The story IN THE DREAMTIME.

Place: TWO chairs somewhere in the room, where all group
           members easily see them.

Chair One:

Invite: Group members to use this chair to comment on the
           creation of light, speaking as one of the characters in the
           myth,
           eg - Kookaburrah
               - Emu
               - Baiame
               - one of the other animal beings.
           Start your speech/comments by saying:
               eg 'I, Kookaburrah..' or 'I, Baiame...'
           And finish with:
               'Thank you for listening.'

Chair Two:

Invite: Group members to use this chair to speak about their
           experience of waking up that very same morning.

Finish your sharing with:
'Thank you for listening.'

nb: Encourage group members to maintain a quiet focus whilst waiting for someone else to come forward to use one of the chairs. Inform the group in advance that the entire exercise will last no more than FIFTEEN minutes.

Return: To the circle.

Reflect: On the exercise.

Think: Of something you find particularly difficult about 'waking-up' these days. When everyone has identified something, ask each group member to speak.

Speak/:   One person voices their difficulty. When this person has
Chorus   stopped speaking, the group responds by saying: 'Yes, it is.' Everyone is responded to in this way.

nb: Though this exercise seems contrived, it works well.

Silence: Stillness is likely to arise when this exercise is finished. Let this be for a little while.

Encourage: Eye-contact. Reach out. Hold hands. Then let go.

Paint: Give each group member a grey or brown piece of paper.

Fingerpaint the image evoked by the words:
Darkness - Light - Dusk - Dawn.

Share: Your paintings with each other.

Reflect: Upon the entire session.

Text:	IN THE DREAMTIME
Focus:	Why it had to be 'just so'
Time:	90 minutes

Recall: Remind yourself of a favourite object.

Share:	Describe this object to the group.
Recall:	Remind yourself when/where you saw this object for the first time.
Move:	Think of what happened when you first saw the object. Maybe this included: seeing/looking away/approaching/holding. When you remember your experience, try to express it in movement. Do this in the following way. The first person to begin turns to his/her neighbour on the left hand side. The 'neighbour' watches carefully, as the story is told in movement form. Then he/she mirrors it, so that the 'teller' has a chance to see his/her story. Then the 'neighbour' tells his/her story to the person on his/her left hand side, who mirrors it, etc.
	The exercise ends when the person who first shared a movement-story, mirrors the tale told by the person who sits on his/her right hand side.
Tell:	The story IN THE DREAMTIME.
Think:	About everything you like and dislike about this story.
Share:	These likes and dislikes, and record the group's ideas on
Write:	a large sheet of paper.
	eg: LIKES - the world was beautiful when Baiame saw it.
	DISLIKES - the destruction of Emu's eggs.
Select:	Each group member selects one of these statements.
	nb: group members may choose the same one.
Write:	A statement. Imagine that you are writing to the early people, and have been asked to explain to them WHY this issue (which has been noted as either a like or a dislike) had to be the way it was. What the value is of it being this way. Which consolation they may derive from it being 'just so'.
Share:	Your writings.

Response-task:	Use small musical instruments, such as bells, whistles, drums and rattles, and/or spoons, finger-tapping, humming. When each person has read his/her writing, the group creates a brief sound response.
Connect:	Reflect on this session's journey: your favourite object, the movement-stories, the myth, the likes and dislikes, the writings and the sound-making.
Reflect:	On the links with your life-experiences.
Share:	One or two of your thoughts with the group.
Closure:	If you know the round, you may choose to sing: 'Kookaburrah sits in the old gum tree.' If not this one, end with another song, such as: 'Oh Freedom', 'All things bright and beautiful' etc.

Mantis and the eland

Mantis, the Maker of Fire, finds Kwammang-a's shoe. His son's shoe. He picks it up, for he wants to make something. By the side of the pool, near the rushes, Mantis sits and thinks. Then he makes a new being, an eland-being. The eland hides amongst the rushes. Mantis names this one: 'Kwammang-a's shoe's piece.' He cuts honey for the eland, and puts it near the water. He returns home.

Then, before the sun rises, he goes back to the pool. He calls: 'Kwammang-a's shoe's piece.' The eland comes from the reeds and walks towards his father. Mantis strokes him and rubs his skin with honey, making the eland, whom he made from his son's shoe, look beautiful. Mantis goes to cut more honey, which he leaves with the eland. Then he returns home. Once more Mantis goes to the pool to call the eland-son whom he made from Kwammang-a's shoe's piece.

The eland stands shyly, whilst his father strokes him gently. And Mantis weeps, for he grows fond of him.

For three nights Mantis does not return, and for three nights the eland grows.

Again Mantis goes and calls Kwammang-a's shoe, the one he has grown fond of. He rubs his skin with honey. Then he goes home. The next morning he asks young Ich-neu-mon to come with him to the pool. Mantis speaks to Ich-neu-mon. He says 'Go sleep now', but young Ich-neu-mon deceives him, and looks whilst Mantis caresses the eland.

Mantis knows Ich-neu-mon has seen Kwammang-a's shoe's piece, his eland-son. And he tells young Ich-neu-mon, that it is but a very small thing. Something Ich-neu-mon's father Kwammang-a had dropped.

But young Ich-neu-mon tells his father Kwammang-a. And Kwammang-a is taken to see the eland. Mantis is not there then, he is in another place. Young Ich-neu-mon knows the call which Mantis used to see the eland. The eland, hearing his father's call, comes from the rushes. The people look at it.

Then Kwammang-a kills the eland. He cuts it up, while Mantis is not there.

When Mantis arrives, this is what he sees. He sees his people cutting the eland, the one he made and rubbed to look beautiful. He says: 'Why could you not first let me come?'

He scolds his people. They have killed the eland, and they did so without him telling them. Kwammang-a says, Mantis must gather wood, for this is meat and the people must eat.

But again Mantis says that if the eland had to be killed, he had wanted to tell them to do so. He had wanted to be there with the eland whom he himself made. Then his heart would not have been sore. Now there is nothing left but bones and gall. Mantis hurts. He is wounded.

He says to himself that he will pierce the gall. The gall speaks, warning him that it will burst and blind him.

Mantis goes away to gather some wood. But again he returns to the place where the gall is. He says that he will pierce it open.

Young Ich-neu-mon and Kwammang-a know that Mantis must leave the place where the gall is. They ask him to go along homewards. But Mantis says, that he must turn back. They try to say, that 'no; they really must go home now.' But Mantis says that he must go back to the place where the eland was killed.

He returns. Then he pierces the gall. It covers him. He can no longer see. Darkness is everywhere. He goes groping along. Groping, groping along. Groping along, until he finds an ostrich feather. A feather of the bird who gave him fire. Then he wipes the gall from his eyes with the feather. He throws it into the sky and says:

'You must now lie up in the sky. From now on you must be the moon. You shine at night, and by your shining lighten the darkness for all people till the sun rises to light up all things. It is he under whom we hunt, walk about, and return home. But you are the moon; you give light to people, then you fall away. You return to life again.'

This the moon does; it falls away and returns to life.

Retold. Principal source: Radin, P. & Sweeney, J., (1952) *African Folktales and Sculpture*. New York: Bollingen Foundation.

Text:	MANTIS AND THE ELAND
Focus:	In the darkness
Time:	120 minutes

List:	Free-associate around the word 'night'. List your associations.
Select:	One of these.
Group Finger-Painting:	Use a large roll of paper. Delineate fair-sized spaces. your chosen word beneath one of these spaces. Look at all the words. Choose one of these (not necessarily your own). Inside the bordered space, paint the image evoked by the word which is beneath it.

Return to the circle

Recall:	Allow your thoughts to meander. Ask yourself which memory is evoked by this exercise.
Write:	About the experience.
Read:	Your writings.

nb: Do not discuss these writings at this stage.

Tell:	The story MANTIS AND THE ELAND.
Select:	One moment in the story which is most poignant to you.

nb: Several group members may choose the same moment.

Record:	The sentence which encapsulates this story-moment.
Write:	Free-flow write whatever emerges in relation to this particular story-moment. You may find yourself writing about a personal experience, registering ideas, or expressing the feelings of one of the story characters. Give yourself permission to write whatever comes to mind.

Share: Mention the specific moment in the story which you have selected. Sequence these moments in accordance with the story's development.

In this sequence

Read: Your story-writing. Stand apart from the group. Establish eye-contact with everyone. Then read your words. Re-establish eye-contact. Return to the circle. Then the next person addresses the group in this manner, etc.

Look/paint: At the group-painting. Select one of the images, which reflects most accurately the way you now feel. Then work with this image. Paint slowly, and work until you feel satisfied.

Return: To the circle.

Share: Your paintings.

Connect: Establish links between the various tasks you engaged with during this session, the story and your actual life-experiences.

Reflect: Upon the entire session.

Text: MANTIS AND THE ELAND
Focus: Taking and making
Time: 90 minutes

Place: A very smooth ball of modelling clay (10" diameter) in the centre of the circle.

Focus: Look carefully at this smooth ball of clay. Breathe quietly.

Take: One by one take a handful clay. Witness the taking-away process and the feelings it evokes.

Clay-model: Make a ball out of your own piece of clay. Hold this ball in the palm of your hand. Look at it carefully.

Clay-model: Then quickly make something out of this ball of clay.
              Place whatever you have made in front of you on a white
              sheet of paper.

                        Before telling the story

              Place a new ball of clay in the centre of the circle. Each group
              member takes another lump of clay.

Tell: The story MANTIS AND THE ELAND.

Response- As you listen to this story, make something out of the piece
task: of clay. When the story is finished, stop modelling. Place this
              sculpture near the previous one.

Walk: Around the room. Look at everyone's sculptures.

Write: Take several pieces of paper and a pen with you. When
              you look at a sculpture, think of a name you might give it.
              Leave this name by the side of each sculpture,
              eg: Protest
                  Contentment
                  Agony

Return: To the circle and choose a partner.

In pairs: Look at the names which your sculptures were given.
              Then

Talk: talk with your partner about the sculptures and about the
              feelings which the names evoke in you. Reflect on the way
              these relate to your current life-experience.

Return: To the circle.

Share: Some of your thoughts, experiences and feelings with the
              group.

Reflect: Upon the entire session.

Text: MANTIS AND THE ELAND
Focus: With bitterness
Time: 90 minutes

Contact: Hold hands. Establish eye-contact. Let go.

Focus: On whatever is evoked by the word 'bitterness'. Note the memories/feelings which present themselves. Do not discuss your experience at this stage.

Create: An area in the room which will be the 'walkabout' space. Make sure that everyone knows the boundaries of this space.

Instruction: 'First I'll explain this exercise. Look at the walkabout area. I shall later ask you to enter this space. As soon as you are inside it, close your eyes and walk around. When you bump into people, note it and continue your walking. Then remind yourself of your associations with the word bitterness. Try to let your walking express the way you feel.

The exercise lasts five minutes. Then I shall ask you to leave the space. Five minutes is a long time to stay with the theme of bitterness and to keep your eyes closed. If you find this is too long for you, leave the area, when you feel you must and sit down. Do you want to clarify anything...? Then, please, enter this space, and walk about with bitterness.

Walk: And remind yourself of the associations this word evokes. Let your posture express your feelings.

Return: To the circle.

Reflect: Briefly reflect on your experiences.

Show/Mirror: Remind yourself of a key-posture, which encapsulates your bitterness experience. Show this posture to the group. The other group members copy it. Relax, and look carefully at what they are doing.

You may wish to ask them a question, such as:
- what do you feel you are carrying on your back.
- what is most painful about this.
- how could you make it a little better.

The answers the other group members give might be helpful to you.

Then the next group member shows his/her posture, it is copied, etc.

Return: To the circle.

Reflect: Briefly reflect on your experience.

Tell: The story: MANTIS AND THE ELAND.

Paint: As you listen to the story, feel free to draw or paint. When the story is finished, continue to draw/paint/be silent for five minutes.

Share: Your paintings with each other.

Reflect: On the connections between this story, the various tasks you engaged in and your actual life-experiences.

Contact: Hold hands. Establish eye-contact. Let go of hand-contact.

Prince Lindworm

Once there lived a King and a Queen who were much sorrowed for they had no child. One day, when out walking, the Queen met an ugly crone. The old woman asked the Queen: 'Why do you look so sad?' And the Queen replied that it was no use telling her, for no one in the whole, wide world could ever help her. 'Never you know', the crone retorted. 'Maybe I can be of use.' The Queen then spoke about the sorrow of her heart. The old woman listened carefully. After having thought, she instructed the Queen to do exactly as she would now be told, and all would be well.

That evening after sunset, the Queen had to take a small cup with two handles, and put it upside down, that is with the bottom upwards, in the north-west corner of her garden. The next morning, at sunrise, she had to lift it up. Beneath it she would then find two roses, a red one and a white one. The old woman said: 'If you eat the red rose, you'll give birth to a little boy, and if you eat the white rose, you'll give birth to a little girl. But, do not eat both roses. If you do eat both of them, great trouble will befall you. Remember what I've said.'

The Queen thanked the crone, and did what she had been told. Early the next morning, upon seeing two roses beneath the cup, she could hardly believe her eyes. Forgetting the old woman's urgent warning, she ate them both.

Sometime later the King had to go to war. When he was still away from home, the queen gave birth to two children, one a beautiful boy and the other a Lindworm, or Serpent. This Serpent scared her very much, but as soon as he had been born, he had wriggled away. Nobody else even seemed to have noticed him. She even thought she had just imagined it.

When the King returned, she never even mentioned the Lindworm to him. The young Prince grew up to become a very handsome Prince.

The time came for him to get married. He set out to find a Princess. But to his bewilderment he was stopped at the first crossroads by a gigantic Lindworm, who cried: 'First a bride for me. Then a bride for you.'

The Prince tried to get past the Lindworm. But he was to fierce for him. Therefore the Prince returned to the castle. He told the King and the Queen what had happened. The Queen immediately remembered the old crone's warning and how she had seen the Lindworm wriggle away just after she had given birth. She knew that the Lindworm really was her eldest child. She had to tell them the truth. The Lindworm did have the right to be married before the youngest of the two.

Thus the King and the Queen set out in search of a bride for the Lindworm. A Princess was sought in distant land. Because she was not allowed to see her groom until the wedding-day, the Lindworm married her. But the following morning the Lindworm was found sleeping alone in the Marriage-bed. He had obviously eaten his bride.

A while later the Prince tried once more to go in search of a bride. Again the Lindworm blocked his path. Dolefully the Prince returned to the Castle. There was nothing else to it, the King and Queen would have to find another bride for the Lindworm. This Princess came from a land far, far-away. The wedding took place. But the next morning, alas, the Lindworm had obviously eaten his bride.

When the Prince set out the third time, he again heard the Lindworm's words: 'First a bride for me. Then a bride for you.' The King and the Queen were at their wits' end.

Now, there lived deep in the forest an old shepherd, who had one daughter. The King decided that he would go and ask the Shepherd to let his daughter marry the Lindworm. Of course the old man would not hear of it. But the King did not accept his refusal. The old man had to consent to his daughter's marriage.

The girl was beyond herself when she heard the news and walked deep into the woods, where she met an old woman, who asked her: 'Why do you look so sad.' The girl replied that it was no use telling her, for there was no one in the whole, wide world who could help her. 'Never you know', the crone retorted, 'maybe I can be of use.'

Then the girl told her about having to marry the Lindworm, who had already married and eaten two beautiful princesses. The old woman listened carefully. Having thought, the crone instructed the girl to do exactly as she was told, and all would be well.

She said: 'Just after the wedding-ceremony, when you get ready to go to the bed-chamber, you must ask to be dressed in ten snow-white layers of clothing. Then you request a tub full of washing water which is prepared with woodashes, as well as a tub full of milk. Then you also ask for all the whips a boy can carry in his arms. All of these, the tubs and the whips, you request to have brought to the bedchamber. When the Lindworm asks you to remove a layer of clothing, you tell him to shed a skin. When all his skins are gone, you dip the whip in the washing water and you whip him. Having whipped him, you wash him in the fresh milk. Having washed him, you must hold him in your arms. This will be difficult. But you must do as I tell you. Hold him; if only for a moment. And remember, do as I say, and all will be well.' Then the old woman disappeared into an oak-tree.

The wedding-day came, and the girl married the prince. Before retiring to the bedchamber, she remembered to ask for everything the old woman had said. Everyone thought that these were peasant customs, but the King made her have whatever she wanted. Thus she was dressed in ten snow white shifts, and the tubs and the whips were taken to the bedchamber.

When they were alone, the Lindworm spoke to her, and said: 'Fair Maiden, shed a shift.' But the girl replied: 'Prince Lindworm, slough a skin.'

He was angered, saying that never before had anyone dared to tell him to do such a thing. She simply replied: 'I tell you now.' He wriggled and moaned and sloughed a skin. The girl removed her top-most snow white robe and laid it upon the skin. Again, the Lindworm spoke: 'Fair Maiden, shed a shift.' Again she replied: 'Prince Lindworm, slough a skin.' He was greatly angered, but she stayed firm. He sloughed a skin; she took off a robe, and covered the skin with it.

When the Lindworm had sloughed nine skins, and his bride had removed nine robes, he had no more skins left. He was but a skinless, horrible, mass. Then the girl whipped him with the whip dipped in the washing water. Next she gave him a milk-bath. Then came the most difficult task of all; she pulled him towards the bed and held him in her arms. That same moment she fell into a deep sleep.

When the King and the Queen came to the bedchamber the following morning, they saw the girl, looking fresh and beautiful, and by her side lay a most handsome Prince. The whole palace rejoiced. There was no end to the love for the girl who had the courage to marry Prince Lindworm.

Retold. Principal source: Henderson, J. L. & Oakes, M., (1963), *The Wisdom of the Serpent, Collier Books.*

Text: PRINCE LINDWORM
Focus: The fight between opposites
Time: 90 minutes

Talk: Free-associate images and ideas evoked by the word
                'courage'.

Move: Stand in a circle. Hold hands. One person lets go of hand-
                contact and starts weaving through the line of people, trying
                to create as tight a human knot as possible. Be careful and
                work with concentration. Then slowly undo the knot.

Reflect: Briefly on this exercise.

Move: Find a comfortable space on the floor. Lie on your back.
                Relax. Imagine that your right hand wants something which
                your left hand wants to prevent. Allow your hands to fight
                with one another. Rest a little. Then fight again. This time
                imagine that your left hand wants something which your
                right hand tries to prevent. Fight until you are tired. You
                may also wish to do this exercise with your feet and legs.

                Rest a little. Allow your thoughts to meander. Then sit up,
                look around, and choose a partner.

Move: Sit opposite your partner. Take turns in doing this exercise.
                Decide who will go first. Then allow your face to express
                this very same battle between wanting and not wanting, be-
                tween caring and not caring. Try to let your face express the
                full intensity of possible emotions. You will probably feel
                'really' tearful, angry, or start to laugh. Let this be.

                Change roles.

                          Return to the circle

Share: Your experiences with this exercise.

Tell: The story of PRINCE LINDWORM.

Select: An episode in the story, with which you wish to work. Several group members may choose the same episode. Everyone will work individually.

Choose: An area in the room which will be your workspace. Take any materials you wish to use to this area: paint, paper, pens, musical instruments, scarves. Delineate your workspace clearly.

Rehearse: You have ten minutes during which to explore your episode through movement, sound, painting, writing, silence, and to prepare a brief presentation which contains key-elements of the episode, which in your opinion, are IGNORED at one's peril.

Present: Delineate an area in the room for performance. Arrange audience places. Sequence the individual presentations in accordance with their place in the story. Invite each presenter to begin and their presentation with the words: 'Listen to these tidings. . .' This enhances the continuity of performance.

Return to the circle

Connect: Remind yourself of the work you have done during this session, the word-associations, the fight between your hands, your memories and reflections and then the story plus the presentations. Make connections with your actual life-experience.

Focus: On one thought/idea which you especially wish to remember from today's work.

Share: This with the group.

End: The session.

Text: PRINCE LINDWORM
Focus: Unknotting our fears
Time: 90 minutes

Talk: Free-associate around the word 'Fear'.

In pairs

Move: Stand opposite your partner. Decide who will go first. A
             has three minutes during which to instruct B verbally to
             make all kinds of movements: to stretch/jump/touch
             toes/crawl/yawn, etc. Use your voice in different ways:
             kindly, forceful, pleading. Then change over.

Return to the circle

Share: Something about your experience.

Talk: Whilst standing in the circle, acknowledge through eye-
             contact that you have found a new partner, preferably some-
             one who is standing opposite you. Without moving any
             closer, start talking to him/her about the weather and the
             way it affects you.
             Meanwhile your partner is speaking to you. Don't listen -
             keep talking. Then start moving backwards. Do this slowly
             and maintain eye-contact. The noise will be great. Try get-
             ting your own voice heard. End the exercise when the
             group is tired.

Return: To the circle.

Share: Something about your experience.

Response-: Before telling the story, give each group member a 3" length
task   of rope, which is suitable for knotting and unknotting.
             Skipping ropes are fine. Whilst the story is told group
             members are encouraged to play with the rope.

Tell: The story of PRINCE LINDWORM.

In pairs

Talk: Take your length of rope, as it is right now, with or without knots. Place it in front of you. Look carefully at it. Consider the possibility that the rope is a fairly accurate representation of the way you experience life at this moment. Speak about your situation. When listening to your partner, try to listen as attentively as you can. Undo all the knots when you've finished speaking. Then change over.
Each person has three minutes during which to speak.
When both have spoken, reflect on any similarities/differences during four more minutes.

Return to the circle

Share: Some of your experiences.

Write: Remind yourself of the Peasant-girl in the story. Imagine that you have been invited to write the poetic text of a memorial plaque, which honours her courage. This text is also meant to inspire future generations of visitors to the town. Please write your text.

Share: Your writings.

Reflect: Upon all you have experienced during this session.

Text: PRINCE LINDWORM
Focus: Tell me what bothers you
Time: 90 minutes

Recall: The way you felt when you woke up this morning. Think of what bothered or concerned you.

Write: Your concern on a small piece of paper. Do not sign it. Fold the paper double.

Collect: These papers in a basket. Place it in a corner of the room.

Move: Stand in a wide circle. One group member makes a step forward into the circle and begins a small movement. Keep this going. The next person steps into the circle and slightly enlarges this movement. When the last person steps forward the movement has become very large. Then the first group-member steps back, then the second, etc.

Sound: Remain in the circle. One-by-one step forward, saying with as much conviction as possible 'No'. When everyone stands in the inner circle, look around and again say 'NO'. Alternate with saying 'Yes'. Repeat this 'Yes-No', until you are tired. Take a step backward to the large circle, and share whatever you wish to share.

Contact: Stand in circle. Hold hands. Take a few steps backward. Still

Jump: Holding hands, surge forwards. Jump up and exclaim whatever feels right. Do this several times.

Response-task: As you listen to the story, allow yourself to draw/doodle.

Tell: The story of PRINCE LINDWORM.

Talk: Bring the basket into the centre of the group. One at a time, a group member takes one of these pieces of paper. Reads the concern. Then imagine yourself to be the wise woman of the forest. Think seriously about the predicament. You know that such concerns are likely to be shared by several group members. Think of possible ways in which help may be found with this predicament. Then the next person takes a piece of paper, etc.

Look: At your doodle/painting. Reflect on the words you have just heard. You may wish to record some of these on your doodle/painting. Take some time to do this.

Share: Your paintings/doodles with one another.

Reflect: Upon your actual life-experiences, the story, the response-paintings, the concerns as well as the words of wisdom and advice.

Select: One phrase which you wish to remember.

Share: This phrase with the group.

End: The session.

The Silent Princess

Once upon a distant time Luck met Wit, who was sitting on a short garden-bench. 'Make space for me!', said Luck. Wit wasn't very clever yet, and he didn't know what the rules were, so he said: 'Why should I. You're no better than I am.'

'Well,' retorted Luck, 'He's the best one, who is called upon most and does most. Do you see that young farmer, who is working the field? You get inside his head, and if he fares better in the world through you than through me, then I'll always give up my seat whenever and wherever we meet.'

Wit accepted the challenge, and at once he popped into the young farmer's head.

As soon as the young farmer knew that he had Wit, he thought: 'I could do something better than this, and make my fortune more easily.' He decided that he wanted to learn to be a gardener. His father was stunned at the change in his son, but not being one to keep him back, he gave young Vanek his blessing, and with a God Speed, send him on the road. The young farmer's son made straight for the King's Gardener. Only the best would do. And sure enough, he talked his way into the palace gardens, and was allowed to start work immediately. He learned, and he learned, and he learned. The gardens became wondrous to behold. The King himself delighted in his fresh, abundant gardens. He often walked there with his queen and their only daughter.

This princess was very beautiful. But, alas, since she was twelve years old, she had stopped talking. Not a word had passed her lips. The King was much sorrowed by her silence. He proclaimed that whosoever helped her to regain the power of words, would be her husband.

Many kings and princes and other nobleman came to the court. But none succeeded. Vanek thought that he too would try. Maybe he could find a question, that would vex her so, that she would want to answer it. Now the princess had a young puppy-dog, whom she loved greatly. This dog was very clever and was the only one who understood everything she wanted. When our young gardener made his entry into her room, he ignored everyone, the king, the queen, the courtiers, even the princess. He went straight to the puppy-dog and spoke, saying:

Doggie, I know that you are very smart and therefore I have come for guidance. I am travelling with two friends, one is a sculptor, the other a tailor. Some time ago we had to pass the night in a forest. For fear of wolves, we lit a fire, and kept watch. The sculptor was the first to stay awake, and in order to while away the time, he carved a damsel out of a block of wood. When he had finished it, he woke up the tailor, whose turn it was to keep the fire going. The tailor saw the damsel, and took a fancy to dressing the wooden creature. Then my turn came, and by morning I had actually taught her to speak. At that point each of us wanted to own her. The sculptor made her, the tailor dressed her, and I too thought that she was mine. Doggie, advise me, whose damsel is she?

The dog held his tongue, but the Princess spoke. She said: 'To no one else but you. What is a wooden statue without life? What good is a dress without speech? By rights she is yours.'

Vanek looked at her, and said: 'Well, so indeed it is. I have given you your speech, and by rights you now belong to me.' The King's councillors were not pleased. He was a man of lowly lineage. Money, they offered him; land, they offered him, but not the beautiful princess. Vanek would not accept any of it. Had not the King said that anyone who helped the Princess to regain her speech could marry her? Was the King going to break his promise? The King must let him marry her. This angered the King's soldiers. They seized him, and asked that the insolent man be executed. The King consented.

When Vanek was taken to the place where he was meant to die, Luck was there, waiting for him. Without Vanek even noticing, Luck whispered to Wit: 'Get out of his head, and let me take over.' Then the strangest coincidence happened. The executioner's sword broke, and just at that moment a royal carriage arrived to beg Vanek to return to the court. The King had changed his mind. The Princess and Vanek could marry after all.

A little while later Luck and Wit happened to meet again. Wit bent his head and quickly passed by. Ever since that day Wit has avoided Luck. And who knows, that might be why...

Retold. Principal source: Wratislaw, A. H., (1926) *Sixty Folktales from Slavonic Sources*, Elliot Stock.

Text: THE SILENT PRINCESS
Focus: Giving form to feeling
Time: 90 minutes.

Paint: An image of the way you feel right now.

Move: Show the group your painting. The other group members
                  will then take up a posture which reflects their interpreta-
                  tion of your painting. Look carefully at what is done. Then
                  ask the group to drop their postures. Another person shows
                  his/her painting, etc.

Write: Remind yourself of WHAT you saw when you looked at
                  the group's body-sculptures of your painting. Write about
                  your thoughts/ feelings/ideas.

In groups of two or three:

Share: Your writings.

Select: A theme which you have in common.

Sculpt: 15 mins. Explore this theme through the use of 'group stills',
                  which are like snapshot family-photographs. Experiment
                  with different 'photographs.' Take time to talk about some
                  memories which the work evokes.

Return: To the circle.

Share: Some of your experiences.

Tell: The story of THE SILENT PRINCESS.

Response-   Try to paint images of Luck and Wit, as the story is told.
task:

Select: A specific memory which is evoked by the story and the
                  work so far.

Write: About this event in some detail.

Read: Your writings to the group.

Response-task:	As you listen to the event, think of a wish, which you have for this person. Write your wish on a piece of paper.
Give:	Your wishes to the people for whom they are meant.
Read:	The wishes you have just received.
Select:	One which feels particularly pertinent at this moment.
Share:	This wish with the group.
Reflect:	Upon the entire session.

Text:	THE SILENT PRINCESS
Focus:	The untold
Time:	120 minutes
Voice:	Group sits/stands in a circle. A small ball is thrown from one group member to another. As the ball is thrown, complete the sentence: 'I am...'. Add whatever words you want to say.
Finger-paint:	The image evoked by the words 'The Untold'.

Walk/Look at all the paintings.

Write:	Leave a word-association near each painting.
Return:	To your own painting. Collect and read the words left with your painting.
Select:	Three words which jump at you. You may not know why, but they stir something inside you.
Write:	These three words on a new sheet of paper. Then connect each word with an as yet 'untold' experience/event/ longing in your life. Write about these.
Share:	These writings with each other.

Response-task: After each group member has spoken, ask yourself what you value about having heard these 'untold' experiences/events/ longings. Write this on a small piece of paper.

Give: Your statements to the group members concerned. Do not yet read what you have just received.

Tell: The story of THE SILENT PRINCESS.

Read: The responses you have received.

Write: Use the responses you have received as a basis, and write a letter of encouragement to the Princess who was silent for so long.

Collect: The letters and distribute them randomly.

Read: The letters of advice.

Connect: When all letters have been read, take your time to think back to the 'I am statements, the finger-painting, and the 'untold' writings/responses, to the story and to the letter you have just received.

Maybe further memories are evoked. Maybe you perceive a connection between the various activities/contributions. Share some of your ideas with the other group members.

Reflect: On the entire session.

Text: THE SILENT PRINCESS
Focus: Withholding explained
Time: 120 minutes

Write: Word-associations around 'withholding'.

Write: A brief statement about 'withholding', such as: 'I withhold because I do not trust.'

Response-: Having listened to a group member's statement, write a brief
task response on a piece of paper and hand it to this person, eg

- and then what?

- how do you know you can trust someone?

Distribute the responses, but do not yet read what you have received.

Choose: Three numbers below 18. Write these numbers on a piece of paper.

Tell: The story of THE SILENT PRINCESS, up to: 'The king was much sorrowed by her silence.'

Write: Take your three numbers. Each number represents an age at which something happened to the Princess which explains her silence, as well as her decision to remain silent. Describe these events.

Share: Your writings.

Response-task: Listen carefully to the description of the three events. Ask yourself how this particular Princess might be helped/healed even further. Then create a gift for her which conveys your knowledge/advice. When everyone has shared their writing, distribute your healing gifts.

Look at these 'gifts' and at the responses to your withholding statement.

In pairs:

Talk: Decide who will start, who go second. Take all the responses with you. Each of you has five minutes to explore the importance of these gifts for you in your actual life-situation.

Return: To the circle.

Paint: The images evoked by the words 'luck' and 'wit'.

Tell: The remainder of the story of THE SILENT PRINCESS.

Connect: Reflect on all you have done/received during this session. Consider any links with your actual life-experience.

Select: One withholding statement and one healing gift, which are important to you right now. Share these with the group.

End: The session.

The mirror of Matsuyama

A long time ago there lived in a faraway part of Japan a man and a woman, who had a young daughter. They both loved this child with the greatest of love.

One day the man had to go away. He had business to do in a distant town. Before he went, he told the girl that he would bring her a present which she would grow to value greatly. This caused her much wonderment. But before she could ask what it might be, her father took his leave. His wife and daughter watched as he disappeared from sight.

Some time passed, and the man returned. They were all very glad to see each other again. After the weary traveller had refreshed himself, they sat down on the white mats in the centre of the room. The little daughter looked with eager eyes at a beautiful basket, which her father had brought back from his journey. And indeed, he drew the basket towards himself, whilst he gave her a promising look. Then he carefully opened the basket. Out came a most wonderful doll, as well as a box filled with cakes. She was delighted with her presents. Once more the basket was opened. This time it offered a mirror, which the good man presented to his wife. On the back of the mirror there were elegantly painted pine-trees and storks. Never before in her life had the woman seen herself in a mirror, and certainly not one which had a rounded, slightly bulging surface. She gazed upon herself with growing excitement. Was this she? Was this another woman? Her pleasure was great, and she decided to take precious care of her gift.

Not long after this happy return, the woman became seriously ill. When she knew that she was soon going to die, she asked to see her little daughter. Looking at her, she said: 'Dear child, when I am dead, please look after your father. You will miss me so when I have gone. But here is my mirror, and at times when you feel very alone, look into it. I promise you, that you will always see me.' As soon as she had finished speaking, she died.

Time passed, and the man married again. His new wife did not like her stepdaughter. This was difficult for the young girl. But she had always remembered her mother's last words, and when she felt most lonely she would huddle into a corner to take comfort from looking into the mirror, in which she saw her mother's face, not pained and sorrowing like when she was dying, but once more young and beautiful.

One day the stepmother saw the little girl as she sat, gazing intently at something, murmuring to herself. This frightened the woman. As she did not like the child, she was convinced that the girl was planning something against her. Maybe she was sticking pins into a little doll, trying to do her harm, or something like that. She spoke to her husband and told him that his daughter wanted to kill her.

The man went straight to his daughter's room. As soon as the girl saw him, she slipped the mirror into the sleeve of her dress. Though he had never felt angry with her before, the father now felt bitter sorrow rise within him. He feared that his new wife had spoken the truth. 'What have you got in you sleeve?' the father demanded. Before the girl had time to answer, the whole story, which his new wife had told him, tumbled out. Then the girl reached into her sleeve, showing him her mother's mirror. She spoke quietly, painfully. She told her father how she had been given the mirror just before her mother had died, and also the words her mother had spoken. How her heart ached for her mother, and nowadays it hurt so often. Then she would hold the mirror to see her mother's sweet-smiling face. It helped her to live with the coldness which these days crept through every wall.

The man understood and he too ached. Even the girl's stepmother felt the pain when she heard the child's full story. She was ashamed and asked to be forgiven. The girl, who had seen her mother's face in the ancient mirror, did forgive. Then trouble departed from this home in faraway Japan.

Retold. Principal source: Hadland Davis, F., (1923) *Myths and Legends of Japan*, Harrap.

Text:	THE MIRROR OF MATSUYAMA
Focus:	In search of consolation
Time:	90 minutes
Recall:	When you last saw yourself in a mirror. Maybe this was earlier today or sometime yesterday. Focus on what you noticed.
Describe:	Your experience to the group.
Response-task:	Write at the top of a sheet of paper, the words 'I saw....' When a group member has finished speaking, write the essence of what you heard:

eg - grey hair
- sorrow
- my mother
- sunlight

Tell: The story of THE MIRROR OF MATSUYAMA.

Paint: An image of the way you feel right now. Use finger-paints.

Write: Imagine that the girl herself had told you this story, and that you write her a letter to thank her for sharing the experience with you. You may wish to refer to some events in your own life.

Share: Your letter with the group.

Response-task: Listen to each letter. Imagine that you wish to give a gift to the GROUP MEMBER who has just read the letter. Create through painting/writing an image of this gift.

nb: If a group member chooses not to read the letter, still create gifts for the letter-writer.

Distribute: These gifts.

Look: At the gifts received. Also look at your earlier 'I saw...' writings.

Select: One gift and one 'I saw. . .' statement which are pertinent to your current life-experience.

Share: These with the group.

Reflect: Upon the entire session.

Text: THE MIRROR OF MATSUYAMA
Focus: From another point of view
Time: 120 minutes

Recall: Think of ways in which you resemble your parents/ grandparents.

In pairs

Talk: Discuss these visible and invisible similarities.

Return: To a standing circle.

Share: Some of the similarities with the group.

Move/sound   After you have spoken, enter the central space and express
imitate: through movement and sound what you feel about these
             similarities. The group will then imitate your movement/
             sound. Then the next person shows what is felt, etc.

Tell: The story of THE MIRROR OF MATSUYAMA.

Select: Decide who you identify with most strongly:
             - the father
             - the stepmother
             - the girl.

             Then join the other group members who have chosen the
             same character as you.

Create: A presentation of the story from the perspective of your
             group's character. Discuss what kind of feelings/ experien-
             ces this story-person is likely to have had, which are not
             mentioned in the story. Then find a dramatic form to repre-
             sent the story from his/her point of view.

Show: Your dramatisations.

In pairs

Talk: About the similarities between your own life-experiences,
             and what you have just witnessed/performed.

Return: To the circle.

Share: Some of your ideas/concerns/insights.

Reflect: Upon the entire session.

Text: THE MIRROR OF MATSUYAMA
Focus: Enduring gifts
Time: 120 minutes

Notice: Establish eye-contact with all group members. Look carefully at everyone. Reflect on that which all/some group members have in common. Observable: eg wear glasses. Known: eg a child who lives abroad.

Share: Your observations/ideas.

Recall: Make sure you sit comfortably. Allow yourself to think back to a (special) gift you once received. It may not have been particularly remarkable to anyone else but yourself. Maybe the circumstances were memorable, or the purpose of the giving, or the time/way in which you had longed for this gift. Maybe it was a real surprise. There are many possibilities. Maybe several gifts/presents come to mind. Or you draw a complete blank. This will pass. When everyone has decided upon a certain gift, continue.

In pairs

Talk: Decide who is A, who B.

B: Imagine that you are a journalist, who has heard that A once received a special gift. You know that B's story will be of interest to your reader. Interview your partner. Make notes. Try to get a very full story.

A: Allow yourself to enjoy the interview.

     Then role-reverse.

Write: Remaining faithful to your partner's story, write your magazine article.

Share: Your writing with the group.

Response-task: Having heard the story, create a simple illustration, as well as an appropriate headline.

Collect: When all group members have read their 'articles', hand the illustrations and the headline to the group member ABOUT WHOSE GIFT(!) the article was written.

Look: At the material you received.

In pairs

Talk: About the way you feel right now. You may find that the exercise evoked strong feelings. Share these if possible.

Return: To the circle.

Tell: The story of THE MIRROR OF MATSUYAMA.

Select: One of the illustrations and headlines you received, which to you seem to encapsulate an aspect of this Japanese story.

Write: Using the words of the headline as your point of departure, write a three-line consolation poem.

Use: A small bell.

Read: Use this bell with a fine sound. Hand the bell to the person who is about to read their poem. Read the consolation poem. Then ring the bell several times. When the sound has faded away, hand the bell to the next person.

Connect: Make connections between this session's material and your actual life-experience.

Reflect: Upon the entire session.

The battle with Snow

A very long time ago, in the days of the animal people, snow was sent to earth by the fierce Snow Brothers, who lived far away in the sky-world. There were five of them. One winter so much snow fell that all the houses in the village disappeared beneath a thick layer of whiteness. The animal people had to burrow their way towards one another. If they wanted to visit their friends, they cut a tunnel through the frozen darkness, which surrounded them everywhere.

This winter lasted a long, long time. The animal people became frightened. They said: 'We must do something. If we have another winter like this, we will all starve to death.' The Chief heard them speak, and he said that there was nothing they could do if they stayed where they were. If the Battle with the Snow Brothers was to be won, they had to travel to the fields where snow began. The animal people replied: 'Then we shall go there.'

At last Spring came, and the Chief addressed his people, saying: 'Winter shall come again, and before it comes, we must travel North to the land where snow begins, to the home of the Snow Brothers.'

During the first days of Autumn they started preparations. When at last all were ready, the animal people set out on the far trail which went north - Rattlesnake, Mouse and Frog were there - as well as all the big animals. Three days and nights they traveled on the earth. The evening before the third night, their Chief spoke, and he said: 'Tomorrow we will journey through the air. I tell you, the remainder of our journey is through the air, we shall travel up towards the sky.'

This happened and on the morning of the fifth day, all the animal people arrived up above in the Skyworld. Here they found the house of Snow without much difficulty. Their Chief spoke again, and he said: 'When tomorrow comes, the battle begins.'

Night fell and darkness was thick around them. Mouse crept away. She sneaked into Snow's house. Here she saw the bows, which the Snow Brothers use to send their snow to earth. Very gently she tripped towards the bow of the oldest Snow Brother and gnawed it to bits. She hastened to the bow of the second Snow Brother and gnawed it to bits. She gnawed to bits the bows of the third and fourth brothers. But dawn was breaking as she was about to gnaw through the bow of the fifth Brother, and she had to scurry back to her animal people.

'I am only small', she said, 'but I've tried to help you. I know that you can now win the battle.'

Early that morning the animal people began the attack. As soon as the Snow Brothers heard the clamour outside their house, they rushed to get their bows, to find that four had been gnawed to bits. Only the youngest brother could fight. But the animal people from the earth had so many more bows and arrows, that he had to give way, and as fast as he could he sped further North. Mouse's work had not been in vain.

Then the animal people went into Snow's house. They looked in every nook and cranny. Whatever they found, they took. As they set out on their long journey back home, Snake and Rattlesnake trailed the party from behind, so that they might pick up whatever the other animals dropped. Snake found only a few straws. They were red, white and yellow. Later he came across a piece of smoked buckskin. Rattlesnake lost his way home altogether. After a long time Snake did return. Some of Snake's friends had been very sad; they were mourning him, for they thought that Snake had been forever lost in the Skyworld.

Snake's cousin, Waterdog, cried, because he believed Snake had been lost. Snake therefore shared a bit of smoked buckskin with him, which is why Waterdogs nowadays have tough hides. Lizard, who was another of Snake's cousins, also cried, because he believed Snake had been lost. Snake made him a gift of some of the straws, which explains why lizards have a striped skin. Frog, too, was one of Snake's cousins. Frog cried, whilst he sang an unfriendly song:

> Snake is cock-eyed. Snake is cock-eyed.
> Which is how he got left behind.

This made Snake furious. He hissed: 'No present for you, Frog. Our friendship is finished.' This explains how Snake and Frog became enemies, which they are to this day. Whenever a Snake sees a Frog he slithers towards him and devours Frog.

When Snake saw that he had a few straws left he put them on his own back. Because of this Snakes have yellow or white stripes on their back.

At last Rattlesnake, too, found his way back to Earth. However, he landed in Yakima country, which is east of the mountains. He did not return to

Chehalis country. This explains why there are no rattlesnakes to be found in Chehalis country to this very day.

In this way the Snows were defeated and there is little snow in the Chehalis country in these times. Because Mouse gnawed through the bows, the snows are not very deep. Only the youngest of the five brothers sends us the snows of winter.

Retold by the author. Oral source: USA.

Text:	THE BATTLE WITH SNOW
Focus:	Beyond the freezing cold
Time:	120 minutes
Talk:	Free-associate words/images evoked by the word COLD.
Sculpt:	Designate an area in the room which will be the sculpting space. One by one group members enter this space. Adopt a posture reflective of feeling cold. Once this posture is adopted, hold it, until all group members have joined the sculpt. Then imagine that your sculpture can move a little. Intensify your posture to 'freezing cold'. Hold this posture. Focus on the way you feel right now. Do not speak these words. Then, one by one, let go of your 'freezing cold' posture and leave the sculpting area.
Stand:	In a circle, establish eye-contact. Then walk around the room. Remind yourself of the words which came to mind, whilst you held the 'freezing cold' posture.
	Prepare to speak these words. Do this in the following way:
Speak/chorus:	Walk around the room. One person speaks a sentence. The other group members echo the words, mumbling as if they have difficulty speaking due to being tired and cold.
	Sentence-example: Too dark, too lonesome, too long.
Return:	To the circle.

Select: Ask group members to recall some sentences. Record these
             sentences on a large sheet of paper, under the heading *Freez-
             ing cold*.

Breathe: Onto the palm of your right hand. Feel the warmth of your
             breath. Then caress your whole hand with your breath, espe-
             cially the spaces between your fingers. Breathe slowly and
             deeply. Note how the air is warmed by your body. Then
             breathe onto the palm of your left hand. Circulate your
             breath around the left hand.

             You may find that your hands begin to tremble. Allow this to
             be. You may equally find that you become somewhat tear-
             ful. Allow this to be also.

Select: Focus quietly on your breathing. Let your thoughts meander.
             Choose one sentence which expresses what you experience
             right now.

Drum: Use a drum or gong. Beat the drum or gong before you speak
             your sentence to the group. Do this also when you have fin-
             ished speaking. Then pass the drum/gong to the next group
             member. Repeat the same sequence.

Select: Some sentences which have particular relevance for the
             group. Record these sentences on a large sheet of paper
             under the heading *Breath*.

Place: A large bowl (12" diameter) filled with sand in the centre of
             the group. Place a small candle in the middle of the bowl.
             Light the candle.

             Give each group member a candle. Do not yet light these
             candles.

Tell: The story of THE BATTLE WITH SNOW.

Light: The candles and place each candle in the bowl. Do this
             quietly. When all the candles have been lit, prepare yourself
             to reclaim your candle. Think of what you want to say be-

fore you reclaim your candle. Speak these words. Take your candle and blow it out.

The central candle stays alight.

Select: A few sentences which have particular relevance for the group. Record these sentences on a large sheet of paper under the heading *Light*.

Write: Read the group's sentences which were recorded under the headings: *Freezing Cold*, *Breath* and *Light*. Using all or some of these sentences, create your own prose-poem. Add further words where necessary.

Share: These prose-poems with the group. Use the drum/gong between poems.

Talk: About memories/associations/feelings evoked. Extinguish the central candle.

Reflect: Upon the entire session.

Text: THE BATTLE WITH SNOW
Focus: Small courage
Time: 120 minutes

Focus: Choose a partner. Sit opposite your partner. Focus on what you are not yet ready to think about/do/face. Then take turns to speak a sentence. In each sentence use the words 'Not yet'.
eg: - I am not yet ready to look at my husband's
photographs.
  - I can not yet return to the allotment.
  - I can not yet sleep alone in the house.

Return: To the circle.

Share: Your experiences.

Paint:	Use one large sheet of paper for the whole group. Paint the images evoked by the 'Not yet' exercise. Work quickly.
Tell:	The story of THE BATTLE WITH SNOW, up to 'Mouse crept away. She sneaked into Snow's house.'
Write:	Retell the story so far, from Mouse's point of view. Imagine her thoughts/feelings/concerns as she travels towards the Snow Brothers' lodge. Do not continue the story. Prevent yourself from anticipating the rest of the tale.
Tell:	Continue the story up to: 'Snake and Rattlesnake trailed the party from behind.' Continue your tale from Mouse's point of view and create your own ending.
Share:	Your writings.
Response-task:	Upon having heard each story, take a small piece of paper and create a gift for the Mouse in this story. Try to choose a gift which reflects your ideas as to what this Mouse needs/deserves.
Tell:	The end of the actual story.
Distribute:	The gifts.
Pairs:	Return to the partner with whom you did the 'Not yet' exercise.
Talk:	Take your gifts with you. Remind yourself/each other of what you were not yet ready to think about/do/face. Place all the gifts in front of you and talk about the way in which a gift/these gifts may help you in this process.
Return:	To the circle.
Place:	The group painting in the middle of the circle.
Select:	One gift which is particularly important to you at this moment.

Share: This gift with the group and reflect upon your contribution to the group painting.

Reflect: Upon the entire session.

Text: THE BATTLE WITH SNOW
Focus: The struggle with frostiness
Time: 90 minutes

Recall: Remind yourself of an experience with 'Snow'. This may be a long time ago. It may be recent.

Talk/move: Share this memory with the group. Use three or four sentences only. Then enter the group's centre and retell your experience through movement. Do this one by one.

Tell: The story of THE BATTLE WITH SNOW.

In pairs

Discuss: The important stages in this story, eg:
- too much snow
- the awareness
- the decision to act
- the preparation

Write: First list these stages. Then think of a key-sentence for each stage.

Move: Create a movement version of the various stages of the story.

Use your key-sentences to support the movement. Rehearse your presentation.

Show: Your work to the other pairs.

In pairs

Talk: Spend a few minutes talking about the experience.

Connect: Make connections between your work during this session and
               actual life-events.

Reflect: Upon the entire session.

The return of the flowers

When the creator, Baiame, no longer walked the earth, the flowers and trees all died, except for three trees which he had marked as his own. Only here could the bees make honey. Only here could parents show their children how the earth had looked, when the flowers and the trees still graced the earth. The early people longed for the honey, yet they dared not touch these flowering trees, which were sacred to Baiame.

In time, the scent and sight of flowers was but a faded memory, which only the oldest people cherished. Meanwhile, the All-seeing spirit told Baiame how the people revered his trees, touching no part of the honey-combs. As a reward for their respect, Baiame sent the people of those early days goonbeans and manna. Though the children delighted in their newly found food, the older people mourned the flowers and the trees, which had given them so much pleasure.

One day, several wise Elders decided to journey to Baiame, to plead for a return of the trees and flowers to the earth. Just before dawn they slipped away. They travelled for many days, until they came to the foot of the sacred Oobi-Oobi mountain. Patiently they searched for a way up the heights until they found a path of stone steps, cut by the spirits of Baiame.

They climbed the sacred Oobi-Oobi mountain for four days and four nights. When they came to the summit, they were very tired. When they saw a spring of water, they drank from it with great eagerness. As soon as they had drunk the water, they felt refreshed. Then they heard the sound of a Bull-roarer. Its Spirit spoke to them and asked why they had come all this way. Then they told him about the earth and how desolately empty it was since Baiame had left. All the flowers had died. They so longed for the colour and the scents.

The Bull-roarer Spirit then ordered his attendants to carry the wise Elders up towards the resting-place in the great sky, where flowers bloom eternally. Here the Elders were allowed to gather as many flowers as they could hold in their arms. Their arms filled with this abundance of colour and scent, they were lifted back to the top of the great Oobi-Oobi mountain.

Again the Spirit of the Bull-roarer spoke, telling the Elders about Baiame and the seasons and winds. Then the wise old people climbed down the path of stone steps, cradling the colourful tumult of happiness in their arms.

The people hurried towards them. The scent of myriad flowers filled the air. Then the wise Elders spoke and the people listened, after which the Elders went across the lands, scattering flowers far and wide. The first place of flowering is called Girraween.

Since that time flowers and trees and shrubs have covered the earth, as it was in the early days, when Baiame, the creator, walked upon it.

Retold by Nancy King and the author. Principle source: Langloh Parker, K., (1934) *Australian Legendary Tales*, 1934.

Text:	THE RETURN OF THE FLOWERS
Focus:	A world without flowers
Time:	90 minutes

Group/paint: On a large sheet of paper (at least 1 x 2 meters) paint the group's image of a flower garden in bloom.

Individually/   On a small sheet of paper your image of a world without
paint: flowers.

Tell: The story of THE RETURN OF THE FLOWERS.

Write: One sentence at the top of a sheet of paper. Repeat this same sentence at the bottom of the paper. In three minutes write down all the other sentences which belong in between.

Share: Your writings.

Paint: Return to the group painting of the flower garden in bloom and
complete it.

Reflect: Upon the entire session.

Text:	THE RETURN OF THE FLOWERS
Focus:	The recovery of joy
Time:	90 minutes

Remind:	Yourself of something you noticed this morning after you got up and before you left your home.
Share:	Your recollection with the group.
Select:	One of the images a group member has shared and allow your mind to travel back through the past to a time when you noticed something similar.
Write:	About this memory.
Recall:	One of your grandparents. If you never met any of them, imagine what they might have been like.
Write:	Something which they particularly enjoyed (or might have enjoyed).
Imagine:	Yourself as a possible/actual grandparent. Think about something you particularly enjoy. Do you want your possible/actual grandchild to know about this?
Write:	What you enjoy.
Tell:	The story of THE RETURN OF THE FLOWERS.
Write:	What the elders decided to say to the people of the earth, including why they needed to go on this journey, what it had been like and how it feels to return with arms full of flowers. Include in your speech some words of advice for the people of the earth.
Read:	The speeches.
Response-task:	After each speech write a sentence which begins with the words: 'I want...'

In pairs

Talk:	About your speech, the 'I want. ..' sentences, and the memories.
Reflect:	Upon the entire session.

Text: THE RETURN OF THE FLOWERS
Focus: Becoming
Time: 90 minutes

Paint: An image of yourself as a flower.

Write: If flowers gave you a gift, which gift would this be? Write this on your flower-painting.

Write: On a small piece of paper (which can later be identified as yours) answers to the following:
                  - the name and age of a character;
                  - the dwelling-place where he/she lives;
                  - the gift which you have just written down.

Collect: These pieces of paper.

Distribute: The papers.

Write: A brief story under the title: 'How. . . received. . . (gift from the flower). Include in the story some whys and wherefores as well as some consequences of the receipt of this gift.

Read: The stories.

Return: The story to the group member upon whose original details the writings are based.

Tell: The story of THE RETURN OF THE FLOWERS.

Connect: Make connections between your image of 'myself as a flower', your gift story and your response to THE RETURN OF THE FLOWERS.

Reflect: Upon the entire session.

Note: These three story-structures can be found in: Gersie, Alida and King, Nancy (1990) *Storymaking in Education and Therapy*, London: Jessica Kingsley Publishers.

The sacred gift of celebration

In the early days a man and a woman lived near the sea. The man hunted, sometimes on the land, sometimes on the sea. This man and this woman, these two lonely people, had a son, and when he was a young boy, his father made a bow for him. Soon he too hunted most skillfully. One day the son did not return from his day's hunting. His parents searched for him, but they searched in vain.

They conceived another child, another son. He too became a skilled hunter, and one day, he too did not return.

The man and the woman lived alone, and they hurt greatly for their two sons, who were lost.

Then they conceived a third child. He too was a son, skilled in hunting and there was food in abundance in their lonesome dwelling by the sea.

Then one day, the third son was hunting deep inside the forest, when he saw circling in the sky a young eagle. He thought of shooting it, but before the thought reached his hands, the eagle landed near him. The eagle pushed back the hood which covered its eagle-head, and revealed the face of a young man. This young Eagle-man, spoke and he said: 'I am he who killed both your brothers. You too shall be killed, if you do not promise that you shall give a songfeast when you go back home. Tell me: do you make this promise, or do you not?'

The third son replied: 'I know not what a songfeast is. Tell me about song, speak to me about feast. Gladly would I give a songfeast. But tell me what it is.' Again the Eagle-man spoke and he said: 'Will you, or will you not.' And the third son replied: 'I will, but I know not what you mean.'

Then the Eagle-man spoke and he said: 'Come with me, and meet my mother. She will teach you all that you do not yet know. Your two brothers did not accept our gift of celebration. They declined to learn. I therefore had to kill them. You however, may go with me. When you have grasped how to let the words give birth to a song which becomes its own singing, when you know the joy that dances your dance, you may freely return home.'

The young hunter said: 'I shall go with you.'

They travelled towards the high mountains. They travelled a long, long way. At last they came to the great mountain, which they climbed. Eagle-man spoke and he said: 'Our house is on the top of this mountain.'

As they came near the top, the young Hunter heard a strange pounding sound. It was loud, and got louder and louder. The Eagle-man asked: 'Do you hear a sound?' 'Yes, like the sound of hammer,' said the young Hunter. 'It is my mother's heart-beat,' said the Eagle-man.

Then they came to the eagle's dwelling-place. Here, the young Hunter was told to wait, until the Eagle-man had returned from preparing his mother for the visitor. A while later he invited the young Hunter to come and meet Eagle-mother. All alone, on a wooden platform, looking worn-out and deeply sorrowed, sat Eagle-mother. Young Eagle-man spoke and he said:

'This young Hunter has promised that he will hold a songfeast when he returns home. He knows not how to let the words give birth to a song which becomes its own singing. He knows nothing about beating a drum, nor does he know the joy which dances his dance. Mother! Human people do not know how to celebrate, and now this young Hunter has come to be with us and learn all this.'

Upon hearing her son's words, Eagle-mother's face returned to life. She thanked the young Hunter and said: 'First you must build a House of Celebration, so that people may gather in one place.'

The two young men set about the building of a House of Celebration. Old, old Eagle-mother then showed them how to make the ordinary drum, and the special festivity-drum, which has a deeply resonant tone, and evokes the heart-beat of Eagle-mother. Then Eagle-mother led them to the knowing which helps words to become songs, and for the songs to become their own singing. Then she helped them to beat the drum when the singing arises; and finally she taught the dance which the joy dances. When they could do it all, and knew it well, Eagle-mother spoke and she said: 'When you have built the festival-house, and have created songs, then gather food in abundance, and call your people. Hold a songfeast.'

The young Hunter said: 'But we know no-one. We know no-one, apart from ourselves.'

Eagle-mother heard his words. She spoke and she said: 'Because they do not have the sacred gift of celebration, therefore human people are lonesome. Hasten and do as I told you. Make yourself ready, and take care to prepare. Then go and look for people. You shall meet them two by two. You gather them until there are many. Invite them all to your songfeast. You must celebrate.'

As the young Hunter knew all he needed to know, Eagle-mother asked her son to guide their guest back towards the place of first meeting. This time they did not travel on foot. Young Eagle-man asked the young Hunter to climb onto his back, hold firm to his neck, and to close his eyes. They travelled fast, when the flying-sound stopped, the young Hunter opened his eyes. They had returned to the place of first meeting. They bid their farewell.

He returned to his parents dwelling-place. He told them all, and said:

'Human people are lonesome, and therefore they live alone, all because they know nothing of the sacred gift of Celebration. I gave my word to teach the people how to celebrate.'

His father came with him, and together they built the House of Celebration. Then they hunted, until their was food in great abundance. When there was food in abundance, they helped words to be songs, and for songs to become their own singing. They made drums, and beat them, until they knew how to beat the drums. They danced their joy, and to all of this they sang. To their words, their dancing and to the beating of the drums.

Then all was prepared. The young hunter went into the forest, towards the hills and mountains, along rivers and streams. He searched to find guests, for human-people were lonesome and knew no-one apart from themselves.

As Eagle-mother had promised, he met people in twos. Some had the skin of wolves, others the skin of foxes. He invited them all and gathered many. They accompanied him with delight.

Then they gave the songfeast. There was food in plentiful abundance, and presents of meat and fur for every guest. They sang and danced. The old father beat the great festivity drum, which sounded deep and resonant like Eagle-mother's heart. It reminded the young Hunter of the sound he had heard near the summit of the faraway, great mountain. All learned, and sang and danced until dawn. Only then did the guests make ready to leave the House of Celebration.

They fell onto their paws, and the father and the son knew for the first time that their guests had been the wolves and all the foxes, red and white and and silver, in their human shape, for such are the powers of celebration.

Time passed, and a while later the young Hunter was deep in the forest when again he met the Eagle, who at once became young Eagle-man. They made their way to the faraway, great mountain, as old Eagle-mother wanted to see the young Hunter, who had been true to his word and had given humankind's first songfeast.

When they came to the top of the mountain, Eagle-mother stepped forwards to greet the young Hunter. And worn-out old, old Eagle-mother, she had become young again. Whenever human people celebrate, Eagle-mother, the earth's heart-beat, is renewed. Therefore the eagle is the sacred bird of song, dance and celebration.

Retold. Principal source: Ostermann, H., *The Alaskan Eskimos*, as described in the posthumous notes of Dr. Knud Rasmussen.

Text:	THE SACRED GIFT OF CELEBRATION
Focus:	Beyond lonesomeness
Time:	120 minutes

Walk: Through the room as if your feet were writing the word 'lonesome' on the floor. Move slowly and with concentration.

Move: Sit in a circle. Clap a slow, steady rhythm. One group member at a time enters the centre of the circle, and performs a brief 'dance of lonesomeness'. When everyone has danced, the clapping stops. Listen to the silence.

Tell: The story of THE SACRED GIFT OF CELEBRATION.

Write: Imagine that you are the young man and that you want to record your experiences for the sake of other people. Imagine his doubts and hopes. Write his account of the events.

In pairs

Share: Your writings.

Talk: About the elements in the writings which you believe to be of particular significance for yourself and the group.

Create: A brief presentation which conveys what you have gleaned. Maybe you do so by creating a song or a dance, maybe by writing and performing a poem. Work together.

Present: Your work.

Paint: The decorated outline of a shield, which carries your name. Create as many spaces within this outline as there are group members. Pass the paper round. When you receive another group member's shield, paint/draw/write something in one of the spaces, which reflects your protective wish for this person.

Look: At your shield.

Connect: Remind yourself of this session's work. The 'lonesomeness' dance, your writing, the presentation(s) and the shield. Allow associations with actual life-experience to enter into consciousness. Share some of these.

Write: Think of a device for your shield. Write this on your paper.

Complete: The session with the sharing of the devices.

Text: THE SACRED GIFT OF CELEBRATION
Focus: Towards togetherness
Time: 120 minutes

Paint: The image of a cold, old person in a lonesome place.

Move: Leave your painting in a safe place. Walk through the room. Make eye-contact. Then remind yourself of the reality that the other people too know about loneliness. Try to convey this when you meet their eyes.

Walk: Draw your attention inwards. Imagine that you are going along a circular path with many obstacles/obstructions:
- climb a gate
- jump across a wide ditch
- crawl beneath some barbed wire
- struggle through dense undergrowth
- climb across scraggy rocks.
At last you reach the point of departure again. You return to this room. Once more, make eye-contact with the other group members.

In pairs

Move: Stand near your partner; your hands can nearly touch. Look each other in the eye. Now, very slowly, start to move together. Let your movements be small and minimal. Ensure that you develop this slow, quiet dance in unison. Do this for several minutes.

Share: Something about your experience.

Return: To the circle.

Tell: The story of THE SACRED GIFT OF CELEBRATION.

In small groups

Create: Imagine that you too have learned something on top of the Sacred Mountain which involves rhythm, songmaking, friendliness, dance, eating and giving. What is it and how may you share it with or teach it to the others? You have ten minutes to prepare.

Decide: The sequence in which the work will be presented.

Share: Your work.

Paint: Look at your earlier painting of a cold, old person in a lonesome place. Add whatever you wish to this painting.

Share: Your paintings.

Reflect: Upon the entire session.

Text: THE SACRED GIFT OF CELEBRATION
Focus: Strengthening the heartbeat
Time: 90 minutes

Recall: Something 'small' which you do from time to time to cheer yourself up.

Share: Your cheering-up acts.

Walk:	Through the room with your eyes closed. When you bump into someone, stop and carefully touch their face. Try to recognise who he/she is, without opening your eyes. Greet this person and then, without words, say good-bye, and so on. With your eyes still closed, make a circle.
	When the circle is complete, and still without speaking, lie down. Keep holding hands. Rest your heads near each other and listen to the sounds you can hear in the room and if at all possible, to one another's heartbeat. Listen carefully. Keep your eyes closed. When the group is ready, start to move slowly and gently. Let this movement take you back into an upright position. Try to maintain body/hand contact. Then prepare to open your eyes. Open your eyes.
Paint:	Take a large sheet of paper. Remind yourself of all you have heard and felt so far. Use finger-paints and crayons to give form and colour to some of these images. Leave some space on this paper for writing.
Look/write:	Leave your painting and look at the other paintings. When you feel inspired to write some words of understanding or encouragement onto the painting, please do so.
Read:	What has been written on your painting. Then ask yourself which song/poem/story the painting/writings bring to mind. You may find it helpful to make a note of some of these.
Light:	A candle. Place this in the centre of the group.
Tell:	The story of THE SACRED GIFT OF CELEBRATION.
Share:	Your paintings/the writings. Also share one of the songs/poems/stories.
Connect:	Reflect upon the entire session.
Sing/tell:	End by singing/reciting one of the songs/poems, which feels particularly important to the group.

Storymaking in Education and Therapy
Alida Gersie and Nancy King
ISBN 1 85302 519 4 hb
ISBN 1 85302 520 9 pb

'This is an essential and wonderful book for anyone interested in working with stories in education or therapy... It is a true discovery'
— Dr Ofra Ayalon, Haifa University

'This is a lovely book... The quality of the presentation of the book adds to its appeal... this is a book to keep, use and refer back to again and again... In short, this is a publication for nurse teachers, psychiatric nurse therapists, counsellors and anyone interested in exploring the universal heritage that is handed down through story-telling and the sharing of myths.'
- Nursing Times

Symbols of the Soul
Therapy and Guidance Through Fairy Tales
Birgitte Brun, Ernst W Pedersen and Marianne Runberg
Foreword by Murray Cox
ISBN 1 85302 107 5 hb

'the book...has many of the best qualities of fairy tales. Its descriptive style is lucid and simple. It contains many pointers and signposts which provoke the readers curiosity. There is transparency and verbal economy... Because it links the 'once upon a time' world with greater access to that of everyday, [the book] is highly recommended.' *—from the Foreword*

'This is a wide-ranging, eclectic look at the profundity of fairy tales and their ability to draw clients into a secure space in which they can explore their own feelings and preoccupations through the story form. The authors draw on their clinical experiences and describe a number of case studies throughout the text.' *— Contemporary Psychology*

'...much to please the followers of Bettelheim and his classic text in this area...people interested in myth, narrative and archetypes will find much to enjoy...a useful collection for anyone interested in using story in therapy.' *— British Journal of Psychotherapy*

'There are a number of valuabe aspects to this book...the introductory chapters and the discussion of therapy with emotionally deprived children are clear and worth reading.' *— British Journal of Psychiatry*

Jessica Kingsley Publishers, 116 Pentonville Road, London N1 9JB

Dramatic Approaches to Brief Therapy

Edited by Alida Gersie
ISBN 1 85302 271 3 pb

Brief dramatherapy is offered in treatment settings for acute or chronic in-patient populations and out-patient or community health settings with a maintenance, rehabilitation or personaldevelopment purpose. Providers of such treatment want to offer: the briefest possible treatment programmes; which involve optimum numbers of clients; at the most resonable level of cost; with the best predictable outcome, and the clearest, most competent, evaluation of efficacy strategies.

Written by the directors of the world's major training programmes in dramatherapy, this book presents their approach to and theory of brief dramatherapy.

Grief in Children
A Handbook for Adults
Atle Dyregrov
ISBN 1 85302 113 X pb

'Dyregrov's writing is clear in its description, and explicit in its advice, and demonstrates that the daunting task of helping a child through grief is both manageable and rewarding...The book will, I´ m sure, become required reading for all those touched by the care of bereaved children'

> – Bereavement Care

'...a handy, small book ideal for teachers, social workers, counsellors, parents and others faced with the task of understanding children in grief and trying to help them.'

> – Association for Child Psychology and Psychiatry Newsletter

'There is valuable material on grief at various ages and development... The question 'What makes the grief worse?' is neatly answered and a brief, but useful, section alerts the helper to differences in the grief experienced by boys and girls. The chapters on care for bereaved children are packed with good sense and practical suggestions... Many interesting ideas are given on ways to deal with bereavement in the setting of the classroom... There is much to commend this handbook. It is of manageable length, giving information concisely and supplementing it with well-chosen quotations...a valuable book which I would recommend to my colleagues and to parents, to those who run playgroups and to any who seek to help young people in bereavement.'

> – Lifeline (Magazine of the National Association of Bereavement Services)

Jessica Kingsley Publishers, 116 Pentonville Road, London N1 9JB

Dramatherapy with Families, Groups and Individuals
Waiting in the Wings
Sue Jennings
ISBN 1 85302 144 X pb
ISBN 1 85302 014 1 hb

'Not only is it extremely well written, but the theoretical models and issues outlined are worked through with the use of detailed and clear examples... deserves to be widely read by specialists and non-specialists alike.'
— Counselling

'She shows an impressive knowledge of myths and dramatic literature and demonstrates their therapeutic validity. The case examples are wonderful.'
— Dramascope

'This is a clear, well-written text that reflects a dramatherapist who is clinically astute and well-grounded in drama, theatre, and ritual processes... There is no doubt that Jennings is a trailblazing pioneer whose journey makes ours a little easier.' *— The Arts in Psychotherapy*

The Forgotten Mourners
Guidelines for Working with Bereaved Children
Sister Margaret Pennells and Susan C Smith
ISBN 1 85302 264 0 pb

'...a clearly written book. It will be a useful preliminary introduction for anybody wishing to prepare themselves for supporting bereaved children.'
— Community Care

'This book gives clear and concise guidance on how children grieve and well structured advice on how different systems may support children through the bereavement process...a useful and easy read, containing pertinent information for social workers and schools. I particularly like the outlines for the process of grieving for different age groups and the key points contained at the end of each chapter. It also contains a useful resource list for further reading.' *— Professional Social Work*

'provides excellent initial guidelines for anyone dealing with bereaved children.' *— Therapy Weekly*

'this easily readable guide will fill a gap in the literature and will be useful to a wide range of workers.' *— ACPP Review and Newletter*

Jessica Kingsley Publishers, 116 Pentonville Road, London N1 9JB

Drama and Healing
The Roots of Drama Therapy
Roger Grainger
ISBN 1 85302 337 X pb

'The Rev. Roger Grainger's new book is undoubtedly an important contribution to the growing body of literature on the theory of drama therapy. It is at once a Scholarly and an unusually personal discussion of the place of drama in the treatment of severe mental illness.'
– British Journal of Occupational Therapy

'This is by far the most thoughtful book on dramatherapy that I have come across... This book is strongly recommended for creative arts therapists and psychotherapists alike.' *– Group Analysis*

'extremely thought provoking...the links made between different theoretical and creative streams are extremely interesting.' *– Counselling*

Play Therapy
Where the Sky Meets the Underworld
Ann Cattanach
ISBN 1 85302 211 X pb

'...an excellent, stimulating read with a manageable style and numerous sensitive insights into the world of play for the child and how it can become a therapeutic process where children 'play out' their perception of their own experiences...uses clear, straightforward language to discuss the theoretical basis for play therapy... The book does not make great claims as to its powers of healing, but it seems to offer a means towards constructively working through traumatic experiences for children.'
– Nursery World

'Cattanach packs a large amount of theory into this easy-to-read volume, together with practical guidelines on how to be a safe companion for the child's journey.' *– Professional Social Work*

'This is an excellent introduction to an activity whose relevance is increasingly recognised and used, not least in the communication of good health practices.' *– Institute of Health Education*

'This is a short and accessible work on a subject of considerable interest to many professionals... Cattanach uses the language of imagination and myth, rather than the more mundane style we have come to expect in works about therapy and teaching. However, she uses it with authority as an international expert.' *– Child Language Teaching and Therapy*

Jessica Kingsley Publishers, 116 Pentonville Road, London N1 9JB

Play Therapy with Abused Children
Ann Cattanach
ISBN 1 85302 193 8 pb

'...a welcome addition to the sparse literature in this area. I would recommend the book to anyone working in this field but especially to beginners... This is a well presented, clear and easy-to-read book, providing a balanced mixture of factual information and case material.'
— *British Journal of Occupational Therapy*

'...scores highly on clarity of presentation. In this regard, the old adage that 'one picture is worth a thousand words' is borne out by the plentiful reproductions of children's drawings...there is a list of books for younger children with the author's individual comments based on her own experience. Another example of making the invisible child visible.' — *Counselling*

'Her accounts of the way in which play is used to make sense of traumatic experiences are full of insight and often moving. All aspects of the work are covered... This is an exceptional volume...goes far beyond a mere text book.' — *Therapy Weekly*

'This is a wonderfully reaffirming book for play therapists. Ann Cattanach writes with enormous empathy and warmth, and with a refreshing lack of sentimentality... I would recommend this book most highly, both for practitioners of play therapy and those professionals who may need evidence that play therapy is as valid as 'talking' therapy, if not more so... It is an unpretentious and optimistic book, and a very positive addition to recent publications.' — *British Association of Play Therapists*

Arts Approaches to Conflict
Edited by Marian Liebmann
ISBN 1 85302 293 4 pb

'Various attempts at resolving conflict using every conceivable art form: drama, visual arts, music, movement, storytelling and combined arts are described here... This is a magnificent book. An inspiration for mental health workers, teachers, artists and art therapists.' — *Nursing Times*

Christian Symbols, Ancient Roots
Elizabeth Rees, Foreword by Sue Jennings
ISBN 1 85302 179 2 pb, ISBN 1 85302 046 X hb

'...an intriguing and imagination-stretching book... [I] commend this exploration into theology and folklore.' — *Reform*

Jessica Kingsley Publishers, 116 Pentonville Road, London N1 9JB

Art Therapy in Practice

Edited by Marian Liebmann
ISBN 1 85302 057 5 hb
ISBN 1 85302 058 3 pb

'Marian Liebmann's introduction provides a highly lucid and readable account of many of the most important concepts and ideas. It would be a good primer for anyone coming to the subject... All the accounts are clear in themselves, and relate well to one another, giving us a clear image of the range and depth of art therapy practice. The result is an encouraging and stimulating 'progress report' on where we are as a profession...there is a richness and variety of material here that succeeds in offering a perspective on art therapy that has unity without conformity.' – *Inscape*

'The most important message which is conveyed in this excellent collection lies in its demonstration of the way in which art therapists have managed to extend their skills in the service of such a wide variety of human distress... It heralds a call to all art therapists to continue to accept any challenge while at the same time it may help others to consider its possibilities in fields where, up to now, it has not figured.'

– British Journal of Psychiatry

Art Therapy and Dramatherapy
Masks of the Soul

Sue Jennings and Åse Minde
ISBN 1 85302 181 4 pb, ISBN 1 85302 027 3 hb

'The creativity of the authors is testified to by their production of a new form. In addition to being a 'how to' manual for art and dramatherapy, this book is a melange of autobiography, anthropology, psychoanalysis, case reports, cross-cultural analysis, art reproduction, poetry, literary quotation, and mythology.' – *The Lancet*

'There is energy, creativeness and richness of imagery in this book... The book is well referenced and relevant theoretical concepts are explained. ...there is some very good sound advice...on many different issues.'

– Inscape

'will prove useful to both beginning and advanced art therapists... The authors, whose passion for their work is obvious, are creative and generous in providing a text rich in methodology for arts therapists interested in expanding their practice.' *–American Journal of Art Therapy*

Jessica Kingsley Publishers, 116 Pentonville Road, London N1 9JB

Interventions with Bereaved Children

Susan C Smith and Sister Margaret Pennells
ISBN 1 85302 285 3 pb

'If you have ever floundered when faced with a grieving child, this book is for you. Equipped with a wealth of practical and compassionate responses, 20 contributors describe their work with bereaved children, sharing effective ways of supporting and helping them in their loss. Case studies are sensitively given, and there are moving accounts of individual, family, group and whole school work. This is an empowering book, which should be accessible to all those who come into contact with children.'
—Nursing Times

'This book should be available to all members of multidisciplinary child mental health teams – The strength of this book is that it ranges from individual grief, through family and societal settings linking grief and disaster, patterning the varying responses of children according to their age and life circumstances and providing a mosaic of assessment and therapeutic techniques – This book is one important step in improving our ability to communicate with the young about death.'
—Journal of Adolescence

'The 26 contributors to this book share a wide experience of childhood and adolescent grief... Differences in culture are sensitively outlined in a chapter on transcultural counselling...a thoughtful contribution to the growing literature on children's bereavement.' *– Community Care*

The Glass of Heaven
The Faith of the Dramatherapist

Roger Grainger
ISBN 1 85302 284 5 pb

'...a book which offers conclusions in an original field...explores the connections between dramatherapy and religion, no easy task since the two are not only scientific disciplines to investigate but also experiential activities to be lived. Dr Grainger achieves this by moving between theoretical analysis and lively case studies. This juxtapositions engages both mind and imagination, and gradually draws us into the faith of the dramatherapist.' *– Counselling*

'This is a book which offers exciting conclusions in an original field... The author examines the dramatherapist's role as one who facilitates both faith and healing, at the point where religion and medicine meet.'
— Catholic Herald

Jessica Kingsley Publishers, 116 Pentonville Road, London N1 9JB

Good Grief 1
**Exploring Feelings, Loss and Death
with Under 11's, 2nd ed**
Barbara Ward and Associates
ISBN 1 85302 324 8 pb

Good Grief 2
**Exploring Feelings, Loss and Death
with Over 11's and Adults, 2nd ed**
ISBN 1 85302 340 X pb

'These books not only provide excellent ideas and guidance for helping grieving people, they also illustrate the huge diversity of human experiences which can be put under the heading of loss... I was so impressed by these books that I felt it was a privilege to be asked to review them.'
— Community Care

'The 22 cooperating contributors provide a superbly constructed resource of information, activities and ideas... Incredibly sensitive in every way... Barbara Ward...is to be congratulated and commended.'
— Journal of the Institute of Health Education

'...the authors have managed to produce an excellent aid to dealing with these very difficult and painful subjects within the national curriculum framework, and in a sensitive and imaginative way that will enable children, their teachers and parents to develop their understanding of loss and its impact. I would strongly recommend these volumes to all professionals working with children. They are also an invaluable source of information about self-help groups, useful literature for children of all ages and a variety of religious and cultural backgrounds.'
— Assoc of Child Psychology and Psychiatry Newsletter

'...ideal for creative inspiration...there are many varied ways of teaching children about the concept of death as a project subject at school, with the involvement of parents carefully noted which I felt was essential... The practical and factual information across differing religious creeds and cultures, and those of no faith, give plenty of scope for teachers and other carers to give information to children growing up in our multi-racial/multi-cultural society... I would recommend both these books for teachers/trainers/carers who look for information and inspiration.'
— Lifeline (Magazine of National Association of Bereavement Services)

Jessica Kingsley Publishers, 116 Pentonville Road, London N1 9JB